COUNTY GOVERNMENT

IN

AMERICA

County Government

In America

by HERBERT SYDNEY DUNCOMBE

Associate Professor, Political Science
University of Idaho

NATIONAL ASSOCIATION OF COUNTIES

Research Foundation

1001 Connecticut Avenue, N.W.
Washington, D.C. 20036

Foreword

COUNTY GOVERNMENT has been undergoing a dramatic change during the past decade. The "Dark Continent" of H. S. Gilbertson's day is becoming a Land of Opportunity. In this book Professor Duncombe documents this transformation and describes the existing and potential uses of the county structure in governing our metropolitan areas, as well as providing local rural government services in a professional and economical manner.

Since its inception in 1959, the Advisory Commission on Inter-governmental Relations has devoted a great deal of attention to Federal-State-local relations in metropolitan areas. At no point in the structure of the American federal system of government are problems of intergovernmental relations so marked, varied, and difficult as in the large metropolitan centers. There Federal, State, county, and municipal agencies, often supplemented by a small host of special purpose units of local government, must carry on their functions in close juxtaposition, subject to an extremely complicated framework of laws and administrative regulations. Within this welter of overlapping local governmental jurisdictions the county emerges as a distinctly favorable and politically feasible structure for providing regional-type services.

Technological changes which have the effect of "collapsing time and space," growing population, and increasing demands for scarce resources, all tend to make the planning and administration of urban services more and more areawide. In addition to "space," the county has high political feasibility (it exists, therefore it is feasible). It is directly accountable to an electorate that, under recent court decisions, will be reasonably representative. Finally, it has a broad tax base and well established working relations with the State and Federal governments on the one hand, and the cities on the other.

A reorganized urban county is likely to make any urban area more manageable, though its utility is probably greatest in the small and medium size metropolitan areas which are undergoing population growth at twice the rate of metropolitan areas as a whole. Reorganized county government vested with the authority to perform municipal functions is responding vigorously and imaginatively to meet urban needs in many parts of Virginia, California, Tennessee, Florida, Oregon, Maryland, New York, and other States. An increasing number of counties now have elected chief executives, counterparts to the city's focal point of politics and administration—the mayor. Indeed, the two major metropolitan governments in the United States—Dade County, Florida and Nashville-Davidson County, Tennessee—are essentially reorganized county governments.

Even in multi-county metropolitan areas the county is frequently a preferred device for extending utility and other urban services over a wide geographic area. Areawide coordination among units of government with regard to such services is facilitated as the number to be "coordinated" with one another becomes smaller. In the Washington metropolitan area, for example, on both the Maryland and Virginia sides of the Potomac River, strong county governments are providing a whole range of urban services. The major participants in areawide coordination are confined to the District of Columbia, and to Prince George's, Montgomery, Fairfax, and Arlington Counties, plus the city of Alexandria.

Except in those States sufficiently small in geographic area for the State government itself to assume responsibility for providing local government services outside the incorporated places, the county has been and will continue to be a dominant form of local government. In many areas of the Midwest and Far West, rural counties have lost population at a rapid rate, making unnecessarily expensive the traditional structure of county government with its retinue of elected officials.

Several of these States have enacted an Interlocal Cooperation Act along the lines proposed by the Advisory Commission, enabling county governments to contract with each other for the provision of joint services. This permits effective functional consolidation among adjoining counties where legal and political consolidation would not be feasible because of local pride and prejudice. In other rural areas, county government has been streamlined to provide the necessary services with a minimum of personnel. In the chapter of this book dealing with Petroleum County, Professor Duncombe documents the economies—both fiscal and functional—which can be achieved through modernizing the traditional form of county government.

It is clear that county government in the United States is on the move and is headed for a much greater role in our federal system than it has ever enjoyed in the past. The "renaissance" of American county government cannot be precisely dated, but future historians are likely to record as one of the significant turning points, the 1958 award of a Ford Foundation grant to support an expanded and revitalized National Association of County Officials, subsequently changed in name to the National Association of Counties.

Under able and aggressive leadership NACO has propelled county government into a significant place at the council tables and in the committee hearing rooms in Washington. It has also given strong support and leadership to the work of many State associations of counties which have resulted in a more active role for the county within the overall structure of State government. It is significant to note that those State associations which are more successful in capturing the respect of State legislatures and governors are also those which are dedicated to a modernization of county government and to an increasing attention to the role of the county in urban affairs.

This book by Professor Duncombe is not only excellent in content, but most timely in the evolution of local government in the United States.

WM. G. COLMAN
Executive Director
Advisory Commission on
Intergovernmental Relations

June 1966

Preface

THE TRENDS IN COUNTY GOVERNMENT FUNCTIONS and intergovernmental relations that have occurred in the past two decades are among the most significant in the thousand year history of counties. The piecemeal transfer of functions from cities to counties in many metropolitan areas and the emergence of the urban county will have far-reaching impact on local government. Surprisingly, there has been no book devoted entirely to county government in the United States since Paul Wager's County Government Across the Nation, published by the University of North Carolina Press in 1950. The important trends that have occurred since 1950 have been reported in excellent articles, chapters in books on local government, and studies of county government in specific states, but gaps still exist in published data on America's three thousand counties.

This book was written primarily to meet the needs of instructors in local government for a short textbook useful in acquainting undergraduate students with current trends and the current status of the organization, functions, financing, and intergovernmental relations of county government. It was written also to provide county officials with a description of county organization, services, and problems beyond the borders of their own states. Although a single volume study of county government is obviously too brief to fully describe county government today, it is hoped that this book will fill some of the voids in published data. Further books on county government are needed, particularly case studies of the county decision-making process, behavioral studies of county boards, and studies of the dynamics of the interrelationships between county political and county governmental leaders.

The significant differences among county governments in organization, services, financing, and intergovernmental relations pose difficult problems for writers on local government. It is impossible, within a single volume, to describe at length each one of America's

3,049 counties. However, lack of emphasis on the differences among counties leads to the false assumption that all counties fit into the same basic mold. The individuality of counties is depicted in this book in two ways. References to individual counties are used extensively throughout the first six chapters and the final chapter of the book to show differing county practices. Chapters 7 through 11 illustrate these dissimilarities more graphically by providing case studies of five, very different counties.

The stress placed upon urban counties and their problems in this book requires an explanation. The traditional functions and organizational structure of rural counties have received adequate coverage in prior books on local government. County court systems and political organizations have also been well described in previous books. The most extensive gaps in published material on county government have been in the more recent changes in the organization, services, and intergovernmental relations of counties with a population of 50,000 or more. In 1960, 72% of the people in the United States receiving county services lived in these counties, and this percentage will increase in future decades. My values which have influenced this stress on the urban county should also be acknowledged. I believe that in the coming decades county government will meet its greatest test in the metropolitan areas of our nation, and that urban counties have the potential to assume local leadership in many areas in a joint federal-state-local partnership to solve the serious urban area problems of our time.

This book would not have been possible without the assistance of the National Association of Counties and county officials in many states. The National Association of Counties made available its files and statistics, and drafts of the book were reviewed carefully by Bernard Hillenbrand and Alastair McArthur, the Executive Director and Deputy Director of the Association. I am also indebted to officials in Petroleum County (Montana), Latah County (Idaho), Montgomery County (Maryland), Davidson County (Tennessee), and Milwaukee County (Wisconsin) for their assistance during my trips to these counties and for their painstaking review of the case study chapters. Officials in Los Angeles County (California), Dade County (Florida), and East Baton Rouge Parish (Louisiana) are to be thanked for their careful review of sections of chapter 6. The detailed comments of Kenneth C. Tollenaar, Research Associate of the Bureau of Municipal Research and Service at the University of Oregon, and the review of the manuscript by Mr. Hill Healan, Executive Director of the Association of County Commissioners in Georgia, are also appreciated.

I am also indebted to the other authorities on local government who reviewed this manuscript before publication. W. Brooke Graves contributed valuable comments and additional bibliographic entries. Norman Beckman, Assistant Director of the Advisory Commission on Intergovernmental Relations, and his staff provided valuable suggestions for further research. Professors Robert Smith of Drew University, Alan Campbell of Syracuse University, Daniel Grant of Vanderbilt University, George Condon of Washington State University, and Robert Hosack of the University of Idaho reviewed all or portions of the manuscript and contributed ideas and information that were incorporated in the book. If errors of fact and judgment remain, they are my responsibility and not that of the many persons who have given their time and effort to reviewing the manuscript. Finally, I am indebted to my wife, Mary Conklin Duncombe, for her many hours of proofreading and typing and for her patience and understanding during the three years in which this book was written.

HERBERT SYDNEY DUNCOMBE

University of Idaho
Moscow, Idaho
March 1966

Table Of Contents

1/INTRODUCTION

"A person traveling across the continent by plane must be impressed with the magnitude, the beauty, and the variety of this great country of ours. He cannot fail to sense its wealth and vigor. Most of all he must thrill at the thought that it is a land of freedom, each man pursuing his work and pleasure, worshipping God, and retiring in his home at night unfettered and unafraid. That is the crowning glory of America, far more to be prized than its material or cultural attainments. . . .

As the traveler looks down on the quilted landscape, he is mindful too that the states are subdivided for purposes of government into smaller blocks, called counties. He reflects that a typical county is about 600 square miles in area which, if the air is clear, is about the area he can see from the two sides of the plane."

Paul W. Wager,

County Government Across the Nation

(Chapel Hill: University of North Carolina Press, 1950), p. 3.

Chapter 1

America's Three Thousand Counties

COUNTIES, LIKE PEOPLE, have differing characteristics. There is as much difference between sparsely populated Mason County on the southern slopes of Washington's Olympic Mountains and suburban New York's Nassau County as there is between the plaid-shirted logger of Mason County and the gray-suited banker of Nassau County. There is a similar diversity in American county government. Those who have described all county governments as basically similar have understated the accomplishments of American county officials in adapting the services of their county governments to the needs of their citizens. The loggers, sawmill operators, and oystermen of Mason County need, and have, a far different form of county government than the bankers, accountants and office workers of densely populated Nassau County.

CHARACTERISTICS OF AMERICAN COUNTIES

The county is the basic geographic subdivision of the state. There are 3,080 counties in the nation including areas similar to counties which are called parishes in Louisiana and boroughs in Alaska.(1) The entire nation is covered by these 3,080 counties except: 34 cities in Virginia, the cities of St. Louis, Baltimore, and Washington, D. C., a section of Yellowstone National Park, and 19 Alaskan election districts largely outside borough limits.

There is organized county government in 3,049 counties;(2) only 31 counties are without county government.(3) Although Connecticut

3

and Rhode Island are divided geographically into counties, they do not have county government. A few counties are governed by city-county or metropolitan governments which are neither city nor county but a combination of both. The Metropolitan Government of Nashville and Davidson County, Tennessee, for example, provides both city and county services for the entire Davidson County area. The number of county governments per state varies from 3 in Delaware to 254 in Texas.

Size and Population Differences

America's three thousand counties differ greatly in size. San Bernardino County, California has 20,131 square miles in land area. It is almost double the size of Holland and larger than the combined area of Massachusetts, Connecticut, Rhode Island and Delaware. Crossing the county by highway from Blythe to Red Mountain is a trip of nearly 270 miles. Arlington County, Virginia, in contrast, has a land area of only 24 square miles, and its six mile length can be crossed in a few minutes by car. The average county contains about 1,000 square miles and is small enough to permit residents in the extremities of the county to drive to the county seat, transact their business, and return in three or four hours.

Counties also vary greatly in population. In 1960, Los Angeles County, California had a population of more than 6 million while Loving County, Texas had a population of 226. The average county falls in the 10,000 to 25,000 population range but, as Table 1 shows, 44% of the people living in areas with county government reside in the 108 most populous counties. While only 18% of the counties had

Table 1
NUMBER OF COUNTY GOVERNMENTS IN 1962
BY POPULATION GROUP(4)

Population-size group	County Governments		Percent of Population served by County Governments 1960
	Number	Percent	
250,000 or more	108	3.5	43.6
100,000 to 249,999	169	5.6	16.7
50,000 to 99,999	283	9.3	12.3
25,000 to 49,999	584	19.2	13.1
10,000 to 24,999	1,081	35.5	11.2
5,000 to 9,999	544	17.9	2.6
Less than 5,000	274	9.0	0.5
United States, total	3,043	100.0	100.0

a population of 50,000 or more people in 1960, 72.6% of all county residents lived in these counties. Most Americans live in urban, not rural, counties.

Economic Characteristics of American Counties

The economic base of American counties differs. Many counties depend primarily upon agriculture, and their villages and cities are marketing centers for the surrounding areas and processing centers for agricultural products. Petroleum County, Montana is such a county; the population of its county seat and largest municipality is 360. Wheat raising Adams County, Washington, cotton raising Sharkey County, Mississippi, corn and livestock raising Guthrie County, Iowa and many other counties across the nation have predominantly agricultural economies.

Lumbering and allied industries form the economic base of many other counties. Mason County, Washington depends, for example, upon timber cut from the southern slopes of the Olympics, from its sale of Christmas trees, and from the Simpson lumber mills in Shelton. There are counties which depend heavily upon mining such as Silver Bow County, Montana and Shoshone County, Idaho. Other counties such as Vilas County, Wisconsin, which is famous for muskellunge fishing, and Clark County, Nevada, with its gambling and resort areas, depend heavily upon the tourist dollar.

The more populated counties tend to depend upon manufacturing, distribution or government as the mainstays of their economies. Some depend upon a large manufacturing plant; some upon an insurance company or a wholesale distributing center; some upon an air base, naval depot, army base, university or state capitol. The most heavily populated counties have economies not overly dependent upon a single corporation or industry. Some of these heavily populated counties are the centers of metropolitan areas while others serve mainly as bedrooms and living rooms for the thousands of commuters who stream into metropolitan cities each day.

The median family income of America's counties also differs greatly. The highest median incomes tend to be in suburban counties. Nassau and Westchester Counties in New York and Montgomery County, Maryland had median family incomes of more than $8,000 in 1959.(5) The lowest median family incomes tend to be in rural southern cities. Tunica County, Mississippi had a median family income of $1,260 in 1959.(6)

The economic characteristics of American counties greatly affect the types of services provided by county government and the ability of the citizens to support these services. Counties with high levels of family income, such as Montgomery County, Maryland, Arlington County, Virginia and Westchester and Nassau Counties in New York are able to support relatively high levels of county services and to provide many urban type services.

Other Differences Between Counties

Counties differ also in climate and topography. A few are so split by high mountain ranges that it is difficult for some county residents to get to the county seat during the winter. Counties differ in the racial, religious, and national origins of the majority of their citizens, and these differences can have a significant effect upon elections in the counties and may also affect the way county business is conducted.

More significant is the variation in the number of local government units within counties. In the average county, the county government is only one of 29 units of local government.(7) Other local governments within counties include municipalities, school districts, special districts and townships. There are significant variations among states and counties. In Virginia, there is an average of three local governments within each county. In some Virginia counties, such as Arlington, the county is the only unit of local government. Virginia was the first of the colonies in America to use the county form of government, and Arlington County is one of the number of Virginia counties providing strong, capable governmental leadership in county-wide areas. In Pennsylvania, there is an average of 93 units of local government per county. Although county government has an illustrious history in Pennsylvania, it has been weakened by a multiplicity of special districts and other small governmental units.

Variation among counties in density of population is also of great significance. Petroleum County, Montana and Nye County, Nevada are among the most sparsely populated counties in the nation with about one-half person per square mile. Cook County, Illinois and Milwaukee County, Wisconsin are among the most densely populated counties in the nation with about 5,000 persons per square mile. Citizens in densely populated metropolitan counties, such as Milwaukee and Cook, receive different types of services from their county governments than citizens in sparsely settled rural counties. The citizens in metropolitan areas face particularly difficult governmental problems, and county governments are in an excellent position to help resolve these problems particularly where the entire metropolitan area is encompassed within a single county.(8) When a metropolitan area extends into more than one county, cooperation between counties can help provide a unified approach to area problems.

County Case Studies

Case studies are used in this text to show more fully how counties differ. Five distinctly different counties were selected for study. Petroleum County, Montana, described in chapter seven, is a rural county with a population of 894.(9) Latah County, Idaho, described in chapter eight, is a partly-urban, partly-rural county with a population of 21,170. It is closer in area and population to the statistically average county in the United States than the other four counties.

Three differing large counties are described in chapters nine, ten and eleven. Montgomery County, Maryland, with a population of 340,928, is an example of a predominantly suburban county. Davidson County, Tennessee is a county of 399,743 which contains urban, suburban, and rural areas. Milwaukee County, Wisconsin, having a population of 1,036,041, is a metropolitan county having no unincorporated areas.

COUNTY POLITICAL ORGANIZATION

In most of the United States, the county is the main political base for party organization.(10) The county chairman is usually the key figure in local political organization.(11) Elective and appointive positions in county government have been a stepping stone to state and national office and a source of patronage for local party organizations. The county is a convenient area for political fund raising. Election statistics are compiled on a county basis, and the boundaries of state legislative districts and Congressional districts are often drawn along county lines.(12) County officials frequently are responsible for determining election precinct boundaries, appointing election precinct registrars and judges, and canvassing election returns. Politically powerful interest groups, such as the American Farm Bureau Federation, the American Bar Association, and the American Medical Association, have county based organizations.

The precinct is the basic unit in county politics. A precinct is the area served by a single polling place and may contain as few as a dozen voters in a sparsely settled rural area or as many as several thousand voters in some urban areas.(13) Party organization within precincts varies widely. In some states, such as Idaho, a single precinct committeeman is elected by the party voters of the precinct at the biennial primary election. In other states, the precinct party organization is jointly headed by a precinct committeeman and precinct committeewoman or is run by a precinct committee.(14) During the hectic general election campaign, precinct committeemen are busy organizing party workers, contacting potential voters, distributing campaign literature, attending rallies and meetings, arranging transportation to the polls, and trying to secure as large a vote as possible for the party.(15) During slack periods, the precinct committeeman may contact new voters who have moved into the neighborhood, receive complaints from constituents about government services, and intercede with local government officials on behalf of constituents. In many states, precinct committeemen are also members of their party's county committee.

There are one or more levels of political organization between the precinct and the county in many of the nation's more populous counties. In large cities, precincts are frequently combined into wards and ward leaders play an influential role. The city party chairman and committeemen are also influential particularly where the mayor and the city councilmen are elected on a partisan ballot. Where a county has a sufficiently large population to be divided into state legislative or Congressional districts, each of these districts may have its own political organization. In most of the nation's rural and semi-rural counties, however, there are no intervening levels of political organization between the precinct and the county.

The county political organization is normally headed by a county committee and a county chairman. The county committee is often composed of all the precinct committeemen in the county, but in some cases it is composed of party members elected in the primary or chosen at party conventions. The principal function of the county committee is to organize the party campaign, but it serves also to raise funds, consider patronage matters, endorse candidates, and select delegates to the state party convention. The chairman of the county committee is normally the executive head of the party organization in the county and frequently represents the county on the state central committee. The county chairman may be elected by the precinct committeemen in the county or may be elected by party voters.(16) His duties frequently include directing the election campaign, raising campaign funds, presiding over the county committee, securing candidates for vacant precinct and county posts, and serving as a clearinghouse for patronage matters. Individually, and as a group, county chairmen exercise extensive influence in state and even national party committees.

Control over county political organization varies widely. There are counties in which a county chairman controls party decision-making through a well-organized political machine. There are other counties in which a county commissioner, mayor, or other prominent party member wields the real political power with the county chairman having little power. In other counties, political power may be widely shared within the county with no single dominant individual. The individuals and groups who control county political organization may be motivated by an interest in higher political office, an enjoyment of politics, a sense of civic responsibility, or a desire to protect or advance business interests. Whatever the motivation, it is important to remember that their interests in politics do not stop at county boundaries. County political leaders are vitally interested in the outcome of state and national elections.

The fact that the county is the main political base for party organization is both a liability and asset to county government. It is a liability because many people associate "politics" with smoke filled rooms, spoils, and corruption and are hesitant about giving county government additional power. It is an asset because the strong political base of county government enhances the responsiveness of county government to popular control through the party system.(17)

COUNTY GOVERNMENTAL ORGANIZATION

There are so many different variations in the organization of county government that scholars on local government disagree on how to characterize them. The traditional county plan, the no executive plan, the county manager plan, the quasi-manager plan, the elected executive plan, the administrative assistant plan, and the county clerk plan are just some of the many terms used by political scientists to describe differing forms of county government. This text, somewhat arbitrarily, divides county governments into two groups: counties having the traditional plural executive form of government and counties having a single executive or administrator who has an important degree of supervision or control over most aspects of county administration. There are wide variations within these two general classifications of county government which will be described in detail.

Traditional Plural Executive Forms of County Government

About 85% to 90% of all counties in the United States have a traditional plural executive form of government.(18) The governing body of these counties is most frequently called a Board of Commissioners but it is sometimes called a County Court, Board of Supervisors, or some other term. In most counties, the county board members have no other governmental function; in others they also serve as supervisor of a township, judge, or justice of the peace.

The county board is a plural body with predominantly administrative functions. It has the power to appoint certain employees and board members, approve accounting documents, and take administrative actions such as reviewing applications for liquor licenses.

As an individual, the county commissioner may directly supervise the maintenance of county roads or the administration of poor relief in his district. County boards usually have the legislative power to adopt the county budget and to enact such ordinances and regulations as are permitted under state law.

The plural executive form of county government, illustrated in Chart 1, is also characterized by the election of a number of other officials by the voters of the county.

Chart 1
**THE PLURAL EXECUTIVE FORM OF GOVERNMENT
IN A TYPICAL IDAHO COUNTY**

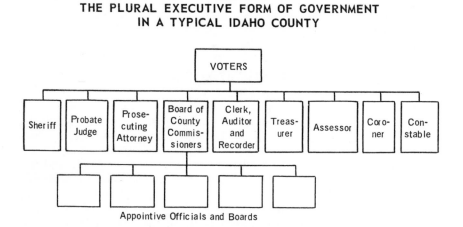

Appointive Officials and Boards

In most states, these independently elected county officials include: the sheriff, the treasurer, the attorney or solicitor, the assessor, the auditor or clerk, the coroner, and county judicial officials. These elected officials are responsible for administering many important functions of county government. Since they are elected separately from the county board, the voters of the county cannot justifiably hold the county commissioners responsible for the conduct of many county functions. One of the problems faced by county commissioners is the tendency of many voters to hold them responsible for all county functions including the work of independently elected county officials.

Executive and Administrator Forms of County Government

The main characteristic of the executive and administrator forms of county government is the fact that a single official has a significant degree of supervision, control, or influence over most aspects of county administration. This form of county government is usually preferred by political scientists because it is easier for the voters or the county board to hold this official responsible.

There are many variations in this general form of county government.

Under the county manager plan, pictured in its simplest form in Chart 2, the county board serves as a policy-making body for the county and employs a manager to be responsible for the administration of most, if not all, county functions. Under accepted practice, the manager is a professional person selected on the basis of his ability and experience rather than his party affiliation. The manager leaves policy making to the board, and the county board, in turn, leaves responsibility for day to day administrative matters to the manager. Usually the manager may be removed by a simple majority vote of the county board, and the manager has the power to appoint most, if not all, subordinate county officials. The manager also has the power to prepare the county budget and to execute the budget after it has been adopted by the county governing board.

Chart 2
THE COUNTY MANAGER PLAN

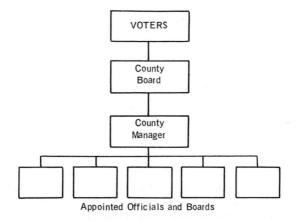

Appointed Officials and Boards

The quasi-manager, administrative officer, and the administrative assistant plans are modifications of the county manager form of government. These types of county government, described in greater detail in chapter three, all provide for the appointment by the county board of a full-time professional to assist it in its administrative functions but without the full appointive and administrative powers of a county manager. In some quasi-manager forms of county government, the manager or executive has full administrative powers except the power to appoint most of his department heads. Department heads are usually appointed by the county board. In some administrative assistant plans, the county board appoints an assistant who is responsible to the county board for the staff functions of budgeting, purchasing and administrative management and has an important influence over most aspects of county administration.

The elected county executive plan, shown in Chart 3, is another form of county government. The chief executive is elected by the voters of the entire county and heads the executive branch of county government. The county board has few, if any, administrative powers and is in the same position as the council in a strong mayor-council form of city government. The county executive has the power to veto legislation of the county board, and the board usually has the power to override the county executive's veto with a two-thirds majority. The county executive appoints all, or nearly all, department heads and is responsible for submitting a budget to the council and for the general administration of county government. Under one variation of this plan, the county executive is elected by the county board, not the voters, but retains some of the power of the elected county executive. Under a second variation of the plan, the elected chief executive is required to appoint a professionally qualified administrator to assist him.

Chart 3
THE ELECTED COUNTY EXECUTIVE PLAN

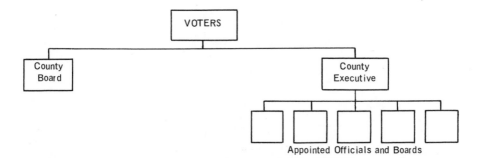

Appointed Officials and Boards

In other counties, the county clerk or some other elected county official has a significant degree of supervision over many aspects of county administration. Some county clerks serve as secretary to the county board, and also as county auditor, budget officer, chief accountant, and purchasing agent for the county. In this position, strong county clerks have become, in effect, administrative assistants to the county board and have assumed supervision over a number of county departments. In some states, substantial administrative powers are granted to a county judge, a commissioner of roads, or a probate judge.

Although the executive and administrator forms of county government are used in only about 10% to 15% of American counties, they are widely used in the more populous counties. A survey made by the National Association of Counties in 1964 indicated that about half of all counties with a population of 100,000 or more had a variation of the executive or administrator form of county government.(19)

SERVICES PROVIDED BY COUNTY GOVERNMENT

For generations counties have provided a number of traditional services for their citizens. These include: the assessment of property, the collection of property taxes, the recording of deeds and other property documents, the maintenance of rural roads, poor relief, law enforcement, and the administration of electoral and judicial functions. These are services that are, for the most part, required of counties by state law. County governments serve somewhat as an arm of the state in providing these services.

County governments also furnish a number of newer services which are generally not required by state law but are undertaken by counties to meet needs expressed by their citizens. These services include: fire protection, water, sewage disposal, parks, recreation programs, airports, and other services frequently provided by cities. County governments, in many urban areas, are providing some or all of these services for densely populated unincorporated areas of the county. Some county governments are administering one or more of these functions for the entire county area.

The county has long been termed a quasi-municipal corporation because it is organized by the state and its traditional functions are generally required by state law. In 1857 when counties had many fewer functions than they have today, the Ohio Supreme Court made a significant legal distinction between a municipal corporation and a quasi-municipal corporation such as a county.

"A municipal corporation proper is created mainly for the interest, advantage, and convenience of the locality and its people; a county organization is created almost exclusively with a view to the policy of the state at large, for purposes of political organization and civil administration, in matters of finance, of education, of provision for the poor, of military organization, of the means of travel and transport, and especially for the general administration of justice. With scarcely an exception, all the powers and functions of the county organization have a direct and exclusive reference to the general policy of the state, and are, in fact, but a branch of the general administration of that policy."(20)

The county retains its quasi-municipal character when it performs the traditional state required functions. When providing urban services, however, the county has increasingly assumed characteristics of a municipal corporation.

The types of services provided by counties vary with density of of county population.(21) Thinly populated, rural counties tend to furnish only traditional services. When the stock raiser of some small western county tramps into the county courthouse, the odds are that he is there to pay his property tax, buy his auto license, complain about his assessment, get the deed of his south forty recorded, or see his county agricultural agent. His wife may visit the county courthouse or county building only rarely, but their children's births will be recorded by the county, their children will receive school health check-ups from the county public health nurse, and her elderly aunt may receive emergency public assistance. Each year the entire family will enjoy the county fair.

Partly urban counties usually furnish a wider range of services. They may provide the part-time services of a psychiatric social worker to staff a child guidance clinic. They may operate a county nursing home or a county library system with a bookmobile reaching the outlying parts of the county. A number of middle sized counties have a county planning commission, and some administer a county zoning ordinance.

The metropolitan and suburban counties tend to provide an even wider range of services. The banker, mechanic, or contractor entering the county courthouse might be: making arrangements for water main connections for the house he is building, presenting arguments in favor of a new park to the county board, getting information on charges for keeping an airplane at the county airport, or obtaining a copy of the county subdivision regulations. The urban and suburban county resident generally needs, and receives, the benefit of far more county services than the resident of a small rural county.

SUMMARY

A significant characteristic of American counties is their diversity. It is important to remember that there are metropolitan and suburban counties as well as the more numerous rural and partly rural counties. Counties are the main political base for party organization, but counties vary widely in party structure. Counties are governed by a variety of forms of government with the traditional plural executive forms predominating. All counties provide traditional, state required services, and many counties (particularly large urban counties) also provide municipal type services.

How did American county government develop its diverse characteristics? Why is it that county government is much stronger in some parts of the nation than in others? The answers to these questions lie in historical forces that go back a thousand years — forces that are described in chapter two.

REFERENCES

1. U. S. Bureau of the Census, Governing Boards of County Governments: 1965 (Washington: U. S. Government Printing Office, 1965), pp. 4, 5. These 3,080 county areas include 3,049 areas having county government and 31 areas without county government.

2. Ibid., p. 4. The U. S. Census Bureau calls these "areas with an independently organized county government."

3. These 31 counties include: 8 counties in Connecticut, 5 in Rhode Island, 3 counties in South Dakota which are attached to other counties for governmental purposes, 3 city-counties, the Metropolitan Government of Nashville and Davidson County, and 11 other counties. The 11 other counties include some of the most populous areas of the nation such as New York, Boston and Philadelphia. In these areas certain types of county offices exist, but they are part of another governmental unit such as a city.

4. U. S. Bureau of the Census, Census of Governments: 1962, Vol. I. Governmental Organization (Washington: U. S. Government Printing Office, 1963), p. 2. By 1965, the number of county governments had increased to 3,049.

5. U. S. Bureau of the Census, U. S. Census of Population: 1960, Vol. I, Characteristics of the Population, Part 34, p. 383 and 386, Part 22, p. 156.

6. Ibid., Part 26, p. 200.

7. U. S. Bureau of the Census, Census of Governments: 1962, Vol. I, Governmental Organizations, p. 10. This publication is the source of all statistical data used in this paragraph.

8. There were 219 standard metropolitan areas in the United States in 1963, and 111 of these areas lay within single counties or county type areas. William G. Colman, "Revision of Standard Metropolitan Statistical Areas" (memorandum to Members of the Advisory Commission on Intergovernmental Relations, Washington, D. C., November 13, 1963). A standard metropolitan area is a single county area or a group of contiguous counties which includes one central city of at least 50,000 persons or (in a few cases) twin cities of 50,000 or more persons. In New England, an exception is made so that a standard metropolitan area is composed of contiguous cities and towns having at least one city of 50,000 persons or more.

9. Population data used in this paragraph are from the 1960 census.

10. In much of New England, cities and towns are more important political units than counties. In a few metropolitan areas, such as Chicago, the city rather than the county is the center of political organization.

11. Hugh A. Bone, American Politics and the Party System (third edition; New York: McGraw-Hill Book Company, 1965), p. 170. Hugh Bone supports this statement with illustrations of the power of county chairmen and analyses of the role of county chairmen.

12. When state legislative districts are drawn along county boundaries, there is a greater tendency for state legislators to work through regular county political organizations instead of creating their own campaign organizations. State reapportionment in the past few years has eliminated the county as a legislative district in some states and may have weakened some county political organizations.

13. George S. Blair, American Local Government (New York: Harper and Row, 1964), p. 127 estimates that there are approximately 130,000 precincts in the nation and that they have an average of 600 voters.

14. Ibid., p. 127. George S. Blair describes these as the predominant types of precinct organization. Texas has both a precinct chairman elected in the primary by the party voters of the precinct and a precinct convention. At the precinct convention, resolutions supporting specific candidates may be passed, and delegates are selected to the county convention. Wilbourn E. Benton, Texas, Its Government and Politics (Englewood Cliffs, N. J.: Prentice-Hall, Inc., 1961), pp. 121-128.

15. The precinct committeeman may also find primary election campaigns a hectic period particularly in the South. For brief descriptions of the work of precinct committeemen, see Hugh A. Bone, op. cit., pp. 168-170, George S. Blair, op. cit., pp. 127-129, and Clyde F. Snider, Local Government in Rural America (New York: Appleton-Century-Crofts, Inc., 1957), pp. 262-266.

16. In Idaho, the county chairman is elected by the county committee. In Texas, he is elected in the primary by party voters of the county. For a description of the work of the county chairman in Texas, see Wilbourn E. Benton, op. cit., pp. 128, 129. General descriptions of the work of the county chairman may be found in Hugh A. Bone, op. cit., pp. 170-172 and George S. Blair, op. cit., pp. 130, 131.

17. This point has been frequently made by Bernard Hillenbrand. See Bernard Hillenbrand, "County Government is Reborn" in Readings in State and Local Government by Joseph F. Zimmerman (New York: Holt, Rinehart and Winston, Inc., 1964), p. 263.

18. The writer's estimate is based on a study of the organization of county government in 1,667 counties made by the National Association of Counties in 1964.

19. This survey showed that among 208 reporting counties with a population of 100,000 or more, there were 101 counties with a plural executive form of government and 107 counties with a variation of the executive or administrator form of government. These 107 counties included: 16 with an elected executive, 15 with a county manager, 54 with an administrator or appointed clerk, 11 with a strong county clerk having extensive supervisory powers, and 11 with a county judge, chairman of the board of county commissioners, or other official assuming strong executive powers. Table 4 in chapter three lists counties of 250,000 or

more people having a variation of the executive or administrator form of government.

20. Commissioners of Hamilton County v. Mighels, 7 Ohio St. 109, 118–119 (1857).

21. George S. Blair, op. cit., pp. 173–179, has developed a classification of counties based on their population density and has skillfully shown the changes in county functions as counties increase in population density.

Chapter 2

The Historic Role
Of The County
In American Government

THE COUNTY, LIKE OTHER INSTITUTIONS of American government, has its roots deep in English history and has been molded by generations of Englishmen and Americans to meet the needs of changing times. To understand the American county today, one must understand the forces that have shaped its structure and determined its functions over the centuries and the forces that are changing county government at the present time.

ENGLISH ORIGINS OF AMERICAN COUNTIES

The origins of the American county can be traced back 1,000 years to shires that formed the apex of local government in Anglo-Saxon England.(1) The shire of that period performed judicial, police, public works and military functions. The legislative and judicial body of the shire was a shire-moot which met twice a year. The earl, an important landowner of the district, presided over the shire-moot and was the leader of the king's military forces in the shire. A shire-reeve, or sheriff, was initially an assistant to the earl but gained increasingly important police, financial and judicial powers. The bishop was the judicial official in ecclesiastical cases. The shire provided Anglo-Saxon England with a government which met the limited needs of the times.

William the Conqueror and his successors changed local government in England to provide for greater central control. The shire came to be called the county. The shire-moot evolved into a county court, consisting of large landowners, that had little real authority. The earl lost power and held only a title of nobility. The bishop no longer tried eccelesiastical cases in the county court. The sheriff gained increasing influence as the king's military representative, chief of county police, and steward of the royal estates. The county became a unit of royal administration rather than a relatively autonomous unit of local self government.

The county was the main unit of English local government at the time the first British colonists landed in Virginia. Under James I, English counties were largely an arm of national government but retained a slight, but significant, element of local autonomy. The most important administrative functions of the counties were performed by justices of the peace who were appointed by the king and supervised by the royal Privy Council. Although these justices were subject to dismissal by the king, the wealthy landowners who were frequently appointed to these positions had significant elements of discretion. The sheriff, an appointee of the king, had lost some of his former power but still retained a position of importance in the court system.

The parish and the borough, other important units of English local government in the early 1600's also provided an element of local autonomy. The parish was a unit of church and civil government which usually encompassed a small rural area and provided mainly for church affairs and for the administration of elementary education, highways and poor relief. It was governed by an assembly of freemen who met at vestry meetings to decide important issues and elect officers. In urban areas of England, the borough had a significant role in providing police and judicial functions. The borough was usually ruled by a small self-perpetuating oligarchy.

THE COLONIAL COUNTY IN AMERICA

The English colonists brought to America many of the local government institutions of their homeland and adapted these to meet the needs of their new environment. The systems of local government that developed in the Virginia, Massachusetts, New York, and Pennsylvania colonies were to have a lasting effect on county and township government.

The Strong County System in Virginia

The colonists found, in the Virginia tidewater region, an area well suited to small agricultural settlements and dispersed plantations and farms.(2) The climate was mild; the soil was fertile; and rivers provided convenient transportation inland. The system of dispersed farms and plantations was encouraged by the fact that land grants were commonly made to individuals, rather than to groups, and by the number of English landed gentry that settled in Virginia. After the early years the development of large, closely knit agricultural communities was not necessary to protect the colonists from Indian attack.

The first units of local government in Virginia were called plantations, hundreds, cities, and parishes. They had many of the characteristics of the English parishes of the time and served both ecclesiastical and civil purposes. The parish never gained the importance in Virginia that the town gained in New England. The plantations, farms, and small agricultural settlements were too widely dispersed to be readily governed by a parish form of government.

Virginians recognized the need for a form of local government encompassing a wider area than a parish, and in 1634 the settled part of the colony was divided into eight shires or counties. New counties were gradually organized. Counties served as election districts for the colonial House of Burgesses with the sheriff acting as election officer. They were military districts, and a county lieutenant appointed by the colonial governor had the power to call to duty all males over 18. Counties were judicial districts with the county court having original jurisdiction over all civil and criminal cases except felonies. They were an important unit of civil administration responsible for the construction and repair of highways and bridges, keeping rivers navigable, and controlling the erection of water mills, the location of tobacco warehouses, and the licensing of private ferry keepers. The passage of the Virginia Highway Act of 1657 placed much of the responsibility for highways and bridges in the hands of a surveyor appointed by the county court.(3)

The Virginia colony had a plural executive form of county government. The county court, composed mainly of large landholders commissioned by the colonial governor, was the governing body of the county. The justices of the county court levied county taxes, acted as a county judicial body, and had major administrative responsibilities. The colonial governor appointed a sheriff from a list of persons nominated by the county court. The sheriff was executive officer of the court, collected county taxes, and acted as county treasurer. The county coroner, surveyor, lieutenant, and justices of the peace were appointed by the colonial governor on the recommendations of the group of aristocratic planters who composed the county court. The Virginia system of local government, with its emphasis on strong county government, influenced the development of county government in America, particularly in the South.

The Massachusetts Town System

The forms of government which the early Massachusetts colonists brought with them from England and adapted to meet their needs also had an important influence on local government in America.(4) In Massachusetts, the colonists found a colder climate, rockier soil, and hostile Indians. They relied upon shipping and fishing as well as agriculture for a livelihood. They tended to live in compact communities that could more easily be protected against the Indians, rather than in the dispersed plantations and agricultural settlements that were common in early Colonial Virginia. The Massachusetts settlers found that the smaller and more compact English parish government was best suited to their needs. They formed towns of about 20 to 40 square miles in area which included a village that could be fortified and the surrounding rural area.(5) The selectmen and other major town officials were elected at the town meeting. The town performed a number of functions which in Virginia were county functions.

The town never gained the prominence in Massachusetts that the county gained in Virginia. In 1643, Massachusetts was divided into four counties which were governed by a county court composed of justices appointed by the governor and by a treasurer and sheriff also appointed by the governor. The county court, like its counterpart in Virginia, had administrative functions such as highway maintenance and licensing as well as judicial functions.

The colonial system of local government in Massachusetts spread throughout New England. The town, although diminished in importance, is still stronger in New England than are towns and townships in other areas of the country. The county has never had the prominence in New England as in other areas, and in Rhode Island and Connecticut counties do not now exist as organized units of government.

County Government in the Middle Atlantic Colonies

The Middle Atlantic colonies of New York, New Jersey and Pennsylvania developed forms of local government that differed from the Massachusetts and Virginia systems.(6) New York, under Dutch rule, had a number of self-governing villages. After the English conquest in 1664, both counties and towns were established. (7) In 1691, the county governing body became an elective board of supervisors. One supervisor was elected from each town to levy and assess local taxes, and this supervisor automatically became a member of the county board of supervisors. The county board of supervisors gradually took over control of highways and other county administrative functions. Towns in New York were stronger than parishes in Virginia and were governed by an elected supervisor and elected clerks, constables, surveyors, and overseers of the poor. The municipal corporations of New York and Albany developed a significant degree of self-government during the 1700's, and by 1770 they were establishing markets, managing ferries, building docks, laying out streets, and providing wells, fire protection and police services.

In New Jersey, assessors were elected in each township to help assess property. These elected assessors developed into a county board of freeholders similar to the county board of supervisors in New York.

Pennsylvania developed a still different pattern of local government. The population in many areas of the colony was dispersed, and counties developed as administrative units before towns. In 1724, the county governing body became a board composed of three county commissioners each elected at large from the county. Pennsylvania townships were not represented in the county governing body as in New York and New Jersey. Townships in Pennsylvania were less important than they were in New York and New England although they did have elected highway supervisors and appointed overseers of the poor. Philadelphia was largely self-governing and provided many of the same urban services as New York City.

The Middle Atlantic colonies developed two forms of county government that were destined to be widely used. The county commissioner system presently found in Pennsylvania and most Mid-Western and Western states is a direct descendent of the form of county government established in Pennsylvania in 1724. In most Western states today, there are three county commissioners elected by the voters at large. The supervisor form of county government in which the county governing body is composed of supervisors elected by towns or townships is found today in New York, Michigan and other states.

THE STATUS OF THE COUNTY AFTER THE AMERICAN REVOLUTION

The American Revolution and Constitutional Convention did not produce a radical change in American county government. The newly adopted Constitution of the United States did not specifically mention local government. Control of local government is not one of the enumerated powers of Congress in the Constitution and is not one of the powers prohibited to the states. It is, thus, one of many powers reserved to the states and the people by the tenth amendment of the Constitution. The United States Constitution established a federal system of government with two centers of power — the national government and the state governments. State governments were not required to make similar distribution of power between themselves and local units of government.

Most early state constitutions continued colonial forms of local government without great change. Article 29 of the New York Constitution of 1777, for example, enumerated a number of town officials whose offices were to continue without change until the Legislature acted.(8) In Virginia, as had been the case before the American Revolution, county officers were commissioned by the governor after nomination by county court justices.(9) However, there were some important changes in the manner of selecting county officials. In New York, county officials formerly appointed by the governor were now appointed by a council of appointment consisting of the governor and four members of the state Senate.(10) Sheriffs and coroners were made elective in New Jersey and sheriffs were made elective in Maryland.(11) The state constitutions tended to reduce the power of state governors in making appointments to county positions.

The early state constitutions continued the status of counties as an arm of state government. As Kneier points out, the county (or shire) came to be considered as an administrative district for the national government in England after the Norman conquest, and did not have the legal status of a municipal corporation when the English borough received this status.(12) Familiar with British practice, the American colonists thus tended to think of the county as part of state government. It was natural then for the early state constitutions to establish the structure of county government while remaining largely silent on municipal government.(13)

The legal distinction between counties and cities recognized during the 1700's was made more explicit during the 1800's. In 1845, Chief Justice Taney of the Supreme Court stated that: "The several counties are nothing more than certain portions of the territory into which the state is divided for the more convenient exercise of the powers of government."(14) In 1857, the Ohio Supreme Court made an important distinction between a municipal corporation (created for the convenience of the locality) and a quasi-municipal corporation such as a county which was created with a view to the policy of the state at large.(15) This legal view of the county as a mere arm of the state had a stultifying effect on the powers of county government throughout the 1800's, and it has hindered counties in providing municipal services in the present century.

COUNTY GOVERNMENT UP TO THE CIVIL WAR

The American settlers who crossed the Appalachians in the 1790's and 1800's brought with them the familiar forms of local government of the eastern seaboard colonies. Kentucky and Tennessee adopted the strong county form of government of Virginia in which county court justices played a prominent role.(16) Ohio adopted the county-township system of Pennsylvania with a three member elective board of commissioners exercising extensive fiscal and administrative authority.(17) Like Pennsylvania, Ohio established the independently elected offices of sheriff and coroner. Generally the strong county systems of colonial Virginia, the Carolinas, and Georgia were adopted by the newer southern states, while the Pennsylvania or New York county-township systems were adopted by the mid-western states.(18)

During the early 1800's, a number of appointive county offices became elective. In 1821, New York abolished the state legislative council of appointment and made a number of appointive county positions elective.(19) The governor of Pennsylvania was stripped of his remaining discretion in the appointment of county sheriffs and coroners in 1838.(20) When new states were created in the Mid-West and South, county officials were generally elected rather than appointed by the state governor or legislature.

Another significant trend in the early 1800's was the creation of many new elective offices such as county treasurer, assessor, surveyor and prosecuting attorney. The first constitution of Indiana in 1816, for example, created only two independently elective offices — sheriff and coroner.(21) The 1851 Indiana Constitution required the election of an auditor, recorder, treasurer, surveyor, and clerk of the circuit court as well as sheriff and coroner.(22)

Why did state constitutions and state laws establish many independently elective officials during the early 1800's thus weakening the power of the county governing board? Gilbertson blames the Jacksonians.(23) When the appointive system in operation in New York and other eastern states did not work well, the Jacksonians concluded that state officials should be stripped of their powers to appoint county officials. They did not consider having officials such as the sheriff and coroner appointed by the county board but instead made the positions elective. They reasoned, according to Gilbertson, that the problem with county government was the appointment of officials.(24) The cure was to have as many officials as possible elected directly by county residents for short terms and thus keep democracy close to the people. The period of the greatest increase in the number of independently elected officials coincided with a period of extension of suffrage through abolition of property and taxpaying qualifications. Both movements may have been associated in the minds of many with the extension of democracy.

The multiplicity of independently elective county offices undoubtedly appealed to the Jacksonian frontiersman with his suspicion of aristocratic cliques and expertness. The independent farmer and frontiersman was a jack-of-all-trades — farmer, carpenter, mechanic, hunter, Indian fighter — and considered himself capable of holding any county elective office. He rejected the notion that specialized skill and training were necessary for county government or government service at any level. A large number of elective county offices and frequent rotation of these officeholders, he felt, would insure that a small clique would not hold power in the county and that county jobs would be passed around so that many would have a chance to receive them.

The development of national and state conventions as a means of selecting party candidates in the 1820's and 1830's also had an influence on county government. The county became the election districts for members of the state legislature in many states and became the natural unit for party political machines.(25) Securing nominations at state and national conventions required a faithful following of party adherents, and county positions became important political plums. The county became the base for both local political policy-making and the spoils system.(26)

By the beginning of the Civil War, the structure of county government had established its present, traditional mold. An elective county board was found in nearly all states.(27) In most states, this board consisted of a small number of commissioners elected at large or by district. In a few states, the counties had larger boards elected from townships or other subdivisions within the county as in New York. By the Civil War, counties had many independently elective officials such as sheriffs, coroners, auditors, treasurers, clerks, assessors, prosecuting attorneys, and surveyors, thus reducing the powers of the county board. State control of counties through selection of county officials had largely ceased, but state constitutions became increasingly detailed covering such matters as the qualifications, powers, and manner of selection of county officers.

COUNTY GOVERNMENT FROM THE CIVIL WAR TO WORLD WAR I

The Civil War produced no significant change in county government. During the reconstruction period, there was an attempt to transplant the northern system of townships into southern states.

This attempt was largely unsuccessful. Virginia, for example, established a township system in 1870 and replaced it two years later with magisterial districts for the election of justices, constables and overseers of the poor.(28) By 1880, counties had been established across the nation. Townships were established in the North as far west as the plains states of the Dakotas, Nebraska, and Kansas. West of these states, settlement was sparse, and the township form of government was unsuited to local needs. The predominant form of county government in the Rocky Mountain and West Coast states was the Pennsylvania form with a small board of county commissioners and many independently elected county officials.

The tremendous growth of urban centers from the Civil War to World War I brought significant changes to city and county government. In 1860, there were 6.2 million people living in urban centers; in 1880, there were 14.1 million; in 1900, 30.1 million and in 1920, 54.2 million.(29) Cities were faced with great increases in demands for services at a time when city government had been weakened both by extensive use of the spoils system and by the weak mayor-council system of government. Large groups of immigrants moved to the larger cities, lived in slum neighborhoods, and were swayed by political leaders of the same nationality. The absence of comprehensive social welfare programs left the immigrants and other low income city residents vulnerable in case of illness, unemployment, or death of the head of the family. In urban centers, political machines developed which provided patronage positions for the unemployed, food for the needy, and medicines for the sick. The political boss and his ward leaders expected and received political support from those they helped and, once entrenched in city government, enriched themselves through fraudulent practices such as kickbacks on purchases and selling land to the city at exorbitant prices. New York had its Tweed Ring, Philadelphia had its Gas Ring, and other cities had administrations fully as corrupt. Concerned with municipal corruption and ineffectiveness, city residents often turned to the state, and boards or commissions were often created to take over functions previously performed by city agencies.

County governments faced the same pressures and problems as cities and succumbed to the same political machines. The political boss of a large urban area ruled both city and county and frequently used county political office as a springboard to power. In his rise to power, William March Tweed became leader of a volunteer fire company, alderman, Congressman, commissioner in the Board of Education, and finally a member of the Board of Supervisors of the County of New York.(30) In the latter post, he enriched himself through shady financial transactions and soon rose to head Tammany Hall and to control both the city and the county of New York.(31) To the reformers of the late 1800's and early 1900's, the county (like the city) appeared to be a jungle of inefficient, irresponsible, and corrupt government. One of these reformers, Henry S. Gilbertson, called the county "the dark continent of American politics."(32)

Gilbertson's criticisms of county government have influenced many writers on local government, and his phrase "dark continent" has been extensively used by writers to characterize county government as archaic, inefficient, or not well known to the public. Gilbertson was a reformer as well as a critic, and his suggestions for reform and his vision of the county of the future have not received the attention they deserve.

The problems of county government stemmed mainly, Gilbertson thought, from a long " 'bed-quilt' " ballot of county officers that "deceived, misled and disfranchised the 'average citizen.' "(33) As the populations of urban counties grew, few people knew elective county officials personally and few could evaluate their qualifications.(34)

Boss rule was the inevitable outcome of the splintering of political responsibility in county government, Gilbertson believed. (35) In a government without a single legal head, the political boss provided needed stability and made "an altogether unworkable system .... tolerably workable."(36) The boss controlled the party machine, and the people, unable to know the qualifications of the large numbers of elective officials, tended to vote the straight party ticket.(37) The voters' only real choice was between party machines. The real allegiance of the independently elected officials was to the party boss, not to the people.

Gilbertson documented the inefficiency and corruption of county government of his day and charged that counties were failing to meet the program needs of urban areas. He described the evils of the fee system in which the sheriff of New York County pocketed fees of $60,000 a year as well as a $12,000 annual salary.(38) He depicted the workings of the spoils system in many counties and showed the inefficiency it caused and the salary kickbacks that sometimes resulted.

He attacked the system of fee-paid overseers of the poor, the unsanitary county penal institutions, and the poorly planned county public works projects.(39) He pointed out that competent professional administration was needed in county functions, and that the many independently elected county officials of the time did not provide the professional leadership needed. While he provided some examples of inefficiency, corruption, and poor administration in rural counties, he stated that "without a doubt, the urban, and particularly the metropolitan county, is the county at its worst."(40)

In his attacks, Gilbertson was not trying to abolish county government but to reform it. He was a staunch advocate of county home rule and favored permitting counties to adopt special home rule charters in which they could choose one of several optional plans for county government.(41) He saw advantages, in some urban counties, of consolidating city and county government.(42) He favored greatly reducing the number of elected county officials and making a single official or group of officials responsible to the voters for the conduct of county government.(43) One can find in his book favorable comment on a county mayor (or county executive) plan of government in which the entire power to appoint department heads is vested in a single elected county official.(44) Gilbertson commented even more favorably on the county manager plan in which the county board selects a professional administrator as manager and delegates to him the appointment of department heads and the details of administration.(45) Gilbertson also advocated a comprehensive merit system for county employees, a modern executive budget, a professional accounting system, purchasing standards and bid procedures, and citizen organizations that would take a greater interest in county government.(46) His final chapter was a picture of the county of the future in which "the county politician of the conventional type has been extinguished."(47)

Gilbertson's book, written during World War I, provides a convenient dividing line between what might be termed the middle ages of American county government and the renaissance. Significant changes were taking place in the urban areas of the nation in the early 1900's that would have a profound impact on the functions and structure of metropolitan county governments. These changes were just beginning to have an effect by 1917. One trend was the population explosion which was to engulf metropolitan areas and bring new problems and program needs. A second trend was suburbanization and the inability of cities to extend their boundaries to include all the densely populated areas surrounding them. Suburbanization was to bring counties into the field of providing municipal services to unincorporated areas. A third trend was the reform movement which has brought changes in the administration of county government.

COUNTY GOVERNMENT SINCE WORLD WAR I

The renaissance of county government has come largely since World War I. It has begun in the metropolitan counties and is spreading to many of the middlesized and some of the smaller counties. Government in the modern county is far different from that in Gilbertson's day.

One significant change in county government has been the slow, continuing increase in county services. The most important county functions in 1913 were general governmental services such as judicial administration, assessment and collection of property taxes, election administration, and the recording of legal papers. More than a quarter of all county expenditures were for general government.(48) The other major county expenditures in 1913 were for the maintenance of county roads, the operation of schools and county school superintendents' offices, the maintenance of charitable and correctional institutions, and the provision of police protection through the sheriff's office. In most functions, the county served mainly as an administrative arm of the state.

Since World War I, responsibility for some traditional county functions has shifted to the state and national government. By 1930, Kneier reports, there had been a shift in police and highway administration from county to state control.(49) During the 1930's a few states assumed almost complete responsibility for highways and schools. The inability of local government to finance relief costs during the 1930's resulted in the passage of the Federal Social Security Act and the shifting of control over public welfare policy to the national and state level.

A compensating trend has been the transfer of responsibility from township and special district governments to counties.(50) There has been increasing recognition that townships and small special districts are too small geographically to provide economic units for highway administration.(51) All township roads were transferred to county jurisdiction in Michigan and Indiana before 1952. (52) In other states, such as Kansas and Texas, individual counties have assumed control of road administration from townships or special districts. In 1952, Snider estimated that one-half the total highway mileage of the nation was under county jurisdiction as compared to one-fourth under county jurisdiction thirty years earlier. (53) Assessment of property and judicial administration are other functions that are gradually being transferred from townships to counties.

The most significant change in county services since the 1910's has been the growth of newer services in which the county acts, not as an administrative arm of the state, but as a more independent arm of local government. There has been a tremendous expansion in county park and recreation programs. The first county park was established in Essex County, New Jersey in 1895,(54) but county park and recreation expenditures reached only $419,000 by 1913. Expenditures for parks reached $7.6 million in 1928, $67 million in 1957 and $123 million in 1962. In many counties today, the operation of the major park system is a county responsibility. Cities have found that undeveloped land suitable for larger parks is usually located beyond city limits. The residents of many areas have found it more equitable, therefore, for the county to run the park system thus distributing the cost to all county residents.

County libraries, airports, hospitals, health services, and utility systems are other examples of county functions which have expanded tremendously since World War I. County library systems are now found in all but a few states, and county expenditures for libraries have risen from $364,000 in 1913 to $59 million in 1962. The first full time county health department was established in 1911 in Yakima County, Washington and by 1926, there were 307 full time county health departments.(55) Health and sanitation expenditures were $2.8 million in 1913; and health expenditures alone were $193 million in 1962.

Technological changes are responsible for the growth of some county functions. Before World War I, airports were small and relatively inexpensive; today's jet airports are costly and often not self-supporting. More and more airports are being run by counties or by joint city-county agencies, because city residents have grown tired of subsidizing a service used by all residents of the area.

The inability of cities through annexation to extend their boundaries to encompass all densely populated areas is another reason for the extension of county functions. As automobiles and highways improved, persons could commute to the heart of the city from greater distances. More people moved to the suburbs and opposed annexation attempts by the central city. In a number of counties, governmental services were not provided to the largely unincorporated suburban areas or were provided by a proliferation of weak special districts. In some counties, residents found county government the natural unit to provide services such as water, sewer, garbage disposal, street construction, street maintenance, fire protection and many other urban servies.

The increase in the number of county functions formerly performed only by municipalities has led to a gradual change in the status of the county. In practice, county government in many urban areas of the nation has changed from the status of a quasi-municipal corporation to one more nearly resembling a municipal corporation. Legal thinking has not fully caught up to this change in practice, however.

As county functions have expanded, counties have hired more and more professional employees and have adopted civil service systems for all or part of their employees. Centralized purchasing, automatic data processing, and modern budget and accounting systems are used extensively by larger counties.

Changes in the organizational structure of counties have come more slowly than changes in functions. In 1917, nearly all counties had the traditional, plural executive form of county government which Gilbertson criticized. Only a few counties, such as Los Angeles County, had reduced the number of independently elected county officials.(56) California and Maryland were the only two states having constitutional provisions which permitted home rule charters, and only four counties (all in California) had home rule charters. During the 1920's there were hardly any changes in the structure of county government with no additional states adopting constitutional home rule provisions and only one county (Alameda County, California) adopting a home rule charter. Although the city manager form of government had been adopted by more than 100 cities, not a single county had adopted this form of government before 1930.

The 1930's brought some significant changes in county government. Ohio and Texas secured home rule constitutional amendments. (57) Four more California counties adopted home rule charters. Six counties changed to the county manager form of government beginning with Durham County, North Carolina in 1930.(58) Westchester and Nassau Counties in New York secured special legislative charters enabling them to adopt an elected county executive form of government.

Since 1940, changes in county government structure have come more rapidly. Missouri, Washington, New York and Oregon secured constitutional home rule provisions. Twenty-nine additional counties adopted the county manager form of government bringing the total manager counties to 35.(59) The county executive plan spread to more than a dozen large counties including St. Louis County, Missouri, Davidson County, Tennessee, Milwaukee County, Wisconsin, Baltimore County, Maryland and Erie, Oneida, and Onondaga Counties in New York. The chief administrative officer plan was first adopted by Los Angeles County in 1948 and has spread to sixteen other large California counties. Seven out of ten of the nation's most populous counties now have a county executive, county manager or some other type of the county administrator form of government. While the traditional, plural executive form of county government is still used by most counties, it is being abandoned by more and more of the nation's largest counties.

Studies of metropolitan area problems have had an indirect effect on county government. Paul Studenski, Albert Lepawsky, Victor Jones and others had, prior to 1945, pointed out the growing number of governmental problems in metropolitan areas. One of the most serious of these problems was the multiplicity of special districts and other small local government units which were too small for effective administration. Coordination of these small local governments was difficult, if not impossible, and piecemeal solutions to serious, area-wide problems were being attempted. The growing concern of political scientists, sociologists, city planners, public administrators and local government officials has resulted in the preparation of studies listing possible solutions to these problems.(60) Several of these solutions involve an expanded role for county government.(61)

One means of solving metropolitan problems is through a service contract by which persons in the unincorporated areas of the county can purchase water, sewer, police and other services from the county or from a city. Los Angeles County has contracted to provide specific services since 1907, and in 1954 the county offered to provide full municipal services by contract to any city.(62) From 1954 to 1962, 29 cities in Los Angeles County chose to receive all or most of their services under contract from the county. Use of the service contract has enhanced the role of the county in resolving area-wide problems.

City-county consolidation and city-county separation are two methods of solving metropolitan problems through combining city and county government. Under city-county separation, the urban area of a county separates from the remainder of the county. In the urban area, there is one government which performs both city and county functions. In the rural area, a second unit of government is formed to provide county functions. City-county separation was used around 1900 to form the city-county governments of Baltimore, Denver, St. Louis and San Francisco.(63) However, the urban area has expanded beyond the limits of these city-counties leaving the areas with almost as many metropolitan problems as before. City-county separation has been used recently only in Virginia and has been criticized as "a product of a bygone rural age."(64) City-county consolidation involves combining city and county government in an entire county area. This plan was used in Boston, Philadelphia, New Orleans, and New York more than fifty years ago but there were no additional city-county consolidations for many years. The mergers of Baton Rouge with East Baton Rouge Parish in 1949 and Nashville with Davidson County in 1962 have caused a renewal of interest in city-county consolidation. About half of America's metropolitan areas lie within the boundaries of single counties, and city-county consolidation may be particularly suited to many of these counties.

Functional consolidation is another metropolitan solution affecting county government. An example is the action by Campbell and Kenton Counties in Kentucky to entrust their planning to the intercounty Northern Kentucky Area Planning Commission.(65) This solution may be particularly useful in metropolitan areas that span county boundaries.

A more commonly used solution to metropolitan problems is the transfer of functions from city to county level. There are many examples of the transfer of metropolitan airports, park systems, expressways, and institutions from city to county jurisdiction. Such transfers usually result in a more equitable distribution of costs over the area in which the services are used. Moreover, the county provides a larger area within which to work out area-wide solutions to these problems.

As these solutions are adopted in many areas of the country, the role of the county is expanding and the image of county government is changing. The average citizen is less likely to picture county officials as political hacks sitting around pot-bellied stoves in the county courthouse today than thirty years ago. The citizen is more likely today to envision capable local officials working in modern office buildings with the latest data processing and other equipment. County government is doing its part to help resolve the serious urban problems facing our nation.

REFERENCES

1. Smaller units of local government in the Anglo-Saxon period included the small rural communities called townships and the hundred composed of several townships. The writer is indebted to John A. Fairlie and Herman G. James for their descriptions of the development of the English county. John A. Fairlie, Local Government in Counties, Towns and Villages (New York: The Century Company, 1914) and Herman G. James, Local Government in the United States (New York: D. Appleton and Company, 1921).

2. Henry S. Gilbertson, The County, The 'Dark Continent' of American Politics (New York: The National Short Ballot Association, 1917), pp. 16 and 17, and Herman G. James, op. cit., pp. 76-82 were used as sources on Virginia colonial local government.

3. George R. Long, "The History of Virginia Highway Administration" (Unpublished paper loaned by the author).

4. H. S. Gilbertson, op. cit., pp. 17, 18; Herman G. James, op. cit., pp. 72-76; and John A. Fairlie, op. cit., pp. 20-26 were used as sources on colonial government in Massachusetts.

5. The New England town differed from the towns or townships that developed in the Middle Atlantic States and Mid-West. The New England town was the unit of government which served the village and rural areas of the town thus usually making unnecessary a separate village government. In the Middle Atlantic States and Mid-West, the township (or town as it was sometimes called) generally was a unit of rural government. Villages within each township usually had their own separate government.

6. John A. Fairlie, op. cit., pp. 27-30 and Herman G. James, op. cit., pp. 82-90 were used extensively as sources for this section.

7. In New York, towns had characteristics more similar to the townships of the Mid-West than the towns of New England.

8. Francis Newton Thorpe, The Federal and State Constitutions, Colonial Charters, and Other Organic Laws of the States, Territories and Colonies (Washington, D. C.: U. S. Government Printing Office, 1909), Vol. 5, p. 2634.

9. John A. Fairlie, op. cit., p. 33.

10. Ibid., pp. 33, 34.

11. Ibid., p. 34 and Francis Newton Thorpe, op. cit., p. 2597.

12. Charles W. Kneier, "The Legal Nature and Status of the American County," 14 Minnesota Law Review 141 (1930).

13. The 1776 Constitution of New Jersey and 1777 Constitution of New York do not specify the structure or functions of city government. A copy of these constitutions may be found in Francis Newton Thorpe, op. cit., pp. 2594-2598 and 2623-2638.

14. State of Maryland v. Baltimore and Ohio RR. 44 U. S. 534,550 (1845).

15. Commissioners of Hamilton County v. Mighels, 7 Ohio St. 109 (1857). This case is quoted at greater length in chapter one. The importance of this legal distinction between cities and counties should not be overemphasized since both are created under state constitutions and laws. The home rule movement has been a struggle by both cities and counties for a source of power more independent of state constitutions and laws.

16. Herman G. James, op. cit., pp. 94, 95.

17. Ibid., p. 100.

18. Indiana modeled its local government after Ohio. Illinois came to establish a system similar. to Ohio's but permitted counties to determine by vote whether to establish townships. Michigan established the New York type of county-township government in which the township supervisors formed the legislative body of the county. Herman G. James, op. cit., pp. 100-102.

19. Article 23 of the 1777 New York Constitution had established a council of appointment composed of the governor and state senators selected by the state Assembly. Francis Newton Thorpe, op. cit., p. 2633.

20. Article 6, Section 1 of the Pennsylvania Constitution of 1790 provided that the voters of each county elect two men for sheriff and two for coroner. The governor then appointed the sheriff and coroner from those elected. In the Pennsylvania Constitution of 1838, the sheriff and coroner were to be elected directly by the county voters. Francis Newton Thorpe, op. cit., pp. 3098, 3111.

21. Francis Newton Thorpe, op. cit., p. 1065.

22. Ibid., p. 1083.

23. Henry S. Gilbertson, op. cit., p. 30.

24. Ibid. A further reason for the election rather than appointment of many county officials was the widespread dislike and distrust of executive authority which went back to the colonial era.

25. Herman G. James, op. cit., p. 96.

26. The fact that the county has formed the base of political parties in most states has given strength to county government. However, excessive use of patronage has plagued county government particularly in the late 1800's and early 1900's.

27. Herman G. James, op. cit., p. 110.

28. James A. Fairlie, op. cit., p. 49.

29. U. S. Bureau of the Census, U. S. Census of Population, 1960, Volume I, Characteristics of the Population (Washington: U. S. Government Printing Office, 1964), Table 3, p. 4.

30. Seymour J. Mandelbaum, Boss Tweed's New York (New York: John Wiley and Sons, Inc., 1965), p. 67.

31. For example, William Tweed purchased 300 benches for $1,500 while a member of the Committee on Armories of the County Board of Supervisors. They were later sold to the county by Tweed's associates for use in county armories at a price of $169,800. Denis T. Lynch, "Boss" Tweed (New York: Boni and Liveright, 1927), p. 241.

32. Gilbertson used this phrase in the title of his book but did not define it.

33. H. S. Gilbertson, op. cit., p. 34. Gilbertson was quoting a Chicago newspaperman whom he did not identify by name.

34. Ibid., p. 44. Gilbertson stated: "In their theory of pure democracy via the ballot, they spread out their interest in county officers so thin that no single officer got sufficient attention to make him realize their influence."

35. Ibid., pp. 49, 50. Gilbertson reasoned that to survive as a functioning unit of government with a splintered executive, counties adopted a boss system.

36. Ibid., p. 50.

37. Ibid., pp. 62, 63. Gilbertson cites a number of examples in which long ballots made it impossible for voters to know the qualifications of county officials. Cook County voters in Illinois at one time voted for 25 elected county officials.

38. Ibid., p. 51.

39. Ibid., pp. 85-93. The overseers of the poor sometimes received a fee for each committment to a county institution and were overzealous in their committments.

40. Ibid., p. 65.

41. Ibid., Chapter 15.

42. Ibid., Chapter 16.

43. Ibid., pp. 169, 170.

44. Gilbertson, for example, comments favorably on the mayor system in the city and county of Denver. Ibid., p. 174.

45. Ibid., p. 175.

46. Ibid., pp. 181–192 and pp. 203, 204. Gilbertson described a case in which good purchasing procedures resulted in a savings of $810,000 in the cost of election supplies.

47. Ibid., p. 193.

48. U. S. Bureau of the Census, Wealth, Debt and Taxation, Volume II, County Revenues, Expenditures and Public Properties, 1913 (Washington, D. C.: U. S. Government Printing Office, 1915), p. 210.

49. Charles M. Kneier, "Development of Newer County Functions," American Political Science Review 24:134, February, 1930.

50. Robert G. Smith, Public Authorities, Special Districts and Local Government (Washington: National Association of Counties Research Foundation, 1964), pp. 180–181 points out the similar, though later, transfer of functions from municipalities to county-wide authorities. These authorities "have called attention to the county as a level for functional integration" and may have had a part in leading to more general acceptance of the county as an effective level of local government.

51. Clyde Snider, Local Government in Rural America (New York: Appleton–Century–Crofts, 1957), p. 366 describes the disadvantages of townships and road districts in highway administration.

52. For an excellent description of changing county functions prior to 1952 see Clyde F. Snider, "American County Government: A Mid–Century Review," American Political Science Review, 46:66–80, March, 1952.

53. Ibid., p. 74.

54. Charles M. Kneier, "Development of Newer County Functions," p. 136.

55. Ibid., p. 139.

56. For a description of the action taken by Los Angeles County in 1912 to reduce its number of elective officials see Richard S. Childs, Civic Victories (New York: Harper and Brothers, 1952), p. 200.

57. Clyde Snider, Local Government in Rural America, p. 106.

58. Ibid., p. 175.

59. Alva W. Stewart, "Well–Managed Counties," National Civic Review, 54:540, November, 1965. Seventeen of these counties are in North Carolina, 4 in Virginia, 4 in Georgia, 3 in California, 2 in Maryland, and 1 in Florida, Montana, Nevada, New York, and Tennessee.

60. These studies are listed in Roscoe C. Martin, <u>Metropolis in Transition</u> (Washington, D. C.: Housing and Home Finance Agency, 1963), p. 3. Perhaps the best known of these studies is Victor Jones, <u>Metropolitan Government</u> (Chicago: University of Chicago Press, 1942).

61. Solutions not described in this chapter will be described in chapter 12.

62. Roscoe C. Martin, <u>op. cit.</u>, pp. 15, 16. In 1966, Los Angeles County provided all municipal services by contract except legal, fiscal, auditing, and administrative services.

63. <u>Ibid.</u>, p. 9.

64. <u>Ibid.</u>

65. <u>Ibid.</u>

2/ THE AMERICAN COUNTY TODAY

"American county government is so complex and lacking in uniformity that its analysis and description become no easy task. County organization varies from state to state, and often among counties of the same state."

Clyde F. Snider,

Local Government in Rural America

(New York: Appleton-Century-Crofts, Inc., 1957), p. 119.

Chapter 3

County Officers

THE MEN AND WOMEN who run our county government come from many different occupations. At a large convention of county officials, one can usually find attorneys, engineers, farmers, physicians, store owners and persons from almost all major occupational groups. County officers, like other local government officials, tend to represent the more important groups in their areas.

There are three types of county officials which will be described in this chapter: (1) county board members, (2) independently elected county officers and (3) elected or appointed executives. The first two groups of officials are found in all counties; the third group is found in a small but growing number of counties. Below these officials on the county organization chart are appointed department heads, unit heads and other county employees.

COUNTY BOARDS

All counties have an official governing body. The most common name for this body is the Board of Commissioners, but it is frequently entitled the Board of Supervisors, County Court, or Commissioners Court.(1) There were thirty-four official titles for county governing bodies in 1965. Despite the variety of official titles, county governing bodies may be divided into three broad categories: the commissioner board, the township supervisor board, and other types of county governing bodies.

The County Commissioner Board

The county board members in about two-thirds of American counties serve primarily as members of the county governing body and do not serve simultaneously as supervisor of a township or in some judicial post.(2)   The commissioner type of county board originated in Pennsylvania in the 1720's and was used in 1965 in 42 states. Three-member county boards are the most common, but five-member boards predominate in California, Minnesota, the Dakotas, North Carolina, Mississippi, and Florida.(3) In Virginia, South Carolina, Georgia, and other states, the size of the county board varies greatly among counties.

The method of electing board members differs from state to state. In Kansas, the three county commissioners in each county are elected by district, and each must be a resident of his district.(4) In Idaho, the three commissioners in each county are elected by the voters of the entire county but must be residents of the commissioner districts that they represent. In Ohio, the three county commissioners are elected at large.(5) The terms of county commissioners vary from state to state with two and four year terms being the most common. To assure greater continuity in county government, many counties have staggered the terms of county commissioners so that only part of the membership of the board faces election each two years. County boards of the commissioner type usually have extensive administrative powers as well as the legislative power to enact such ordninances and regulations as are permitted by state law.

The Township Supervisor Board

The township supervisor type of board originated in New York in colonial times and was found in 1965 in 299 of American counties.(6) It is the predominant form of county government in New York, Michigan, Wisconsin, and Illinois and is found in a few counties in New Jersey.(7) In a county board of this type, the township supervisor acts in a dual capacity: (1) as executive head of his township and (2) as a member of the county governing body. Persons elected or appointed from cities also frequently serve on the county governing body. Thus, most of the members of county boards are both members of the county governing body and officials of other units of local government in the county.

Michigan provides an illustration of the township supervisory board. In Michigan, the board of supervisors consists of one supervisor from each organized township and representatives from the cities within the county.(8) The number of representatives from each city varies with the population of the city, with cities of less than 750 people having one representative and cities of 80,001 to 100,000 people receiving twelve representatives. While representation of city residents on a population basis assures more uniform apportionment, it does result in a large county board of supervisors. The average Michigan county has a 20 to 29 member board of supervisors, and Wayne County (Detroit) has a board of more than 100 members.

The terms of office of the supervisors vary from state to state with one and two year terms being the most common. Large boards of the supervisory type with short terms of office have faced difficulties in performing administrative functions.(9) Frequently, they will rely heavily upon committees of board members to supervise administration. In a growing number of counties, the board has appointed an administrative assistant or administrative officer to help in its supervisory work. In a few counties such as Milwaukee County, Wisconsin, county government has been reorganized so that an elected county executive assumes the administrative functions of the county board leaving the board with its legislative functions.

Other Types of County Governing Bodies

There were 666 counties in 1965 which had neither a commissioner form nor a supervisory form of board.(10) The judge and commissioner board was found in 322 counties in 1965 and is widely used in Alabama, Oregon, and Texas.(11) In many Alabama counties, there are five-member Courts of County Commissioners whose members have no judicial duties.(12) Presiding over this Court of County Commissioners as ex-officio chairman is the Judge of Probate. This judge has no vote in the proceedings of the court except in the event of a tie but is responsible for recording the proceedings of the court, issuing warrants against the county treasury, maintaining financial records, preparing the county budget and performing other fiscal and administrative duties.(13) As probate judge, he has many judicial duties including probating wills and estates and presiding over insanity proceedings. In Texas, counties are governed by a Commissioners Court composed of four commissioners and the county judge.(14) As in Alabama, the County Judge presides over the meetings of the Commissioners Court and may vote only to break a tie. The County Judge has many administrative and financial functions and in some counties has become the unofficial head of county government with many of the responsibilities of a county executive or county manager.(15)

In Oregon, there are 24 counties which have three-member county governing boards composed of a county judge and two commissioners.(16) In seven of these counties, the county judge retains no judicial functions, and these functions in other counties are being transferred to the circuit and district courts. In 1961, the

Association of Oregon Counties secured enactment of a bill which made it permissive for any county whose judge had lost his judicial functions to abolish the position of judge and substitute a third county commissioner. By 1966, twelve Oregon counties were governed by boards composed of three county commissioners.

In 1965, the judge and justice of the peace system was used in 299 counties. In Kentucky counties, the voters elect a County Judge who presides over a Fiscal Court composed of magistrates elected by district.(17) The County Judge acts as chief executive officer of the county and exercises much influence on the actions of the Fiscal Court. As a judicial officer, the County Judge presides over a county court handling minor civil and criminal cases. A somewhat similar system is in operation in most Tennessee counties. Arkansas counties have a variation of this system in which the County Judge has even more power.(18) The justices of the peace, elected from Arkansas townships, compose the Quorum Court which meets primarily to approve the budget submitted by the County Judge and to approve tax levies. Forty-five counties have other forms of county governing boards.(19) These include: boards composed of a single officer as found in some Georgia and South Carolina counties and boards having ex-officio members. In Ramsey County, Minnesota, for example, the Mayor of St. Paul serves as ex-officio chairman of the Board of Commissioners.

One characteristic of nearly all of the 666 counties described in this section is the fact that the county board and/or its presiding officer have judicial as well as legislative and administrative functions. Another characteristic is the strong administrative powers frequently granted the county judge. It is significant that when Davidson County, Tennessee reorganized its judge and justice of the peace form of government to establish a Metropolitan Mayor-Council form, the strong, able County Judge of Davidson County was elected Mayor of the Metropolitan Government of Nashville and Davidson County.(20)

Apportionment of County Governing Bodies

State constitutions and state laws provide the legal basis for the apportionment of county governing bodies. In ten states, the members of the county governing body are elected at large, and apportionment has not been an issue.(21) In states such as California, Kansas, and South Dakota, the members of the county governing body have been elected by district, and apportionment has been an issue. Kansas, for example, requires the board of county commissioners to divide the county into three districts "as compact and equal in population as possible subject to alteration at least once in three years."(22) The Kansas Supreme Court has strictly enforced redistricting particularly in cases in which one commissioner district has contained more than half a county's population. In South Dakota, one study showed that 191 of the state's 282 commissioner districts had a population of more than 15% above or below the national average. South Dakota law provides for districting a county into commissioner districts nearly equal in population but prevents a city from having more than half the commissioner districts. On April 1, 1965, a South Dakota Circuit Court Judge ruled that the later provision of law was in conflict with the Fourteenth Amendment to the Federal Constitution leaving the way open for a change in law or a requirement that all county commissioners be elected at large.(23)

Prior to 1960 in California, the boundaries of supervisory districts had not been changed for sixty years in twenty counties, and there was a significant variation in population between districts in these counties.(24) In Monterey County, California, for example there had been no change in supervisory district boundaries since about 1884, and one supervisory district contained 1.9% of the county's registered voters in January, 1960 while another district contained 48.9% of the registered voters. In August, 1963, the California Supreme Court issued a writ of mandamus ordering the Board of Supervisors in Monterey County to redistrict.(25) Since that time, a bill passed by the California Legislature requires county boards of supervisors to adjust the boundaries of districts so they will be "as nearly equal in population as may be" and establishes guidelines for the county supervisors.(26) If a board of supervisors does not redistrict by a certain date, a commission consisting of the county assessor, district attorney, and county clerk is required to redistrict the county. The new law applied initially to counties operating under general law, but a constitutional amendment passed in November, 1964 extended the law to the remaining counties in the state.(27)

States having a township supervisory board face a particularly difficult problem of apportionment. In Wisconsin, for example, state law provided that each town and city ward elect a representative to the county board. At one time in Dane County, Wisconsin, one supervisor represented 149 persons and another represented 11,634 persons.(28) The Wisconsin Supreme Court invalidated the state law and ruled, in January, 1965, that the "one man, one vote" principle applied to representation on county boards.(29)

Reapportionment of county governing bodies has received support from many county officials. The Board of Directors of the California Supervisors Association endorsed legislation providing for mandatory reapportionment of county supervisory districts.(30) The Wisconsin County Boards Association was reported as favorable to a change in state law which would base county representation more completely on population.(31) Reapportionment has been opposed by other county officials who might be defeated if they were forced to run in more populous districts.

Organization, Meetings, and Compensation of County Boards

Most county boards elect a chairman from among their own members. The chairman has one vote (as do other board members), presides over the board meetings, signs official documents on behalf of the county, and may have other functions which give him a little more prestige and power than other board members.(32) In a smaller number of counties, the presiding officer of the county board is the county judge or a county commissioner elected by the voters. In this case, the presiding officer can usually vote only in case of a tie.(33)

Almost all counties have the staff assistance of a county official who prepares agenda for board meetings, records the actions taken by the board, and performs other clerical and administrative services for the board. Many larger counties have made this the full-time job of an official appointed by the board; in smaller counties the elected county clerk often performs these functions.(34)

Regular sessions of the county board are usually held at least once a month, and adjourned meetings are held if the board cannot dispose of all its business on the regular meeting day. Special sessions of the board are called when action is needed before the next regular board session. In smaller counties, board meetings may be informal with commissioners interrupting the regular agenda when citizens enter to bring information, make requests, or register complaints. In a typical smaller county, Latah County, Idaho, the Commissioners have a small meeting room with a row of chairs on one side and the three commissioners' desks on the other. Whenever a citizen appears at the door, he is courteously asked to be seated, and soon the Commissioners interrupt their agenda to consider his needs — whether it be an application for public assistance, a complaint about his assessment, or a plea for a spraying of weeds along his county road.(35) In more populous counties, the meetings tend to be more formal, and frequently members of the press and a number of administrative officials are present. In metropolitan counties with large boards, the county board room has the appearance of a small state legislative chamber, strict procedural rules govern debate, and the board makes extensive use of committees.(36)

The hours of work and compensation of county board members vary widely. Los Angeles County, California pays its county supervisors $25,000 a year while more than fifty counties pay their commissioners less than $500 a year.(37) Some of the most populous counties pay their commissioners a sufficient amount so that they can devote full-time to county work. In many less populated counties, the salary or per diem allowance of county commissioners is too small to live on, and the commissioners receive their main income from other sources. A 1964 study by the National Association of Counties, shown in Table 1, reports that in nearly half of all counties the members of county boards received $2,500 or less a year. In 172 counties, the presiding officer received a higher salary than the board members. In 15 counties, the presiding officer received over $5,000 a year more than the other board members.

Table 1
ANNUAL SALARY OF COUNTY BOARD MEMBERS, 1964*

Annual Salary	Number of Counties Reporting	Per Cent
Less than $500	51	4.1
$501 – $1,500	240	19.5
$1,501 – $2,500	304	24.7
$2,501 – $4,000	262	21.2
$4,001 – $5,500	142	11.5
$5,501 – $7,000	115	9.3
$7,001 – $9,000	62	5.0
$9,001 – $12,000	51	4.1
More than $12,000	7	.6
	1,234	100.0

*National Association of Counties, *County Officials and Services* (unpublished study), 1964.

The Powers of County Boards

County boards derive their powers directly or indirectly from state constitutions and state laws, and frequently these powers are listed by state law in considerable detail. Since state constitutions and laws vary among states, the powers of county boards also differ. Even within the same state, larger or home rule counties have powers not held by other counties. However, the following general types of powers are granted to most counties.

1. Ordinance-making power. County boards do not have as extensive law-making powers as Congress or state legislatures. Counties are generally limited to enacting those types of ordinances and regulations permitted by state law. In Michigan, for example, counties may pass by a two-thirds vote of the Board of Supervisors "such laws, regulations and ordinances relating to purely county affairs as they may see fit, but which shall not be opposed to the general laws of this state and which shall not interefere with the local affairs of any township, incorporated city or village within the limits of such county.(38) In Idaho, the Board of County Commissioners is given the power to "pass all ordinances and rules and make all regulations, not repugnant to law, necessary for carrying into effect or discharging the powers and duties conferred

by the laws of the State of Idaho.(39) The ordinance-making power
of county governing bodies has generally been narrowly construed
by state Attorney Generals and by courts, but a number of counties
have been able to enact ordinances or regulations on zoning, subdivision controls, trailer courts, and a variety of other matters.
However, lack of a more extensive ordinance-making power is an
important weakness in county government.(40)

2. Fiscal powers. The county board also has a legislative role
in reviewing budget requests of county agencies, appropriating funds,
establishing county tax levies, and incurring indebtedness. However, counties must keep property tax rates and indebtedness within
limits set by state law or constitutions. County boards also have
continuing fiscal responsibilities in the execution of the budget.
Frequently, the county board alone has the power to shift funds
from one appropriation item to another within the county budget.
State law usually gives the county board final responsibility for
allowing claims or bills against the county.(41) The board usually
approves purchases of county land and the awarding of contracts.
The fiscal authority of the county board extends to independently
elected county officers as well as to agencies administered by its
own appointees.

3. Licensing and regulation. County boards in many counties
are authorized to license taverns, carnivals, dance halls, amusement parks, and enterprises of a similar type. Usually this
authority extends only to establishments outside incorporated
municipalities.(42) The license fees collected from taverns and
amusement places help defray the extra cost of policing these
establishments. State law frequently gives county boards other
licensing powers. In South Dakota, the county boards license persons who establish temporary businesses such as fireworks stands
outside municipalities, and in Washington, the county boards are
empowered to license ferries.(43)

4. Appointment powers. The typical county board appoints all
county department heads and officials not elected by the voters. In
less populated counties, most county employees may be appointed
by independently elected officials leaving the county board with the
appointment of only a few full-time employees.(44) As county governments increase in size, county boards usually make more of the
important appointments. Several exceptions should be noted. In
counties having a county manager form of government, the county
board appoints the manager and delegates much of its appointment
power to him. In counties having a county executive form of government, the elected county executive appoints most department heads
subject to confirmation by the county board.

5. Supervision and review of administration. County boards
exercise general supervision over the officials they appoint, and

these officials often appear at county board meetings to report to the board, to describe their problems, and to seek advice. The county board takes a less active role in the supervision of independently elected county officers. County elective officers sometimes appear before the county board to secure additional funds. At meetings of the board, the commissioners may question elective officials about their programs or about some action which has aroused favorable or unfavorable comment in the county.

6. Day to day administrative responsibility. In some counties, particularly small counties, the county board members have day to day administrative responsibility over one or more functions of county government. In a number of Washington counties, for example, the county commissioners have the responsibility for highway administration in their districts and may take direct responsibility for supervising the county engineer.(45) In a number of Idaho counties, the commissioners interview applicants for emergency assistance and issue disbursement orders for food, clothing and other essentials.

7. Judicial powers. Although county governing bodies are not established as judicial agencies, some county boards have minor judicial functions. In Alabama, the Courts of County Commissioners are empowered "to punish for contempt by fine not exceeding ten dollars and imprisonment not exceeding six hours."(46) They may also subpoena witnesses in the same manner as a probate court. The county judge, the presiding officer of the county governing body in several states, does however have significant judicial functions. In many Kentucky counties, the County Judge presides over the County Court, which handles minor civil and criminal offenses, and holds examining trials on more serious cases when the circuit court is not in session.(47)

INDEPENDENTLY ELECTED, "ROW" OFFICERS

In most county governments, administrative responsibilities are divided between the county governing board and a number of independently elected officials. The term "row" officers is sometimes used to describe these officials because their titles appear in a long row in the organization chart of the county. As Table 2 indicates, the most commonly elected row officers are: the sheriff, treasurer, attorney, coroner, court clerk, engineer or surveyor, county clerk, auditor, recorder, assessor and superintendent of schools.(48)

The duties of most independently elected officials are either: financial administration, record keeping, law enforcement, or judicial administration. In many small counties, most county employees are under the supervision of these independently elected

Table 2
INDEPENDENTLY ELECTED COUNTY OFFICES*

Office	Number of States
Sheriff	46
Treasurer	37
Attorney or solicitor	34
Coroner	30
Clerk of court	30
Assessor	26
Surveyor or engineer	25
Recorder or registrar of deeds	24
Superintendent of schools	19
Auditor or comptroller	19
County clerk	18

*Compiled from U. S. Bureau of the Census, *Census of Governments: 1957.* Vol. 1, No. 4. *Elective Officials of State and Local Governments* (Washington: U. S. Government Printing Office, 1957). Not shown on the table are collectors of taxes, registrars of wills, public administrators, constables, elected judicial officials and other county officials found in only a few states.

county officers. As counties grow larger, there is a tendency for a greater proportion of county employees to be under the county governing board or an elected or appointed general executive. The functions of the independently elected county officials are as follows:

County Clerk

An important duty of the county clerk in some counties is serving as secretary to the county board. Frequently he helps compile the budget for the county board. More often he compiles the agenda for the board, records the action of the board, and follows up the meeting by writing letters requested by the board. In a number of counties, the county clerk is the registrar of voters and the recorder of election returns. He may also keep records of births, deaths, marriages, and divorces and may issue licenses. Sometimes the position of county clerk is combined with the position of county recorder, and the individual holding the post will record deeds, mortgages, and a variety of other business transactions. The position of county clerk may also be combined with the position of court clerk and county auditor. (49)

Court Clerk

The court clerk is usually attached to the main trial court of the county. An important function of the court clerk in South Dakota and other states is the collecting and recording of fines, forfeitures, penalties, and costs in criminal cases.(50) The clerk of courts is commonly responsible for keeping records of court proceedings and the actions of the court.(51) The court clerk may sometimes prepare the formal writs and process papers issued by the court. Court clerks usually receive a salary, but some are paid on a fee basis.(52)

Recorder or Registrar of Deeds

The recorder or registrar of deeds has an important role in the orderly transfer of title to property. Persons buying property want to make sure that they will have clear title after their purchase. They will normally request an attorney, abstract company or title-guarantee company to make a title search for them in order to be sure the seller has a clear title. By recording each deed, mortgage, and lease, the recorder or registrar of deeds is providing the records needed for a thorough title search. The recorder also prepares an index to facilitate title searches. In recent years, a number of the larger counties have microfilmed their land records and stored the microfilm in fire-proof vaults.(53)

In many states, county recorders or registrars of deeds also record other important documents such as: marriage licenses, veterans' discharge papers, mining claims, wills, liens, and official bonds. For a fee, a citizen may get a photocopy of these documents from the recorder. In some states, the office of recorder or registrar is combined with another office such as that of county clerk or county auditor.

County Auditor

A common function of the elected county auditor is auditing bills or other claims against the county and preparing warrants in payment of these bills. An audit by the county auditor is made after the goods have been received or services rendered but before payment is made.(54) The auditor will make sure that the goods or services have actually been received, that there is no error in calculating the amount of the charge, and that the agency receiving the goods or services has sufficient funds and the authority to make the expenditure. To insure that county agencies are not overspending their appropriations, it is common for the county auditor to maintain accounting records on all appropriations. County auditors may have a variety of other functions. Some make a post-audit a year or more after payment has been made; others compute or collect property taxes. In some states, the auditor may have all or part of the functions of the county clerk and recorder or registrar of deeds.(55)

County Treasurer

The main function of the county treasurer is to collect county revenues, deposit these funds in banks, and keep records of revenues and bank balances.(56) Frequently the county treasurer will also keep overall records of expenditures by fund. In some counties, the treasurer also participates in the property tax collection process by sending out tax delinquency notices and following up on deliquent taxes. Another function of the county treasurer, which is growing in importance, is the investment of idle funds. Some county treasurers have earned substantial amounts for their counties by carefully determining the amount of idle funds at differing times of the year and investing in government securities.(57) In some counties, the treasurer acts as a public administrator of the estates of persons who die without a will.

Assessor

The county assessor is the key man in the property tax collection process. His principal responsibility is to appraise all property subject to county property taxes.(58) The assessor commonly has extensive maps of all parcels of property in the county and records of the physical characteristics and value of all buildings. When new buildings are built, the assessor and his staff will usually know of this from the issuance of the building permit and will make an inspection to determine the assessed valuation. The assessor frequently is responsible for sending out notices of assessment to property owners so that they may have an opportunity to challenge the assessment if they think that it is excessive. The assessor may also send out the tax notices and collect the property taxes. In some counties, the assessor has numerous non-property tax functions such as issuing automobile license plates and collecting a variety of taxes and fees.

Prosecuting Attorney

The county prosecuting attorney has three main roles. He provides legal advice to the county board and other county officials on a variety of matters and is frequently asked to give an informal opinion on the legality of a proposed action. He represents the county in many types of cases in which the county is a plaintiff or defendent. His third, and probably most important function, is to prosecute in the name of the state persons suspected of crimes. In his third role, the prosecuting attorney commonly calls violations of law to the attention of the grand jury, submits evidence, and draws up an indictment. In some cases, the prosecuting attorney may bring a person to trial without grand jury action.(59) Even more important is the role of the prosecuting attorney in preparing the case against the defendant and conducting this case in the court-room. A number of prosecuting attorneys have won fame through able, energetic prosecution of notorious criminals and have gone on to high elective office.

County Sheriff

The county sheriff and his deputies serve (1) as a police force, (2) as keeper of the county jail, and (3) as officers of the county court system. In many counties, the sheriff's office provides the largest police force in the unincorporated areas and in the small incorporated communities of the county. In most Wisconsin counties, the Sheriff's deputies: patrol highways, streets and parks; use radar to check the speed of motor vehicles; operate the county police radio networks; investigate crimes against persons and property; and maintain systematic records on criminals and juvenile offenders.(60) A number of Wisconsin County Sheriffs also: provide ambulance and rescue services; operate law enforcement training schools; conduct highway safety education programs; and regulate dance halls and amusement parks. In Idaho, the County Sheriff enforces closing hours on taverns, aids in rescuing hunters lost in the mountains, and provides many of the same services as in Wisconsin counties.

The sheriff is usually responsible for the county jail and the custody and feeding of prisoners. In former years, he was commonly allowed a fixed sum per day for prisoners' board and was able to make a substantial profit, but this practice is much less frequent today. In some of Wisconsin's counties, the Sheriff's office provides custody of U. S. prisoners by contract.(61) In many small counties, the sheriff maintains the only jail in the entire county.

The sheriff often acts as a court officer, attending sessions of the court and serving warrants of arrest, summonses to jurors, and subpoenas to witnesses. The sheriff and his deputies may serve process papers on a variety of civil court matters such as divorce or bankruptcy.

In the past two decades, county sheriffs have lost some of their powers in a number of urban counties. In Montgomery County, Maryland, the Department of Police Protection is under a professional police officer appointed by the County Manager. The Montgomery County Sheriff is responsible for serving summons, subpoenas, and other court papers and for transporting prisoners and mental patients to places of trial or confinement. In Nashville-Davidson County, Tennessee, the Sheriff no longer has law enforcement duties but is responsible for process serving and the maintenance of the Metropolitan Jail and Workhouse.(62)

Coroner

The main function of the coroner at the present time is to determine the cause of death of persons who have died by violence, died under suspicious circumstances or died when a physician was not in attendance. In some states, the coroner also holds inquests in accident cases. The coroner commonly examines the body, may have an autopsy performed, and may summon a coroner's jury. In Washington, for example, the coroner is empowered to subpoena witnesses to clear up details surrounding a death and to summon six persons to serve in the coroner's jury at the inquest.(63) The coroner uses the inquest to help him determine the circumstances of the death, and who, if anyone, was responsible. In Washington, the coroner has the power to issue an arrest warrant.(64)

The elected county coroner has been greatly criticized by some writers on government, and the medical examiner system has been proposed as an alternative.(65) Under this plan, the coroner's legal responsibilities are vested in the county prosecuting attorney, and his medical responsibilities, such as performing autopsies, are vested in an appointed medical examiner. The office of coroner has been abolished in a number of counties, or he has been left with nominal duties.

Other Elected County Officials

In states having an elected superintendent of schools, the superintendent serves as a key adviser for the smaller school districts of the county.(66) Financial and statistical reports prepared by these school districts are frequently reviewed for accuracy and completeness by the county superintendent before they are sent to the state department of education. In a number of counties, the county superintendent may provide specialized services for school districts. He and his staff may assist school districts by preparing curriculum guides, maintaining film libraries, and providing remedial reading teachers and other specialists.

The county surveyor is of much less importance today than formerly. His primary duty in the past was to make land surveys and to determine boundary lines upon the request of landowners or the courts. Many states which retain this office have stripped the county surveyor of nearly all of his functions.

Some other elected county officials are found in only a few states. In 1957, there were hide and animal inspectors in a few Texas counties, jailers in many Kentucky counties, and drain commissioners in Michigan counties.(67) By and large, all county "row" officers have one thing in common, they are individually responsible for the administration of one agency of county government. They seldom exercise general supervisory responsibility over all county agencies.

ELECTED OR APPOINTIVE EXECUTIVES

Executive power in most counties is divided between the county board members and "row" officers with no single county official having the executive power that the President has in national government or the governor has in state government. To overcome this lack of unified, executive leadership, a number of counties have adopted a county manager plan, county executive plan, county administrative officer plan or some modification of these plans.

County Manager

In 1965, thirty-five counties had county managers.(68) These counties range in size from Dade County, Florida with a 1960 population of 935,047 to Petroleum County, Montana with a 1960 population of 894. Under the county manager plan, the county governing board appoints a manager as the principal administrative officer of the county. The manager is responsible to the county board and serves at its pleasure. The board retains its legislative and other policy-making functions and delegates a wide range of administrative responsibilities to the manager. While there are differences among counties in the division of responsibility between the county board and the manager, some typical divisions of responsibility are shown in Table 3.

The county manager plan has been credited with bringing greater efficiency to counties using this plan.(69) The success of the plan can be attributed partly to the willingness of the county boards to delegate administrative responsibilities to the manager and partly to the professional abilities of county managers. The county manager profession has attracted a number of able, dedicated men with professional training in administration or engineering and with extensive administrative experience in counties and cities.

County Administrative Officers

A growing number of counties have an appointive executive with some, but not all of the powers of a county manager. Seventeen California counties of over 100,000 population have chief administrative officers. The Chief Administrative Officer of Los Angeles County "acts as over-all manager of county government operations; provides the Board with objective recommendations and data; ....
coordinates, directs, plans and controls administrative operations

Table 3
TYPICAL DIVISIONS OF RESPONSIBILITY
BETWEEN COUNTY BOARD AND MANAGER

	Responsibility of Board	Responsibility of Manager
1. Ordinances	Enacts ordinances and exercises oversight of administration to make sure they are properly enforced.	May prepare drafts of some ordinances. Administers ordinances adopted by the board.
2. Budget	Reviews the budget prepared by the county manager, holds hearings on the budget, and appropriates funds. Establishes tax rates. Exercises general oversight of revenue administration and expenditure trends.	Prepares the annual budget for submission to the board. Provides information and advice to the board during its budget hearings. Administers expenditure controls to keep expenditures within appropriations.
3. Appointments	Appoints and can dismiss county manager. May appoint the members of quasi-legislative commissions and perhaps a few other officials.	Appoints all or most department heads and staff officers.
4. Program administration	Determines broad program policies through the enactment of ordinances, regulations, resolutions, and appropriations. Reviews the operation of programs.	Is responsible to the board for the administration of county programs and reports to the board on these programs. The county manager and his department heads make day-to-day, detailed policy decisions on programs.

pursuant to policies determined by the Board."(70) He has direct administrative supervision over the Divisions of the Budget, Capital Projects, Management, Personnel, Safety, and Special Services. He is directly responsible for the preparation and execution of the annual budget and for maintenance of financial control over departmental activities. He is responsible also for public information services, data processing and management improvement studies, and the coordination of activities of county departments in furnishing contract services to cities.

There are two main differences between the power of California's chief administrative officers and those of county managers. The chief administrative officer usually lacks the power to appoint and remove department heads. His budget powers are generally not quite as strong as a county manager's. Clyde Snider reports that there is substantial satisfaction with the chief administrative officer plan in California, and that it has spread to a number of California cities.(71)

Cuyahoga County, Ohio is one of a number of counties having a variation of the chief administrative officer plan. The County Board in Cuyahoga County appoints an administrative assistant to coordinate the work of county departments and to assist the Board in its budgeting, purchasing and supervisory functions.(72) Hamilton County (Tennessee), Clark County (Nevada), Charleston County (South Carolina) and Lane County (Oregon) are other counties having somewhat similar types of county government.(73)

County Executives

There is an increasing number of counties having some form of county executive. In Milwaukee County, Wisconsin, the County Executive has powers similar in many respects to those of the President or a strong state governor.(74) He is elected by the voters of the entire county for a term of four years and has the power to appoint and remove most department heads. He is responsible for the administration of county government and prepares an annual budget for submission to the County Board. Like the President, he is not a member of the legislative body but does present a recommended legislative program to the Board. He has the right to veto an ordinance or resolution by the County Board, but the Board may repass it over his veto by a two-thirds vote. The Metropolitan Mayor of Nashville-Davidson County, Tennessee and the County Executives of Westchester and Nassau Counties in New York have similar powers.

The county executive plan provides the same strength and stability to county government that the Presidential system provides national government. The office of county executive has attracted a number of able, popular political leaders whose talents compare favorably with the governors of their respective states. Well known in their counties, they have accepted responsibility for the executive branch of county government in a way that enhances the responsiveness of county government to the will of its citizens.

In some counties, an elected executive exercises part of the powers of the county executive but does not have full administrative responsibility. In a few New Jersey counties, the elected county supervisor is the principal executive officer of the county but lacks the power of appointment.(75) He has no staff under his direct control and must depend upon the general county staff to implement

Table 4
COUNTIES OF 250,000 OR MORE HAVING A COUNTY
ADMINISTRATOR OR EXECUTIVE*

	Type of Admin- istrator		Type of Admin- istrator
Counties of over 1 million		**Counties of 250,000 to 499,999**	
Cook (Chicago, Illinois)	BC	Baltimore (Maryland)	E
Cuyahoga (Cleveland, Ohio)	A	Berks (Reading, Pennsylvania)	BC
Erie (Buffalo, New York)	E	Bernalillo (Albuquerque, N.M.)	A
Los Angeles (California)	A	Contra Costa (California)	A
Milwaukee (Wisconsin)	E	Davidson (Nashville, Tennessee)	E
Nassau (New York)	E	Fairfax (Virginia)	M
San Diego (California)	A	Fresno (California)	A
		Kent (Grand Rapids, Michigan)	A
Counties of 500,000 to 1,000,000		Kern (Bakersfield, California)	A
Alameda (Oakland, California)	A	Knox (Knoxville, Tennessee)	J
Bergen (Patterson, New Jersey)	A	Lucas (Toledo, Ohio)	A
Dade (Miami, Florida)	M	Luzerne (Wilkes-Barre, Pa.)	A
Franklin (Columbus, Ohio)	A	Macomb (Michigan)	A
Fulton (Atlanta, Georgia)	M	Mahoning (Youngstown, Ohio)	A
Hamilton (Cincinnati, Ohio)	A	Mecklenburg (Charlotte, N.C.)	M
Hennepin (Minneapolis, Minn.)	A	Montgomery (Maryland)	M
Honolulu (Honolulu, Hawaii)	E	New Castle (Wilmington, Del.)	A
Hudson (New Jersey)	E	Oneida (Utica, New York)	E
Jefferson (Louisville, Kentucky)	J	Onondaga (Syracuse, New York)	E
Maricopa (Phoenix, Arizona)	A	Pinellas (Clearwater, Florida)	A
Monroe (Rochester, New York)	M	Prince Georges (Maryland)	A
Montgomery (Dayton, Ohio)	A	Riverside (California)	A
Montgomery (Pennsylvania)	A	San Joaquin (California)	A
Oakland (Pontiac, Michigan)	A	San Mateo (California)	M
Orange (California)	A	Tulsa (Oklahoma)	CL
Sacramento (California)	M		
St. Louis (Missouri)	E		
San Bernardino (California)	A		
Santa Clara (San Jose, Calif.)	M		
Suffolk (New York)	E		
Summit (Akron, Ohio)	A		
Westchester (New York)	E		

*SOURCE: *The Municipal Yearbook, 1962.* (Chicago: International City Managers' Association, 1962), pp. 74-78 was one source of information for this table. Supplementing this source was information from the National Association of Counties, *County Officials and Services* (unpublished study of 1,667 reporting counties, 1964). The symbols used are as follows:

    A — Chief administrative officer or administrator
    BC — President or chairman of the board who has executive powers
    CL — County clerk or court clerk having executive or administrative powers
    E — Elected county executive
    J — County judge having executive powers
    M — County manager

his directives. Furthermore, the county supervisor is not responsible for preparing the budget or regulating expenditures. The elected county clerks in many Wisconsin counties have informally exercised many of the powers of a county executive. They normally serve as staff to the county board, maintain the accounting records, pre-audit bills for payment, and prepare the preliminary county budget. Strong, able county clerks, who have served several terms of office, have established for themselves a commanding position in many Wisconsin counties. In Arkansas, the county judge has also assumed strong executive powers. In other southern states, the probate judge, board chairman, commissioner of roads, or some other elective official has been given many executive powers.

Trend in Metropolitan Counties

In metropolitan counties, there is an increasing trend towards the use of appointed or elected county executives. Seven of the ten counties in the United States having populations of more than a million people in 1960 have some form of appointive or elective executive. Half of the counties of more than 250,000 population have these forms of county government. (Table 4 on page 58)

COUNTY EMPLOYEES AND COUNTY ASSOCIATIONS

County governments had a total of 752,000 full-time employees and 111,000 part-time employees in 1962 according to the U. S. Bureau of Census.(76) Exclusive of teachers, three per cent of the full-time county employees made $9,000 or more in 1962, 13% made $6,000-$8,999, 59% made $3,000-$5,999, and 25% received less than $3,000.(77) County median salaries are below those of federal, state, and municipal government, and this is one problem faced by many counties in attracting the most capable personnel.(78)

Most counties are without formal civil service systems. The New York and Ohio constitutions require counties to have merit systems. A number of counties in California, New Jersey and Maryland also have civil service systems as well as a scattering of counties in other states. One writer estimated that in 1957 about 10% of American counties had civil service machinery for making appointments on the basis of competitive examination.(79) Some of these counties have civil service commissions; others appoint personnel officers; still others are served by state personnel agencies.

The trend, particularly in urban counties, is toward increasing professionalization of county government and increasing use of merit systems. Montgomery County, Maryland, typical of the many forward looking counties, has a comprehensive civil service system which covers more than 95% of all county employees exclusive of those in the school system. The county has recruited key staff personnel at levels in excess of $10,000 per year and has an outstanding professional training program for police officers. Los Angeles County has a comprehensive civil service system and an employee training program including an exceptional administrative internship program. Graduates of this internship program have had outstanding records in city, county, state and federal positions.(80) Dade County (Florida), Nashville–Davidson County (Tennessee), Milwaukee County (Wisconsin), Westchester, Nassau, Erie, Onondaga, and Monroe Counties (New York) are a few of the growing number of urban counties with professional staffs which would compare favorably with comparable staffs in better state governments.

State Associations of County Officials

State associations of county officials exist in 44 states and have done much to improve county government.(81) They have been instrumental in securing improvements in state laws affecting counties. In 1964, the Oregon Association of Counties developed a county charter, and in 1963–64 it prepared a comprehensive study of road needs. The Maryland County Commissioners Association has worked closely with the Maryland Legislative Council Committee on Local Legislation in its study of local government in Maryland. The County Supervisors Association of California successfully worked to secure legislation providing a more rational county–wide approach to annexation and special district problems in the state.

State associations have been active also in educational and training programs. In 1964, the Association of Minnesota Counties published an Information Manual for Minnesota Commissioners, and the Association of Georgia County Commissioners wrote a forty page budget manual. The Washington State Association of Elected County Officials has published a suggested code of ethics for its members. The California County Supervisors Association has an internship program to stimulate the training of able young men for careers in county government.(82) All of the state associations have annual conferences, and many have had schools and training institutes for county officials. The Florida Association of County Commissioners, for example, had a short course for county commissioners in 1963, and the New Jersey Association had a two day workshop. Washington State University conducted an institute for county commissioners in 1965. The Iowa Association of County Officials has sponsored five district workshops for county officials, and associations in Minnesota, Georgia, Wyoming and Tennessee have helped in sponsoring property tax seminars for local assessors. The Oregon Association of Counties cooperates with universities, community colleges, and state civil service officials to expand in–service training of county employees.

State associations of county officials provide a valuable clearing house for information on county government. Fifteen state associations published magazines in 1962, and twenty-one state associations published newsletters. State associations in California, Idaho, Iowa, Michigan, Minnesota, North Carolina, New York, Oregon, Utah, Virginia, Washington, and Wyoming publish digests of state laws affecting county government immediately following the state legislative sessions. The California Supervisors Association receives and digests important ordinances of California counties.

In many states, each group of independently elected officers has its own association. Most of these associations have annual conventions at which legislation passed at the last legislative session or proposed new legislation is considered. They have an influence on state legislation and provide a clearinghouse for information for their members.

National Association of Counties

The National Association of Counties, the national counterpart of the state associations of counties, has contributed to many improvements in county government since its establishment in 1936. Noteworthy are the publications and information services of the Association which help keep county officials up-to-date on developments in other counties and at the national level. The Association publishes a monthly journal, American County Government which contains news of national legislation and administrative programs having an impact on county government and descriptions of outstanding county programs.(83) With the aid of an $185,000 grant from the Ford Foundation, the Association has greatly increased its research and reporting activities since 1958 and will expand them still further with a $300,000 Ford Foundation grant for 1963-1967.(84) The Association has established a research foundation which has among its accomplishments the publication of Public Authorities, Special Districts and Local Government by Robert G. Smith. The Association presently has a county information service which offers its subscribers ten informational services.(85) These include: a weekly County Letter providing brief news on new county developments; the Washington Report which describes federal legislation of significance to counties; a Public Lands Newsletter; and information reports on nearly thirty subjects such as civil defense, records management, and cooperative purchasing. Subscribers also receive the use of the Association's lending library and research services.

Like the state associations, the National Association of Counties holds an annual conference. Recent conferences have been organized around specific themes such as county planning, the urban county, or county information services. The panel presentations and speeches have usually been published. The conference attracts not only the leading county officials in the nation but national political leaders. President Johnson, Senator Goldwater, and Senator Humphrey spoke at the 29th annual Association conference in August, 1964. Regional conferences are also sponsored by the National Association of Counties, and it cooperates with state associations of county officials in helping to provide programs for state association meetings.

The National Association of Counties has its general offices in Washington, D. C. and represents county government before congressional committees and federal administrators. The Association, in the past decade, has taken a positive approach to national problems and has worked closely with congressmen and federal officials in solving problems of water pollution, civil defense, mass transit, recreation, and poverty. Characteristic of this approach is the series of articles in The County Officer, which describes the economic problems of rural counties and the steps taken by these counties to attract industry and alleviate poverty.(86) This approach is also reflected in the extensive research being carried on by the National Association on water pollution problems and solutions. The National Association is a dynamic organization dedicated to advancing the interests of county government through helping to solve some of the more serious problems facing county government.

Associated with the National Association of Counties are a series of functional organizations for county officials such as the National Association of County Engineers, the National Association of County Administrators, the National Association of County Recorders and Clerks, the National Association of County Treasurers and Finance Officers, and the National Association of County Civil Attorneys.(87) News from each of these associations is printed in American County Government, and each association has its own annual meeting. County officials have also joined other professional organizations such as the American Public Welfare Association, American Public Works Association and National Association of Assessing Officers.

SUMMARY

County officials come from almost all major occupational groups and tend to represent the more important groups in their areas. Two types of county elective officials are found in all counties: county board members and independently elected "row" officers. County board members not only have legislative functions but usually have administrative powers of appointment, regulation and supervision. This administrative responsibility is shared in many counties with independently elected officials such as the county clerk, auditor, sheriff, assessor, treasurer, prosecuting attorney, coroner, and engineer.

An appointive or elective executive holds key administrative powers in a growing number of counties. In thirty-five counties, a county manager has been appointed by the county board and is made responsible for most county administrative functions. In other counties, a chief administrative officer, appointed by the board, exercises many of the powers of the county manager. In still other counties, an elected county executive or mayor has become the chief executive in the county and holds much the same relationship to the county board as the President holds to Congress. Many of the most populous counties in the nation have adopted these newer forms of county government.

The last two decades have brought an extension of civil service and professionalization to county government. This trend has been stimulated by state associations of county officials and The National Association of Counties. These associations are playing a part in helping to solve serious national problems in fields such as welfare, pollution, recreation, and transportation.

REFERENCES

1. A tabulation of the titles of all county governing bodies may be found in: U. S. Bureau of the Census, Governing Bodies of County Governments: 1965 (Washington: U. S. Government Printing Office, 1965), p. 3. The governing body is entitled Board of Commissioners in 1,281 counties, Board of Supervisors in 676 counties, Commissioners Court in 254 counties, County Court in 197 counties, and Boards of Commissioners of Roads and Revenue in 125 counties. Fiscal Court, Quarterly Court, Police Jury and Court of Commissioners are other commonly used titles.

2. This was true in 2,084 counties having boards of commissioners or supervisors in 1965. Ibid., p. 2.

3. Ibid., pp. 3, 14-46 lists the number of county board members in each county. There are 1,330 counties with a three-member county board and 914 counties with a five-member county board.

4. William H. Cape, County Government in Kansas (Lawrence: University of Kansas, 1958), p. 13.

5. Matthew Holden, County Government in Ohio (Cleveland: Cleveland Metropolitan Services Commission, 1958), p. 5.

6. U. S. Bureau of the Census, Governing Bodies of County Governments: 1965, p. 2.

7. Ibid., pp. 14-46.

8. Bureau of Social and Political Research, Michigan State University, The County Board of Supervisors (East Lansing: Michigan State University, 1959), p. 6. On January 1, 1958, there were 1,263 township supervisors and 830 board members representing cities on the boards of supervisors in Michigan's 83 counties.

9. For an extensive discussion of the contrasting advantages of large and small boards, see Clyde F. Snider, Local Government in Rural America (New York: Appleton-Century-Crofts, Inc., 1957), pp. 135-137 and James M. Collier, County Government in New Jersey (New Bruns- wick, N. J.: Rutgers University Press, 1953), pp. 12-14.

10. U. S. Bureau of the Census, Governing Bodies of County Govern- ments: 1965, p. 2.

11. Ibid.

12. James D. Thomas, A Manual for Alabama County Commissioners (University, Alabama: University of Alabama, 1963), p. 10.

13. Ibid., pp. 23, 24.

14. Wilbourn E. Benton, Texas, Its Government and Politics (Engle- wood Cliffs, N. J.: Prentice-Hall, Inc., 1961), p. 422.

15. Ibid., pp. 423, 424. Benton states that "the position of the county judge in county government depends in no small measure, upon the abili- ties and personality of the man who occupies the office."

16. Kenneth C. Tollenaar, Executive Secretary, Association of Oregon Counties, letter dated January 3, 1966.

17. Paul Wager, County Government Across the Nation (Chapel Hill: The University of North Carolina Press, 1950), pp. 390-391.

18. Ibid., p. 528.

19. U. S. Bureau of the Census, Governing Bodies of County Govern- ments: 1965, pp. 2, 46.

20. See chapter 10 on the government of Davidson County, Tennessee.

21. In Maine, Massachusetts, Nevada, New Jersey, Ohio, Oregon, Penn- sylvania, Utah, Vermont and Wyoming, the members of county governing bodies are elected at large in all or nearly all counties. U. S. Bureau of the Census, Governing Bodies of County Governments: 1965, p. 7. In states such as Colorado, Idaho, and Montana, in which county board members are elected at large but must reside in a commissioner district, apportionment may become an issue.

22. Stuart C. Hall, County Supervisorial Districting in California, 1961 Legislative Problems: No. 5 (Berkeley: Bureau of Public Administra- tion, University of California, 1961), p. 165.

23. National Civic Review, 54:264, 282, May, 1965.

24. Stuart C. Hall, op. cit., p. 124 lists twenty counties in which no adjustment of county supervisory boundaries occurred between 1900 and 1959. He also lists, on pages 121 through 123, the number of registered voters per supervisory ditrict in all California counties.

25. National Civic Review, 52:558, 559, November, 1963.

26. Earlier state legislation gave the supervisors discretionary authority to reapportion. Under the new legislation, the population in any three of the five supervisory districts must equal at least half of the total population of the county. National Civic Review, 53:446, September, 1964.

27. National Civic Review, 54:91, February, 1965.

28. Stuart C. Hall, op. cit., pp. 160, 161.

29. National Civic Review, 54:96, February, 1965. Milwaukee and Menominee Counties were not affected by this ruling since they were not subject to the state law that was invalidated.

30. National Civic Review, 53:446, September, 1964.

31. National Civic Review, 54:96, February, 1965.

32. In South Dakota, for example, the board members elect a chairman annually from among their members. The chairman presides at the meetings of the board, casts one vote in board meetings, and signs all orders of the board and warrants drawn on the county treasurer. William H. Cape, Handbook for South Dakota County Officials (Vermillion: University of South Dakota, 1961), pp. 7, 8.

33. This is true in Alabama counties having a judge of probate as presiding officer. James D. Thomas, op. cit., p. 23.

34. Montgomery County, Maryland (see chapter 9) is an example of a county with an appointive county clerk; Latah County, Idaho (see chapter 8) is an example of a county in which the elected county clerk acts as staff for the county board.

35. See chapter 8 on Latah County, Idaho.

36. This is true in Milwaukee County, Wisconsin described in chapter 11.

37. National Association of Counties, County Officials and Services (unpublished study), 1964.

38. Bureau of Social and Political Research, Michigan State University, op. cit., p. 22. The term "purely county affairs" has been given a restrictive meaning in many cases. For example, counties cannot pass ordinances in Michigan limiting the speed of motor boats in lakes within the county. Ibid., p. 24.

39. Idaho Revised Code, Section 31-714. This section of law also gives the Board of County Commissioners broad additional powers to pass ordinances and regulations necessary for the safety, health, prosperity, comfort and convenience of county residents.

40. Bureau of Social and Political Research, Michigan State University, op. cit., p. 24 describes a number of limitations placed by rulings of Michigan Attorney Generals on the ordinance-making powers of the county boards of supervisors.

41. Alabama Law, for example, gives its Courts of County Commissioners the authority to "examine, settle, and allow all accounts and claims chargeable against the county." James D. Thomas, op. cit., p. 15.

42. South Dakota, for example, gives counties the power to license dance halls and establishments selling liquor outside municipalities. William Cape, Handbook for South Dakota County Officials, pp. 26-28.

43. Ibid., p. 202 and Barbara Byers, County Government in Washington State (Olympia: Washington State Association of County Commissioners, 1957), p. 31.

44. In Latah County, Idaho, for example, the county board appoints only two full-time employees but does appoint the unpaid members of a number of commissions and boards.

45. Barbara Byers, op. cit., p. 31.

46. James D. Thomas, op. cit., p. 15.

47. Paul Wager, op. cit., p. 391.

48. County and probate court judges are also elected by the voters of many counties. They are part of the state and local court system and are not usually county executive officials. Their work is briefly described under the heading "Judicial Administration" in chapter 4.

49. In Idaho, the position of county clerk is combined with the positions of court clerk, auditor, and recorder.

50. William H. Cape, Handbook for South Dakota County Officials, p. 63.

51. Barbara Byers, op. cit., pp. 95-108 has an extensive description of the County Clerk in Washington. This official, who acts mainly as a court clerk, is responsible for recording: the names of cases tried, the names of the attorneys in these cases, the witnesses and jurors in the cases, a summary of court action each day, and many other court matters. From his records, the clerk can compute the costs of a case.

52. In Alabama, Clerks of the Circuit Court are elected for a term of six years and some are paid from fees. James D. Thomas, op. cit., p. 26.

53. Some county records have been stored underground. The County Officer, August, 1963, p. 328 describes the use of a former salt mine in Kansas to store public and corporate records. Cook County, Illinois and Shelby County, Tennessee have leased space in the Kansas salt mine. The County Officer, 29:88, February, 1964.

54. This is called a pre-audit in accounting. A post-audit is an audit after the payment is made.

55. In Washington, for example, the county auditor collects the real estate transaction tax and records articles of incorporation, and marriage licenses. Barbara Byers, op. cit., pp. 10-14.

56. Michigan state law, for example, requires the county treasurer to "receive all money belonging to the county and.... to exhibit his books and accounts to the board of supervisors at its annual meeting or such other time as it may determine." Bureau of Social and Political Research, Michigan State University, op. cit., p. 100.

57. The County Officer, 28:388, October, 1963 describes the programs of Ohio county treasurers for investing idle funds. In 1962, Cuyahoga County collected $2,891,000 in interest from its idle funds.

58. A more detailed description of the property tax assessment and collection process may be found in chapter 5.

59. An alternative to grand jury indictment, the information method, is described by Clyde F. Snider, op. cit., p. 338.

60. Bureau of Government, University of Wisconsin, County Government Activities in Wisconsin (Madison: University of Wisconsin, 1961), pp. 41-43.

61. Ibid., p. 43.

62. See chapter 9 on Montgomery County, Maryland and chapter 10 on Nashville-Davidson County, Tennessee.

63. Barbara Byers, op. cit., p. 119.

64. Ibid.

65. Clyde F. Snider, op. cit., pp. 331-335 presents a number of criticisms of the office of coroner and a description of the medical-examiner system. Wayland Pilcher, The Medical Examiner in Texas (Austin: Institute of Public Affairs, University of Texas, 1959) describes the history of the medical examiner system in the United States and its use in four Texas counties.

66. South Dakota encourages its County Superintendents to actively contact schools by requiring them to visit every school under their supervision at least once a year. The County Commissioners are authorized to deduct $10 from the County Superintendent's salary for each school under his supervision that he does not visit each year. William H. Cape, Handbook for South Dakota County Officials, p. 86.

67. U. S. Bureau of the Census, Census of Governments: 1957, Vol. 1, No. 4. Elective Offices of State and Local Governments, pp. 32, 40 and 84.

68. Alva W. Stewart, "Well-Managed Counties," National Civic Review, 54:540, November, 1965.

69. Clyde F. Snider, op. cit., pp. 176-180 provides an extensive description of the advantages of a county manager form of government.

70. County of Los Angeles, <u>Guide to Departmental Organization and Functions</u> (Los Angeles: County of Los Angeles, 1965), p. 21.

71. Clyde F. Snider, <u>op. cit.</u>, p. 185.

72. The responsibilities of the Cuyahoga County Administrative Officer are described by Matthew Holden, <u>op. cit.</u>, p. 7.

73. In Lane County, Oregon, the Director of the General Services Department serves as county administrative officer.

74. See chapter 11 on Milwaukee County government.

75. James M. Collier, <u>County Government in New Jersey</u> (New Brunswick, New Jersey: Rutgers University Press, 1953) p. 16.

76. U. S. Bureau of the Census, <u>Census of Government, 1962</u>, Vol. 3. <u>Compendium of Public Employment</u> (Washington: U. S. Government Printing Office, 1963) p. 19.

77. <u>Ibid.</u>, p. 26. The 1962 salary figures were based on the annual rate of pay in October, 1962.

78. The median annual salary rate in October, 1962 was $5,390 for federal civilian employees, $4,224 for non-teaching state employees, $4,824 for non-teaching municipal employees, and $4,062 for non-teaching county employees. <u>Ibid.</u>, p. 26.

79. Clyde F. Snider, <u>op. cit.</u>, p. 162.

80. Positions held by former interns include: Minnesota Commissioner of Corrections, County Manager of San Mateo County, and Head of the Hospital Management and Planning Unit in the U. S. Bureau of the Budget. County of Los Angeles, <u>Administrative Trainee Biography</u>, 1933-62 (Los Angeles: County of Los Angeles, 1962), pp. 124, 142, 146.

81. Alastair McArthur, "State Associations of County Officials in 1964," in <u>The Municipal Yearbook</u>, 1965, p. 72. The writer is indebted to articles by Mr. McArthur in the 1965, 1964, 1963, and 1962 Municipal Yearbooks for most of the material in this section on state associations of county officials.

82. For a more extensive description of the California internship program, see Bernard Hillenbrand, "California Internship Program Launched in Counties by CSAC," <u>The County Officer</u>, 29:19, January, 1964.

83. The name of the journal, <u>The County Officer</u>, was changed in April, 1965 to <u>American County Government</u>. The history of the monthly magazine is described in <u>American County Government</u>, April, 1965, pp. 12, 13.

84. The grants are described in <u>The County Officer</u>, 28:235, June, 1963.

85. For further information on this service, write to the National Association of Counties, 1001 Connecticut Avenue, N. W., Washington 6, D. C. See also <u>The County Officer</u>, 29:265, June, 1964.

86. The County Officer, 29:209-211, May, 1964, and The County Officer, 29:257-260, June, 1964.

87. Other organizations affiliated with the National Association of Counties include the National Association of County Parks and Recreation Officials, and the National Association of County Planning Directors.

Chapter 4

County Services

HOW MANY SERVICES does your county government provide its citizens? Ask this question of a farmer in a sparsely populated, rural county, and he may be able to name only a dozen services. He will be able to describe the value to him of the county agent, weed control supervisor, 4-H program, and county fair. He will also be able to list some of the functions of the county sheriff, auditor, assessor, treasurer, prosecuting attorney, and public health nurse. Ask the same question of an attorney in a metropolitan county, and he may be able to name several dozen functions ranging from building expressways to operating the county airport, park system, and zoo. Both the farmer and the attorney are likely to understate the actual number of functions that their counties perform since few lists of these functions have ever been compiled.

The exact number of services performed by all counties in the United States is not known. A comprehensive list of the services performed by counties in one state, however, was compiled by the Bureau of Government of the University Extension Division of the University of Wisconsin.(1) The Bureau found 375 identifiable activities performed by Wisconsin county governments as of June 30, 1958.(2) Milwaukee County, the most populous county in Wisconsin, performed 285 government activities, the largest number of any county in the state.(3) The fourteen counties having the next greatest population tended to provide more services than the remaining counties. Florence County, Wisconsin, with next to the lowest population in the state, performed the fewest functions.(4) A similarly comprehensive listing of county services has not been made on a nation-wide basis. It is possible, however, that if officials in all counties were questioned, a list of more than 500 county functions might be compiled.

National surveys have been made of county performance of selected functions. A 1962 survey of 221 county governments showed that: 69% provided police services to unincorporated areas of the county, 51% provided street construction, 45% libraries, and 40% parks and recreation. There were zoning ordinances in 47% of these counties and subdivision regulations in 61%.(5) This study was significant in that most of the functions studied are generally considered by many citizens to be only performed by cities.

A more extensive study was made in 1964 by the National Association of Counties. Questionnaires were sent to 3,043 counties, and county officials were asked to check whether they performed any of a list of 36 selected functions. A total of 1,667 questionnaires were returned and the data was tabulated by county population class.(6)

The study shows (see Table 1) that a surprisingly high per cent of counties perform urban functions such as planning, zoning, industrial development, parks and recreation. A high proportion of counties also provide the more traditional county services such as assessing, tax collecting, welfare, and roads. The study shows also that the practice of a county furnishing services jointly with another unit of government is widespread particuarly in the fields of health, welfare, library, and mental health services.

Table 2 shows the per cent of reporting counties of various population classes which provide services by themselves or jointly with another unit of government. The per cent of counties furnishing each type of service generally varies with the population class of the county. For example, 65% of all reporting counties of 250,000 or more persons report that they engage in zoning; whereas only 15% of those of 10,000 persons or less report that they provide zoning. In seven of the more traditional functions of county government, however, the per cent of counties providing service does not diminish significantly as the population of the county decreases. These seven functions, which counties have performed in rural areas for many years, are assessment, elections, fairs, fire protection, roads, tax collection, and welfare. Thus, there is a tendency for larger counties to provide more services than less populous counties with respect to most, but not all, functions of county government.

Two additional distinctions need to be made to further clarify the role of the county in providing governmental services. There is an important (though overemphasized) distinction between services which counties are required to provide by state law and services which are optional to counties under state law. In almost all states, five of the required functions are administration of justice, care of prisoners, welfare, the recording of deeds, and election administration. Examples of optional functions are air pollution

Table 1

PER CENT OF REPORTING COUNTIES FURNISHING SERVICES IN 1964

| | County Furnishes Service Alone | County Furnishes Jointly With | | | | |
		Cities	Other Counties	State	Other**	Total
Agriculture	60%	*	*	8%	*	69%
Air Pollution	3	1	*	*	*	5
Airports	24	7	*	*	*	32
Assessing	73	6	*	1	*	81
Child Guidance	24	1	2	1	*	28
Civil Defense	75	6	1	3	1	86
Clinics	24	1	1	2	*	28
Education	46	1	*	3	*	51
Elections	82	3	*	2	*	87
Fairs	56	1	*	1	*	58
Fire Protection	34	7	*	1	3	45
Health	58	5	3	7	1	74
Hospitals	42	2	1	1	1	47
Homes for the Aged	35	*	*	1	*	37
Industrial Development	23	4	*	*	*	27
Libraries	47	8	2	1	1	59
Mental Health	30	1	5	4	1	41
Parks	34	2	*	1	*	37
Planning	34	4	1	*	*	39
Ports	3	*	*	*	*	5
Recreation	25	3	*	*	*	28
Refuse Collection	9	3			*	12
Refuse Disposal	16	2	*	*	*	19
Roads	77	2	*	4	*	84
Sewers	13	4	*	*	1	18
Sheriff (court functions)	80	*		*	*	81
Sheriff (police functions)	75	1		*	*	77
Social Centers	6	1	*	*	*	8
Special Purpose Hospitals	12	*	1	1	*	14
Tax Collecting	78	4	*	*	*	83
Traffic Engineering	15	1		*	*	16
Urban Renewal	5	1		*		6
Water Supply	14	4	*	*	1	19
Welfare	74	2	1	14	*	91
Youth Institutions	11	*	*	1	*	13
Zoning	29	4	*	*	*	33

SOURCE: National Association of Counties, *County Officials and Services* (unpublished study of 1,667 reporting counties, 1964).

*Less than .5% of all counties.

**County furnishes service jointly with a city and county, with a semi-independent commission, or with the state and some other governmental unit.

Table 2

PER CENT OF REPORTING COUNTIES OF VARIOUS POPULATION CLASSES PROVIDING SERVICES BY THEMSELVES OR JOINTLY WITH ANOTHER UNIT OF GOVERNMENT

	Population Class of County					
	250,000 and over	100,000 249,999	50,000 99,999	25,000 49,999	10,000 24,999	Below 10,000
Agriculture	79%	75%	74%	74%	70%	60%
Air Pollution	34	11	5	2	2	2
Airports	45	39	27	33	31	27
Assessing	75	74	72	82	82	85
Child Guidance	58	47	40	29	22	15
Civil Defense	93	94	94	85	85	79
Clinics	69	50	38	26	23	17
Education	76	55	45	53	53	43
Elections	88	89	83	87	87	88
Fairs	48	44	54	60	60	61
Fire Protection	47	42	46	41	44	49
Health	82	79	82	81	75	61
Hospitals	75	49	46	52	43	40
Homes for the Aged	70	57	55	45	31	19
Industrial Development	44	40	33	30	26	18
Libraries	72	65	61	64	57	55
Mental Health	67	58	50	39	38	30
Parks	78	50	40	31	34	29
Planning	90	76	58	42	30	20
Ports	10	5	5	4	3	2
Recreation	64	40	34	26	26	19
Refuse Collection	23	13	12	14	12	10
Refuse Disposal	43	27	22	21	17	10
Roads	94	87	79	83	82	87
Sewers	49	25	18	16	15	15
Sheriff (court functions)	95	87	81	85	79	77
Sheriff (police functions)	82	76	76	80	78	70
Social Centers	20	11	8	7	7	4
Special Purpose Hospitals	51	31	19	16	8	4
Tax Collecting	83	81	77	85	84	83
Traffic Engineering	64	38	26	14	9	5
Urban Renewal	24	14	8	7	3	2
Water Supply	40	23	17	18	18	19
Welfare	91	89	87	90	91	93
Youth Institutions	69	41	15	12	5	4
Zoning	65	61	47	36	28	15

SOURCE: National Association of Counties, *County Officials and Services* (unpublished study of 1,667 reporting counties, 1964).

control, zoning, parks, and recreation. While it is not possible to separate mandatory from optional functions in Tables 1 and 2, it is obvious that more counties perform mandatory than optional functions. It is also apparent that a large number of counties are providing services, not because they are required by state law, but because their citizens have felt the need for these optional services.

A second important distinction is between services provided by the county for its entire population and services provided for part of the county — usually the unincorporated areas. The 1962 study reported by the Advisory Commission on Intergovernmental Relations indicates that counties provide some services to the unincorporated areas of the county that they do not provide on a county wide basis.(7) These services are often financed by special assessments, fees, and charges on the residents of the areas served.(8) Although data on this matter is lacking in the Wisconsin study and in the study by the National Association of Counties, it is reasonable to assume that many of the counties covered by these studies provide certain types of services (such as water, sewage, street lighting) only to the parts of the county that need them. In essence, a number of counties are providing city services for densely populated unincorporated areas.(9)

WHY COUNTIES PROVIDE "URBAN" SERVICES

Many of the services that counties provide can be termed "urban" services. They are furnished to meet the urban needs of densely populated areas rather than the general needs of both urban and rural areas. Individuals whose stereotypes of county government date back several decades may be surprised that counties are providing urban services — the same types of services that cities provide. Counties do not furnish these services because city government is inefficient or because county commissioners are empire builders, but simply because cities in a number of areas are financially unable to provide all the services needed and have not been able to expand to the limits of the densely populated areas surrounding them.

Through no fault of city officials, many cities are becoming victims of what might be termed "the urban cycle."(10) In the first stage of the urban cycle in the 1800's, most of these cities were able to keep expanding through annexation so that city limits nearly kept pace with the limits of the urbanized areas. In the second stage in the 1900's, annexations slowed, and satellite suburban cities and villages grew around the central city. As the 1900's progressed, more and more of the upper and middle income business and professional men moved outside the central city to the suburbs. These new suburbanites tended to resist annexation for many reasons such as their fear of higher taxes or loss of their status as suburbanites. The cities lost, not only many able leaders, but also an important tax base. The poorer people who remained in the cities tended to require higher cost health, welfare, and other services. The suburbanites continued to work in the cities and to utilize city services usually without paying any city taxes. Compounding the financial problems of the cities were restrictive state tax and debt limits. After World War II, there was an increased movement of both shopping centers and industry to suburban communities. The deterioration of downtown business districts, traffic congestion, and the need for airport runway expansion, new parks, and urban renewal added to city problems at a time of financial strain.

The third stage of the urban cycle has begun. It begins usually in a single functional area. The city airport is losing money and needs to expand its runways to provide jet service. It is physically outside the city limits, and it receives proportionately greater use from suburban businessmen who pay no city taxes than from city dwellers. When the financial pinch is greatest, city officials may request the county to take over operation of the airport. This is more equitable for the city dweller since he now pays only part of the taxes needed to extend the airport runways for jet service.

The same cycle may be repeated in the park program. As the city becomes densely populated, it tends to purchase land for larger parks outside the city limits where large blocks of land are much less costly. These parks are closer to suburban dwellers who tend to make extensive use of them without paying any fees or city taxes. When the city needs to expand its park system, city dwellers may be unwilling to pay the cost of more parks for use by suburbanites. The stage is set for city officials to turn again to the county or some metropolitan authority to take over the larger city parks and run an area-wide park system.

At the same time as counties (and other units of government such as metropolitan districts) are assuming area-wide functions from cities, the suburbanites are having their governmental problems. They moved to suburban areas to escape city living and taxes, but they frequently find population density rising in their areas to the point where they must have urban water, sewer and other services. Often the suburbanite lives in an unincorporated area, and he may first try a piecemeal solution to his problem through the use of single-purpose special districts. This may provide a partial solution to his problems at a relatively high cost. Suburban dwellers may also form small incorporated communities and try to provide urban services in this manner. In many areas, suburbanites are finding that small special districts and satellite cities are not large enough to offer the economies of mass purchasing, a professional staff, and effective use of expensive equipment. These suburbanites may ask counties to perform urban functions for them.

Thus counties have been requested to undertake "urban" functions by both city officials and suburbanites. Counties, of course, are not the only units of government to be asked to assume new urban functions. State agencies, metropolitan special districts, and federated metropolitan governments such as Toronto have also undertaken these new functions. However, half of all metropolitan areas in the nation are encompassed within single counties and, in these cases, counties are usually considered an excellent area for providing many metropolitan-wide services. In larger metropolitan areas that extend beyond the limits of one county, citizens may prefer that some urban functions be performed on a county-wide basis rather than superimposing a new unit of government on the existing, overly-complex framework of local government in the area.

To understand why counties provide the services they do and to better understand the intergovernmental relationships and problems in the provision of these services, it is essential to briefly describe all important county services. These services will be described in the succeeding sections of this chapter under eight general categories: general government, agriculture, education and libraries, health and welfare, parks and recreation, physical planning and development, public safety, and public works and transporation. These categories are intended only to provide a convenient grouping of similar functions. They will be used again in chapters 7 through 11 to describe the functions of five individual county governments.

GENERAL GOVERNMENT

The term general government encompasses many of the general (rather than urban) services of county government, most of which are mandated by state law. Counties have been performing many of these functions as an arm of the state, for more than 100 years, and state law may prescribe in detail the manner in which these functions are to be administered. The Bureau of Government of the University of Wisconsin lists 107 separate general government activities conducted by Wisconsin counties.(11) A description of some types of general governmental services follows.

Assessment and Collection of Property Taxes

In most states, the county assessor is required by law to assess property. Assessment involves maintaining a current record of property values; inspecting and setting an assessed value on new buildings; periodic reassessing of all property; notifying property owners of assessments; and a variety of other steps.(12) Collection of property taxes (usually by the county treasurer) involves accounting for the money collected, sending out notices to delinquent taxpayers, and other procedures. In assessing and collecting taxes, the county is not only providing revenues for itself but also providing a major source of funds for cities, school districts, and other units of local government within the county. General procedures for the assessment and collection of property taxes are often prescribed by state law, but county officials have discretion in the methods used. Counties such as Bucks County, Pennsylvania, for example, have been able to make effective use of data processing equipment in many phases of property tax administration.(13) Although cities and townships in some states assess and collect property taxes, the trend is toward county administration. Counties can achieve greater economies through large scale administration, and county administration tends to stimulate more uniform assessment on a county-wide basis. Recognizing this, some city officials, such as the Mayor of Milwaukee, have urged a shift in property tax assessment from cities to counties.(14)

Election Administration

Except in New England, the county usually serves as the administrative district for the conduct of state and county elections. Although state law generally sets a maximum size of precinct, it is usually the county governing body which sets the boundaries of election precincts. In South Dakota, as in many states, the county board chooses the election judges, determines whether voting machines are to be used, and takes part in the election canvass.(15) In Idaho, the county commissioners conduct the official canvass of the votes.

County officials have an important role in registration, absentee voting, and other election procedures. In Idaho, for example, the county auditor registers voters who intend to be absent from their precincts during the periods when voters are normally registered. The Idaho county auditor also accepts applications for absentee ballots, issues the ballots, receives the completed ballots, and transmits the absentee ballots to the polls. He is also responsible for having election ballots printed, accounting for these ballots, and distributing voting instructions and supplies. County auditors or clerks in many states have similar duties.(16)

Judicial Administration

County officials play an important role in some levels of the state court system. The highest appellate court in the state court

system is generally the state Supreme Court.(17) Immediately below the state Supreme Court in the judicial systems of fourteen
states are intermediate appellate courts.(18) These courts are used
in many of the more populous states to lighten the appellate workload of the state Supreme Court but are not a part of the court systems in thirty-six states. County officials normally play very little,
if any part in the work of the Supreme Court and intermediate appellate courts.

General trial courts are the next level of the state court system.
In Washington, for example, the general trial court is called the
Superior Court, and almost all the judges of this court are elected
from single county districts.(19) Half the salary of a Superior
Court judge in Washington is paid by the state and half by the county
in which he serves. The Washington Superior Court has original
jurisdiction over serious civil and criminal cases and appellate jurisdiction in cases originating in the justice courts and police courts.
County officials in Washington play a key role in the Superior Court
system. County prosecuting attorneys present the case against the
defendant in criminal cases tried in the Washington Superior Court.
County sheriffs serve legal papers required by court action, see that
court orders are carried out, sell real property to satisfy court
judgments, and transport prisoners to the court. The county clerks
in Washington keep court records, record final judgments, collect
fines, and perform many other functions for the Superior Court.

Idaho and Texas are examples of states whose general trial
courts cover multi-county areas rather than single counties. Idaho
is divided into thirteen judicial districts, and the judges of the Idaho
District Courts travel from one county to another within the district.
Each Idaho county provides a courtroom, office space, and some secretarial assistance, but the state pays the salary of the District Court
judge. The county prosecuting attorney, sheriff, and county clerk
provide much the same services for the Idaho District Court as
Washington county officials provide the Washington Superior Court.
In Texas, District Courts have jurisdiction in serious criminal and
civil cases and appellate jurisdiction over less serious cases.(20)
District Courts make less use of county personnel in Texas than in
Idaho and elect their own district clerks and district attorneys.

Below the general trial courts in the state and local judicial system are the county, probate, magistrates, municipal, and many
specialized courts such as police, traffic, and family relation
courts. In most states, one or more of these courts is a county
based court. In Idaho, there is a Probate Court in every county in
the state, and this court is responsible for less serious criminal
and civil cases, the probating of wills, guardianship matters, and
many proceedings involving juveniles.(21) In Texas, County Courts
have jurisdiction in less serious civil and criminal cases, the probating of wills, appointment of guardians, and the signing of orders
for the temporary hospitalization of mentally ill persons.(22) County

sheriffs, prosecuting attorneys, and clerks have some of the same functions in these county courts as they do in general trial courts.

Many of the lower courts are courts exercising jurisdiction only in a city or limited area of the county. In these courts, county officials normally play a less important part than in county based courts. However, some of these lower court officials, particularly justices of the peace, may be appointed by county officials.(23) Moreover, in a few states, justices of the peace and county court judges may be part of the county governing body.(24)

Recording of Legal Documents

The recording of legal documents such as wills, mortgages, and marriages is a voluminous task mandated by state law. This work was initially made a county function in most states because the state legislature wanted certain legal records maintained and believed they could more conveniently be recorded at the county seat than at the state capitol. The recording, indexing, microfilming, and photostatting of legal documents is usually the job of an elected county recorder or clerk, and general procedures may be prescribed by state law.(25) However, discretion is given county officials in the methods used, and counties such as Sullivan County, Pennsylvania and Spartanburg County, South Carolina have made imaginative use of aerial surveys to map all county property and to check property boundaries for a more accurate recording of deeds. Such procedures have turned up many "lost or unlisted properties" and have been of value to tax assessors as well as to property owners.(26)

Other General Government Functions

The services of the sheriff as process server; the coroner or medical examiner in investigating suspicious deaths; and the prosecuting attorney in his many functions can also be termed functions of general government. The liquor licensing, dog licensing, and auto licensing functions of county government are also services which counties may perform mainly as an arm of the state. There are important areas of county discretion in each of these functions, however, and also some optional general governmental services. In some states for example, counties are permitted to operate liquor stores and use the profits for the county general fund.

AGRICULTURE

The county courthouse in many rural counties is the hub of governmental services to farmers. It frequently houses federal agricultural stabilization and soil conservation officers as well as officials paid partly or entirely from county funds. In many counties, the county agent has emerged as a key figure in coordinating federal, state and local services to farmers. County agricultural services are not only provided for the residents of rural counties, but certain of these services are also provided for residents of metropolitan counties.(27)

Agricultural Extension

Agricultural extension provides an in-service education for farmers and their families. The county extension staff includes one or more county agriculture agents and extension home economics agents. County agents are paid from federal, state, and county funds. A county agent may give demonstrations, teach classes, give advice, and supply free government publications on a wide variety of farm subjects from the spraying of fruit trees to animal nutrition and livestock feeding. Continually on the alert for outbreaks of plant and animal diseases, he provides a vital link between the farmer and specialists at the state agricultural experiment station or federal agencies who can identify these diseases and recommend control measures.

The extension home economics agent provides advice, instruction, government publications, and leadership training for homemakers and 4-H clubs. She assists (and helps establish) extension homemaker groups emphasizing consumer education, for example, food buying; the buying, care and construction of clothing; and family budgeting. A county agent helps organize 4-H clubs in the county and provides advice and encouragement to the leaders of these clubs. The 4-H club movement has encouraged many farm youngsters to become interested in modern practices of gardening, livestock raising, and home economics, and it has spread into urban areas. In Milwaukee County, for example, there are 4-H clubs on electricity, landscaping, and home repair, and the entire county extension staff has redirected its efforts to meet the needs of its urban citizens.

County Fair

The annual county fair gives farmers and other county residents an opportunity to meet friends and discuss common farm problems as well as providing an enjoyable family outing. It is a place where the farmer can see and compare new types of seeds, new strains of livestock, and new types of farm machinery and can discuss their relative merits. The ribbons and prizes provide incentives for 4-H club members. The county fair is usually run by a board, appointed by the county commissioners, and is supported partly by county appropriations and partly from fees paid by concessionaires and, perhaps, admission charges.

Weed and Predator Control

Noxious weeds, such as Canadian thistle, cost farmers millions of dollars a year, and mountain lions, wolves, and other predators cause heavy losses to livestock growers. In many rural and semi-rural counties, the county governing body employs men to spray weeds along the sides of the roads to prevent their spread. Many states have laws requiring land owners to destroy harmful weeds. Owners who fail to comply may have the weeds on their property destroyed by the weed control supervisor and be billed by the county for this expense. In a number of livestock raising counties in the West, the county boards pay bounties or hire professional hunters to reduce the number of predatory animals.

EDUCATION AND LIBRARIES

The role of counties in providing schools, community colleges, libraries, museums and other education services differs greatly from state to state. In some states, such as Idaho and Washington, the county plays a limited part in furnishing these services. In others, such as Maryland, county government plays the leading role.

Public Schools

In 1961-62, 376 counties operated school systems which provided education for 2,419,000 school children. County school systems ranked below independent school districts and municipal school systems in enrollment but ranked ahead of other types of school systems as Table 3 shows. County systems were the predominant form of school system in Maryland, North Carolina, Tennessee, and Virginia in 1961-62 and were also found in nine other states.

Table 3
PUBLIC SCHOOL SYSTEMS IN THE UNITED STATES, 1961-62*

	Number of Public School Systems	Public School Enrollment Number	Per Cent
Independent school districts	34,678	29,387,000	77.7
Municipal school systems	412	4,018,000	10.6
County school systems	376	2,419,000	6.4
Town and township school systems	1,141	973,000	2.6
Pennsylvania "joint schools"	415	839,000	2.2
State school systems	3	166,000	.5
	37,025	37,802,000	100.0

*Adapted from: U. S. Bureau of the Census, *Public School Systems in the United States, 1961-62*, Preliminary Report No. 3 (Washington: Bureau of the Census, 1962), p. 1.

County operated school districts have provided one answer to the problem of school consolidation. Many authorities on education believe there is a minimum size for the effective operation of a school district. Morphet, Johns, and Reller state, for example, that: "Studies of services needed for a satisfactory program of education through the high school grades show that these cannot be provided most economically and effectively by a district having fewer than about 10,000 students."(28) Morphet and associates state that a district of 5,000 students might be reasonably effective and that at a minimum, a school district should have 1,200 to 1,500 students. Most school systems fall far short of desirable size according to these standards with only 1,069 of the more than 37,000 school systems having 6,000 or more pupils in 1962, and only 1,498 having 3,000 to 5,999 pupils.(29) In many areas of the country, there are still many small uneconomically sized school districts within a county area. These could be consolidated into a larger school district such as a single, county operated school district.

Educational authorities are not in agreement as to whether school districts can become too large for effective operation. The Committee for the White House Conference on Education said that: "Citizens of a large city generally have less pride in their schools than those of a smaller school district, and are seldom willing to work as hard for better schools."(30) However, the Advisory Commission on Intergovernmental Relations has cited the Montgomery County, Maryland school system as a large school system which has retained citizen interest. It makes the following statement:

> ".... The school system of Montgomery County, Maryland, illustrates that size alone does not produce the economic and cultural conditions which lead to parent disinterest and apathy. It had a 1960 population of 340,928 and public school enrollment of 80,680, yet is considered by many as one of the outstanding systems of the country."(31)

Where a county does operate its own school system, the system may be administered in one of several ways. In Montgomery County, Maryland, general educational policy is made by a seven member, elected Board of Education, and the system is administered by a professional Superintendent of Schools appointed by the Board. The school budget is reviewed first by the Board of Education and then by the County Council. In counties such as Nashville-Davidson County, Tennessee, the school board members are appointed by the County Mayor.

County Superintendent of Schools

The elective office of county superintendent of schools exists in 19 states.(32) In county unit school systems, the county superintendent of schools has extensive administrative authority, but in other counties he may play a relatively minor role in the educational process. In some states, the county superintendent may serve mainly as an arm of the state education department in reviewing statistical reports prepared by local schools, inspecting local schools to see that state regulations are being carried out, and helping to administer school elections. The County Superintendent in the State of Washington often helps small school districts find new teachers, helps teachers prepare curriculum guides, and may maintain a film library for schools in the county.(33) In some counties in Washington, the County Superintendent provides remedial reading teachers and other specialists that small school districts could not otherwise afford to hire.

Community Colleges

The operation of community colleges is a county function in a number of states. More than a dozen counties in Wisconsin reported that they operated county teachers colleges.(34) In Michigan, the three counties of Saginaw, Bay and Midland jointly operate a community college.(35) Westchester County, New York operates a junior college for 1,100 day and 3,000 evening students.(36) The purpose of the Westchester program is to provide a strong general educational background beyond the high school level and training for a large number of technical and scientific positions. Applied science subjects taught by the college include communications, construction engineering, electronics, metallurgy and radiation. About three-fourths of the graduates enter industry or commerce after graduation. Community colleges on a county level are close enough to the student to permit him to commute to classes. The rapidly increasing number of community colleges fill an important educational gap for students who need a two year program of technical, scientific, and general courses beyond high school. They also provide the first two years of college training for some students who will go on to four year colleges.

Libraries

Library service is provided by cities, counties, joint city-county agencies, private library agencies, special library districts, school libraries and regional library systems. Libraries face some of the same problems as school districts. Small libraries cost more per capita to operate than large libraries, and libraries operating within a unified library system benefit from economies of joint purchasing, sharing of books and other resources, and specialization of responsibility. One authority believes that the minimum population base for a comprehensive library system might be 100,000.(37) County operated library systems in many larger counties may provide one of several good alternatives to a number of uneconomically small special districts and small city library systems. Montgomery County, Maryland and Nashville-Davidson County, Tennessee are examples of counties with excellent county-wide library systems serving the entire county area; Hamilton County, Ohio and Erie County, New York are examples of county areas well served by joint city-county library systems.

Table 4
NUMBER OF PUBLIC LIBRARY SYSTEMS
IN CONTINENTAL UNITED STATES
BY MAJOR SOURCE OF SUPPORT*

	Number	Per Cent
City, town or village	2,826	45.2
Township or New England town	1,050	16.8
County	536	8.6
City and county	453	7.3
School district or county district	378	6.0
City and township	338	5.4
Town and school district	92	1.5
Regional	83	1.3
Independent branch of county library	47	.8
Other	446	7.1
	6,249	100.0

*Source: Adapted from U. S. Department of Health, Education and Welfare, *Statistics of Public Libraries: 1955-56* (Washington: U. S. Government Printing Office, 1959), p. 45. Not included in this table are 1,622 library systems which did not report their major source of financial support.

Museums

A sprinkling of counties across the nation operate museums. Eight counties in Wisconsin, for example, reported operating public museums.(38) County museums often include a collection of historical exhibits and war records and sometimes include natural history and other exhibits.

HEALTH AND WELFARE

The extensiveness of health and welfare services depends to some extent on the density of county population. In sparsely populated counties, such as Petroleum County, Montana, fewer services are provided than in more populous metropolitan counties such as Nashville-Davidson County (Tennessee), Montgomery County (Maryland), and Milwaukee County (Wisconsin). Within the boundaries of a single county, health and welfare services may be provided by state agencies, county government, cities, or other units of local government such as joint state-county or city-county agencies. Where counties directly administer health and welfare services, they frequently do so as an arm of the state and receive federal and state aid.

Health

In 1962, there were nearly 1600 governmental health organizations serving local areas. These included: 914 county health departments, 324 city health departments, 233 local health districts, and 120 state health districts.(39) The Advisory Commission on Intergovernmental Relations has noted a steady trend in transferring health functions from cities to county or joint city-county health departments.(40) Consolidations of city and county health departments occurred in 1961 in Salt Lake County (Utah), Douglas County (Omaha, Nebraska), and Monroe County (Rochester, New York). In 1962, Clark County (Las Vegas, Nevada) was one of several counties assuming former city health services. There are a number of areas of the country, particularly in the plains and rocky mountain states, in which there are no full time local health units.

Most county health departments, regardless of size, collect vital statistics and provide communicable disease control. The county health department receives reports of births, deaths, and many types of diseases. Statistics compiled from these reports are analyzed to determine whether epidemics are developing which will require control measures. If an epidemic develops, mass inoculation, the temporary closing of schools, isolation of certain diseased persons in special hospital wards, and public health education are measures that county health officials might use to combat the epidemic. Larger county health departments have laboratories which they can use to help identify and counteract the spread of disease. Counties also use mobile x-ray clinics which give citizens free chest x-rays as a means of locating persons with tuberculosis.

Almost all county health departments have public health nurses. In Washington and other states, the county health nurses check the health of school children and may test their hearing and sight. They often conduct classes in child care for expectant parents and conduct well child clinics to which mothers can bring their babies for health check-ups. In some counties, the public health nurses visit chronically ill patients and give them needed care and injections. A few counties have public health nutritionists who provide in-service education for nurses, and consultation services for physicians, dentists, and other health workers in the county to help them keep up-to-date on the latest research in nutrition. The nutritionists may (upon the order of a physician) prepare special diets for patients with diabetes, heart conditions, or other diseases. Some larger counties employ public health educators who provide free booklets on a variety of health subjects and may sponsor a radio or television program in which physicians, dentists, nurses, or nutritionists will discuss important aspects of personal health. The public health educator's aim is to help coordinate the health education programs of all agencies in the county to provide a community wide approach to health education.

Most county health departments have sanitarians who help prevent outbreaks of disease by inspecting public water supplies, sewage disposal facilities, garbage disposal, swimming pools and bathing beaches. The sanitarian also makes inspections of hotels, restaurants, food markets, dairy farms, and milk handling plants. (41) The sanitarian may check the breeding grounds of rats, flies, and mosquitoes and take measures, if necessary to wipe out these disease carriers. One Florida county, for example, has used planes to spray mosquito breeding grounds.(42) In some counties, medical and dental x-ray machines are studied for radiation leaks and air and water sources are monitered for radiation.(43)

Air pollution tends to be a serious problem in some areas, and some counties have outstanding programs for its control. A 1961 survey showed that there were thirty-four air pollution control agencies spending more than $25,000 a year.(44) Ten of these agencies were county agencies, 21 were under city government, and three covered more than a single county. Milwaukee County, Wisconsin has an extensive air pollution control program. Air is tested in seventy locations within the county, and samples of air and dust are analyzed for irritants in a specially designed laboratory. A laboratory in a trailer is used also to test industrial chimneys and other sources for pollutants, and the county enforces its pollution control ordinance if pollutants are found.

Welfare Services

The division between state and local responsibility for welfare services differs from state to state. In 1963, there were 23 states in which a state agency provided all or most types of welfare.(45) In Washington, for example, welfare is entirely a state administered function, whereas in Idaho, the state provides most types of public assistance leaving counties to furnish emergency aid and medical care. In 1963, there were 26 states in which welfare was entirely or predominantly a county administered function with a state agency playing a supervisory role. In North Carolina, for example, all public assistance is administered by a county welfare staff. In Maryland, New York, and Virginia, cities as well as counties administer public assistance. In 1963, one state (Massachusetts) provided welfare through towns and district welfare boards.

Almost all welfare recipients receive monthly cash grants. A person applying for assistance is normally contacted by a caseworker who determines whether the applicant meets the requirements for assistance. There are five programs of assistance.

1. Old age assistance (provided for needy persons 65 years of age and older)

2. Aid to the blind (provided for needy blind persons)

3. Aid to the permanently and totally disabled (provided for needy disabled persons who are unable to meet their monetary needs through work)

4. Aid to families with dependent children (provided to needy children under the age of 18 who have been deprived of parental support or care by reason of the death, continued absence from the home, or physical or mental incapacity of the parent. The children must be living with a parent or other relative in a home, and the parent or other relative caring for the child may also receive a grant.)

5. General assistance (provided to other needy persons)

The federal government provides grants-in-aid for the first four categories of assistance. The fifth category, which is called poor relief in some states, is entirely financed from state and local funds. Federal and state governments establish detailed eligibility rules and requirements for aid, so that even when counties administer the assistance programs, they are not free to determine many key public assistance policies.

Public assistance recipients and other needy persons (termed medical indigents) also receive free medical care. This care normally includes care in hospitals and nursing homes and care by physicians, dentists, and other medical specialists. Drugs, dentures, eye glasses, and artificial limbs may also be furnished. In most counties, physicians, dentists, and other medical specialists provide care through a contract with the public assistance agency or on a fee for service basis. However, many large urban counties provide much of this care through the county hospital.

Casework service is a third important category of public assistance. The caseworker, who determines eligibility and re-eligibility for assistance, comes to know the assistance recipient as a person and is frequently able to help him. In some cases, this help may be only answering questions about the community and the services it provides to needy persons. At other times, the caseworker may be able to encourage the recipient to secure training and find work. Caseworkers may also help mothers, who are receiving assistance, plan for the needs of their children.

County public assistance agencies may provide other specialized services. If a child's parents die or desert him, the county may place the child in a foster home and pay the foster parents to raise

him until he is eighteen. If parents have been mistreating or neg-
lecting a child, a court may ask the county public assistance agency
to place the child temporarily in a foster home or have the child
returned to the parents under the watchful eye of the county child
welfare caseworker. Many counties also distribute surplus food to
needy persons, and some provide recipients with disbursement
orders which they can use to purchase food and other commodities.

In line with President Johnson's "War on Poverty" Program a
number of counties, particularly in the Appalachia area, have begun
their own anti-poverty programs. Craven County, North Carolina
has developed extensive programs in cooperation with federal
agencies which include: the establishment of a strawberry marketing cooperative to raise farm income; expanded health education;
day care centers; and training for women to teach home management skills to indigent families.(46) In Kanawha County, West
Virginia, an imaginative attack is being made on the problems of
school dropouts, juvenile delinquency, and high welfare loads.(47)
The City of Detroit has joined six counties in Michigan in a coordinated anti-poverty program.(48)

County Health and Welfare Institutions

Most state constitutions and laws permit the establishment of
county hospitals. In Michigan, the constitution expressly provides
for the establishment of county hospitals by one county acting
separately or in conjunction with other counties.(49) Michigan
counties are authorized also to establish homes for the feeble-
minded, tuberculosis sanitoria, and (in the case of Wayne County)
a large university county hospital.(50) In South Dakota, the county
commissioners are empowered to call an election for the establishment of a county hospital, or they may establish one or more
county wards in any public or private hospital and pay the costs of
these wards.(51) The large county hospitals in many urban counties
have a full range of services. The county hospitals in King County
(Seattle, Washington) and Milwaukee County (Wisconsin) are among
many providing emergency medical services. In Seattle, most of
the accident cases in the city are taken to the King County Hospital.
The Milwaukee County Hospital has 28 outpatient clinics and gives
training to interns, dentists, dietitians and nurses.

Specialized hospitals and institutions are operated by a number
of urban counties. Milwaukee County, for example, has a mental
health center with two large buildings housing an average of 3,700
patients, a psychiatric clinic, child guidance clinics, and other
outpatient mental services. Montgomery County, Maryland has an
alcoholics clinic staffed by psychiatrists, internists and social
workers. Westchester County, New York has a large general hospital and alcoholics clinic. A number of counties have tuberculosis

hospitals, homes for the elderly, homes for children, and other health and welfare institutions. Los Angeles County has a Mental Health Department with a budget of more than $3 million per year.(52)

PARKS AND RECREATION

Parks and recreation are rapidly expanding functions of county government. From 1950 to 1960, the number of county parks increased from 933 to 2,610 and the acreage of county parks reached 430,707 acres.(53) In 1950, only one Oregon county had budgeted funds for outdoor recreation; by 1964, 22 of the state's 36 counties had park and recreation programs. Between 1957 and 1965, Iowa counties acquired 324 parks and other recreation areas with a total of 17,000 acres. Westchester County, New York acquired 3,000 acres of park land between 1960 and 1964, and Berks County, Pennsylvania purchased 900 acres for parks.

County park programs are expanding rapidly because urban residents are demanding more outdoor recreation facilities close to the home.(54) The increased demand for parks comes at a time when choice water and shoreline areas suitable for parks are becoming scarce near large cities. Counties in metropolitan areas have found the need for parks particularly urgent, since cities in these areas often lack the space for large additional parks within their borders. In metropolitan counties, most large blocks of available land lie outside the boundaries of the central city, and county officials are in a good position to plan area-wide park systems, acquire needed sites in advance, and finance these systems.

Counties have taken the lead in many areas to preserve the remaining waterways and forest areas near large cities for recreation uses. In Sacramento County, California, county officials and citizens' committees acted to preserve 23 miles of American River shoreline when it appeared that part of it would be subdivided.(55) County officials purchased 1,182 acres, established two new parks, opened riding, cycling, and hiking trails, constructed an 18 hole golf course, and built boat launching facilities. Westchester County (New York), Essex County (New Jersey), and King County (Washington) are other counties taking steps to preserve waterfront and forest areas. In 1965, the King County Board of Commissioners announced plans to double their existing park facilities at a cost of $9 million.(56) Sacramento and King Counties are among a number of American counties receiving federal aid for the purchase of park land under the Open Space Program.

County park facilities vary widely. The non-urban county may own only a small picnic area or playground. In more populous counties, the facilities may be very extensive. Milwaukee County, for example, owns 13,000 acres of land and has 80 separate parks. Some of its small parks provide only picnicking, shuffleboard, or tot lot playgrounds. Its larger parks include: baseball, football, and soccor fields; bicycle tracks; bridle paths; golf courses; campgrounds; lakes for fishing, boating, and skating; and facilities for picknicking, skiing, tobogganing, archery, badminton, model airplane flying, tennis, and many other sports. Milwaukee County is one of a number of urban counties which have expanded their parks programs to include much more than a park system. The county operates an 174 acre, beautifully landscaped zoo, a botanical garden, a boat marina, and a conservatory displaying large plants found on tropical and desert regions. The county also owns a musical amphitheater used for outdoor concerts and the Milwaukee Stadium with a seating capacity of 47,000.

Counties in other parts of the nation have developed special park and recreational facilities to meet area needs. Bibb County (Macon, Georgia) has begun a $4.7 million recreation project which will result in damming Tobesofkee Creek to provide a 1,755 acre lake with a shoreline of 34 miles.(57) The county will acquire 600 acres of land surrounding the lake and provide campsites, picnic grounds, boat marinas, and other facilities. Fairfax County, Virginia has a large campground close to Washington, D. C.(58) Santa Clara County, California has provided its bicycle fans with a 1/5 mile asphalt bicycle track built to Olympic specifications.(59) Essex County, New Jersey has two 200-foot long skating rinks used for ice hockey, speed skating, figure skating, and instruction for all age groups.(60)

Organized recreational programs are also provided by counties to supplement their park programs. Westchester County, New York established one of the nation's first Recreation Commissions in 1924 and has an extensive recreation program.(61) Westchester operates two camps accommodating 1,200 children, a Civic Center with an audience capacity of 8,000 and arts and crafts workshops which serve more than 2,500 people a year. The county provides technical and consultant services to Westchester communities which furnish their own recreation programs. Montgomery County, Maryland has a recreation program which includes organized baseball, swimming, and other sports for thousands of school children during the summer. In California, the Kern County Parks and Recreation Department includes art, drama, and music among its recreation programs. It sponsors district and county art contests, an annual drama festival, chamber music festival, a series of children's concerts, and folk dancing for children and adults.(62)

Counties have entered the field of park and recreation services for two main reasons. First, no other unit of government was providing these services for densely populated but unincorporated areas. Secondly, there are certain types of park and recreational services that are better provided by a unit of government having a larger area than a city. George Butler, one authority in the park and recreation field, believes that recreational services and facilities benefiting only local or municipal residents should be administered by city officials, and that counties are the logical agencies in many metropolitan areas to provide non-local recreational activities.(63) A policy statement of the National Association of Counties takes a somewhat similar position when it states "The special role of the county is to acquire, develop and maintain parks and to administer public recreation programs that will serve the needs of communities broader than the local neighborhood or municipality, but less than statewide or national in scope."(64) In providing parks and recreation programs, counties are not acting primarily as an arm of the state but as a unit of local government meeting county-wide needs.

PHYSICAL PLANNING AND DEVELOPMENT

Planning, zoning, subdivision control, urban renewal, industrial development and tourist information services are relatively new, expanding functions of county government. In providing these services, counties are acting, not as an arm of the state, but as a unit of local government meeting local needs.(65)

Planning

County planning involves far more than just the physical development of highways, parks, schools, and other physical features of the county. As Donald Webster points out:

"In the broad sense, planning is concerned with the orderly relation of all functions which government performs directly or through regulation. Physical planning and program planning cannot be completely separated. In almost every instance physical planning has a close relationship to the policies and objectives of some functional program or service."(66)

The economic and social objectives of planning include influencing the location of residential, commercial, and industrial areas to promote better living and working conditions and greater efficiency in business management.(67)

The comprehensive plan, the keystone of the planning process, is a blueprint for long range development. The plan predicts future population growth and portrays future residential, commercial and industrial areas. It plots present and future highways, streets, parking and other transportation facilities. It shows existing school buildings, parks and public facilities as well as those which will be needed in the future. When completed and adopted, the comprehensive plan, with its maps and supporting documents, is used by local government officials to help them make decisions about the future location of streets, parks, schools, and other public facilities. It is also used as a basis for zoning a city or county into areas of residential, commercial, and industrial land uses. The comprehensive plan is an aid to builders in deciding where to locate new subdivisions and an asset to manufacturers in planning plant locations. Planning and zoning help prevent industrial and commercial buildings from causing health, safety, and noise problems for residential landowners and help keep residential areas from intruding on industrial and commercial zones.

To be effective, planning cannot stop at city lines. Unplanned, unincorporated areas surrounding well planned cities often act as magnets attracting auto junk yards and other unsightly and objectionable land uses. There is danger that the plans of the different municipalities within a county or metropolitan area may conflict or fail to take into consideration the needs of the entire area. Furthermore, rural areas have special planning needs such as the protection of agricultural and forested areas.(68)

County officials have increasingly recognized that planning is a county as well as a city function. A 1964 study by the National Association of Counties showed that 90% of the reporting counties of 250,000 or more people and 76% of the counties in the 100,000 to 249,999 population class provided planning by themselves or jointly with another unit of government.(69) In many counties, there are both county and city planning commissions with the county planning commission having jurisdiction over the unincorporated areas and smaller cities. In 1962, Orange County, California, for example, had a county planning staff of 31 persons serving an area of 534 square miles of increasingly urban unincorporated territory, while fifteen cities in the county had a total staff of 90 planners for an area of 207 square miles.(70) Where both the county and a number of small cities have planning staffs, there may be relatively high costs on the part of small city planning staffs and danger of an uncoordinated approach to area planning. In Davidson County, Tennessee, a different approach to planning organization was taken in the 1950's. Davidson County and the City of Nashville shared the same planning staff, and this staff coordinated city-county planning and prepared invaluable studies of the entire county area. After the consolidation of Nashville and Davidson County, this joint planning agency became the new Nashville-Davidson County Metropolitan Planning Commission.

Nearly all counties which are engaged in planning place their professional planning staff under an appointed or elected planning board or commission. In Westchester County, New York, the

County Executive appoints the nine citizen members of the Planning Board.(71) To insure representation from differing types of county areas, four members of the Planning Board must be from cities, two from incorporated villages, and three from unincorporated town areas. In Nashville-Davidson County, Tennessee, the Planning Commission consists of the County Mayor, a member of the Metropolitan County Council, and eight persons appointed by the County Mayor.

The county planning commission staff is usually responsible for preparing the comprehensive plan, and this plan must be approved by the planning commission and county governing body before it goes into effect. In Virginia, after the comprehensive plan is approved by the Board of Supervisors, it becomes legally binding and thereafter no road, park, public building, or public utility can be constructed in the unincorporated area of the county unless approved by the county planning commission.(72) County planning boards exercise controls on the location of commercial, industrial and residential buildings through their zoning powers.

Zoning

Zoning has been defined as "the division of a community into zones or districts according to the present and potential use of properties for the purpose of controlling and directing the use and development of those properties."(73) Zoning ordinances may control, not only the use of lands and buildings, but the height of buildings, the proportion of a lot which buildings may cover, the number of parking spaces a building owner must provide, and other matters. The county zoning ordinance is usually prepared by the county planning staff and may be adopted in a variety of ways. In Virginia, as in most states, the county governing board may adopt a zoning ordinance.(74) In South Dakota, however, the zoning ordinance is prepared by the county zoning commission, and 60% or more of the voters in the area must sign a petition approving the zoning ordinance before it can be placed before the county commissioners. The commissioners can adopt or refuse to approve the zoning ordinance.(75) In most areas, the zoning ordinance is enforced by the refusal of county officials to issue building permits for structures which are not built in accordance with the ordinance.

Subdivision Regulations

Subdivision regulations are also a means of implementing the county's comprehensive plan and providing for the orderly development of subdivision. Counties having such regulations usually prohibit the recording of plats not approved by the planning agency. The planning agency may require subdividers to construct streets, install sanitary sewers, provide water mains, and other improvements before the subdivision is approved. The subdivision requirements tend to insure that costly facilities will not need to be installed at a later time and that the streets and other facilities of the subdivision will not deteriorate. Although most counties having subdivision regulations apply them only to the unincorporated areas of the county, some counties such as Allegheny County (Pittsburgh, Pennsylvania), Jackson County (Kansas City, Missouri), and Santa Clara County (San Jose, California) apply these regulations also to cities within their borders which do not have subdivision regulations.(76)

Urban Renewal

The three main elements of an urban renewal program have been described as follows by the Urban Renewal Administration:

"(1) Slum prevention through neighborhood conservation and housing code enforcement.

(2) Rehabilitation of structures and neighborhoods.

(3) Clearance and redevelopment of structures and neighborhoods."(77)

Urban renewal projects, undertaken by city, county, and special district units, may qualify for federal funds if the local unit adopts what is termed a "workable" program. Such a program must encompass enforcement of health, sanitation and safety codes, formulation of a comprehensive community plan, and other measures. Authorities advocate that urban renewal be done on a metropolitan area basis. Victor Jones states:

"The entire community must be considered in planning urban redevelopment projects. There are blighted areas in the suburbs and in the unincorporated fringe as well as in the central cities. ...

Furthermore, the pressures that affect the use of land in a metropolitan area cannot be excluded by the boundary lines of a municipal corporation. ..."(78)

Where county boundaries encompass the limits of a metropolitan area (as they do in half of American metropolitan areas), the county is particularly well suited to undertake urban renewal projects. Allegheny County (Pittsburgh, Pennsylvania), Alexander County (Cairo, Illinois), Jefferson County (Louisville, Kentucky), and Dade County (Miami, Florida) are examples of counties having urban renewal programs.(79)

Building Codes, Housing Codes and Public Housing

Many cities and a small, but growing number of counties are using building codes, housing codes and public housing to assure their residents of better housing. Building and construction codes have been used by some counties in conjunction with subdivision regulations to enforce minimum standards for the construction of new dwellings.(80) Housing codes have been used to require that existing houses meet minimum standards of space per occupant, light, ventilation, fire safety, sanitation, and structural condition. There are advantages to having building and housing codes extend beyond the borders of municipalities to cover an entire county or multi-county area. Builders will have lower costs if one building code covers the entire metropolitan area than if each separate city has a different building code.(81) Moreover, without areawide building and housing codes, there is danger that substandard, unsafe buildings will develop in the unincorporated areas of a county.

Where private housing does not meet the needs of low income groups, a few counties have developed their own public housing programs or created public housing authorities. Fresno, Kern, Marin, and Contra Costa Counties in California have public housing programs.(82) The housing authority of Allegheny County, Pennsylvania is responsible for public housing in twelve localities in the county.

Industrial Development

A survey of 1,667 counties in 1964 showed that 23% of these counties had industrial development programs and 4% worked cooperatively with other units of local government in such programs.(83) To attract new industries, counties have published attractive reports providing information on transportation facilities, utilities, water supply, minerals, and the economy of the county.(84) Counties have expanded airport, highway, water, and sewage services in some instances to attract new industry.(85) Industrial development has become a county function because many new industries are locating in unincorporated areas outside cities, and county government is providing services for these areas.

Industrial development is a function of rural as well as urban counties. Nine rural counties in the slash pine area of southern Georgia have established a planning and development commission to further the economic growth of the region.(86) Rural counties have also been active in promoting tourism.

The national War on Poverty program has brought increased
interest in the possibility of industrialization in rural areas, particularly in Appalachia. Increasing mechanization of agriculture
has thrown many farmers and farm laborers out of work, and in
Craven County, North Carolina 61% of the population live in rural
areas of the county but no longer farm for an income.(87) Loans
and grants are available through the War on Poverty program to
help communities undertake a variety of industrial, health, education and other projects.(88)

PUBLIC SAFETY

Law enforcement, fire protection, and civil defense are the
major public safety functions. In many small, sparsely settled
counties, public safety functions are split between county government, municipalities and special districts. The county sheriff
furnishes police protection in the unincorporated areas of the
county while the municipal police patrol the incorporated areas.
Fire services are provided by fire protection districts in unincorporated areas and by city fire departments in cities and villages.
Civil defense is usually a county function.

In more populous counties, county government may have greater
responsibility for public safety. The county government of Montgomery County, Maryland provides police services for nearly the
entire county, civil defense for the entire county, and a fire dispatching service for the volunteer fire departments of the county.

There are significant benefits from area-wide administration
and cooperation in police services. One authority states that it is
unlikely that a governmental jurisdiction with less than 50,000
people can support a police department which is self-sufficient and
sustaining.(89) A multiplicity of police forces in an area can create
rivalries; cause an overlapping of enforcement powers; and result
in less efficient utilization of police specialists and expensive police
equipment.(90) There is danger also that one community running a
"wide open town" will diminish the effectiveness of police forces in
other communities in the area. One solution to area-wide police
problems is for county government either to provide the major
area-wide police force (as is done in Montgomery County, Maryland) or for county government to take a major role in providing
specialized services for local police forces. The Los Angeles
County Sheriff's Office does this by furnishing, by contract or
agreement, a variety of services to municipalities such as recruitment, training, photography, crime detection, and two-way radio
services.(91)

The multiplicity of fire departments have caused problems in
some metropolitan areas. The Advisory Commission on Intergovernmental Relations reports that: "The small municipality in

an urban or suburban area is often an uneconomical unit of fire defense administration."(92) Larger fire departments are better able to provide adequate training facilities, communications equipment, fire prevention bureaus, and arson squads. In a few metropolitan areas (such as Nashville-Davidson County, Tennessee) almost all fire-fighting forces in the county are united under a single county-wide fire department. In other counties, the county or a joint city-county agency may furnish certain specialized services to the entire county. Los Angeles County, for example, provides fire protection services, such as central communications and dispatching services, to cities under contract.(93)

According to a 1964 survey by the National Association of Counties, 1,233 of 1,661 reporting counties had civil defense programs. In the case of 175 additional counties, the county government had a civil defense program in cooperation with another unit of government. As in fire and police protection, there are advantages of area-wide operation of civil defense programs.

PUBLIC WORKS AND TRANSPORTATION

Public works is a general phrase which is often used to encompass a variety of capital construction and maintenance projects. The farmer in a rural county has little need for county public works programs such as port facilities, airports, expressways or mass transit. He gets his water from a well or cistern, uses a septic tank for his sewage, and disposes of garbage and refuse by burning or burying. His county may undertake the construction of a new wing on the county courthouse, a new building for the county fair, and additions to the county road system. However, the construction of streets, water lines, and sewer systems tend to be municipal functions in small, rural counties.

The citizen of a larger county has greater need for public works services. In urban counties, city and village governments are able to extend water lines, sewers, and streets to all or nearly all inhabitants, but in the unincorporated fringe areas around the cities, these services may not keep pace with the needs of suburbanites. These services are provided in many areas by a number of small special districts, each furnishing one or two types of services often at a high per capita cost. In other unincorporated areas, county government provides street construction, sidewalks, street lighting, water lines, sewage disposal, garbage and refuse collection, and a variety of other services. As counties further expand in population, county government often finds itself in a new role. Officials in some cities may request the county to assume responsibility for the metropolitan airport or an expressway system, because they are no longer able to finance them. It is more equitable for citizens of the entire area to pay the costs of these services than for city residents to support them.

Roads, Highways, and Expressways

The role of county government in road and highway administration varies from state to state as well as within states. Construction and maintenance of roads, highways, and expressways in Delaware, North Carolina, Virginia, and West Virginia are almost entirely a state function.(94) In other states, the state highway department is responsible for the construction and maintenance of interstate highway systems and a number of secondary roads. In 1962, 673,139 miles of highways outside municipalities were under state control. (95) Counties, in 1962, were responsible for construction and maintenance of 1,741,885 miles of roads and highways, while towns and townships were responsible for road systems amounting to 542,189 miles.(96) In states such as Illinois, Minnesota and Ohio where both counties and townships construct and maintain roads, the townships tend to be responsible for farm-to-market roads while the counties are responsible for the more heavily travelled roads.

Clyde F. Snider reports that decentralization of rural road administration among thousands of small districts results in waste and inefficiency.(97) Road construction is a complex task requiring trained engineers and expensive equipment. Some counties and the great majority of townships and road districts cannot easily afford to hire qualified highway engineers or purchase the necessary machinery. There were 5,000 road commissioners, supervisors, and clerks in 1949 in townships and road districts in Illinois. These officials increased local road costs. Expensive pieces of equipment were sometimes purchased that were used only a few days a year; road gangs were poorly supervised; and untested materials were sometimes used. There has been a significant transfer of township roads to county jurisdiction in the past decade, particularly in Iowa, Indiana, Michigan, and Oklahoma. In some states, there has also been a transfer of county highways to the state highway system.

Planning and financing new county road projects is often a problem in both urban and rural counties. Since funds for county roads come from federal and state sources, as well as county sources, county officials have some difficulty in estimating future highway receipts and planning long-range county road programs. In a number of counties, such as Montgomery County, Maryland, county road needs are estimated over a five year period in a capital improvements budget. In 1964, Oregon counties conducted a road survey assisted by members of the Oregon Association of County Engineers and Surveyors and other officials.(98) This survey showed that $621 million was needed to correct county highway deficiencies. The survey was presented to Oregon's Interim Committee on

Highways for use in their study of the distribution of state highway user revenues to cities and counties. One of the greatest benefits of the study was its use by county road departments in establishing priorities for future road projects.

Metropolitan counties face additional problems. One solution to commuter traffic is an expressway system linking the central city with suburban cities and villages. Central cities often have neither the funds nor desire to build expressway systems, much of which would be outside their borders. Counties, such as Milwaukee County, Wisconsin, are constructing such systems. Expressways and interstate highways tend to radically change normal traffic patterns on existing county highways. Hence counties are building many access roads to the new interchanges.

The construction and maintenance of streets is a county function in a few urban and suburban areas. Montgomery County, Maryland constructs and maintains streets in the densely populated part of the county and also constructs curbs, sidewalks, and gutters. The cost of new streets, sidewalks, curbs and gutters is usually assessed against abutting property owners. The cost of street cleaning and roadside tree services is paid through a tax levied against area residents.

Traffic safety has also become a county function. Counties have experimented with reflecterized license plates and highway signs to cut accidents. County highway traffic engineers synchronize traffic lights to produce an even flow of traffic, and sheriffs' deputies patrol county highways.

Mass Transportation

County governments, particularly in metropolitan areas, have become increasingly involved in the problems of commuter railroads, buses, and other forms of transportation. In past decades when most people lived in the city in which they worked, there was less need for county involvement in mass transportation. The proportion of persons commuting into a city from surrounding areas of the county or from adjacent counties is steadily increasing, and the problems of the commuter cannot be solved by the actions of city government alone. Furthermore, the problems of mass transportation have reached crisis proportions in some metropolitan areas requiring the attention of county government as well as national, state, and city governments.(99)

Perhaps, the most publicized crisis in mass transportation is the plight of the commuter railroad particularly in the New York City area. Mounting deficits in commuter railroad lines caused some lines to threaten to abandon service unless they received tax relief or cash subsidies.(100) County officials in metropolitan areas have been concerned about the commuter railroad problem and have supported increased federal appropriations for mass transit.(101) Westchester County, New York has taken part in a tax abatement program for commuter railroads.(102) While counties have assisted in solving the problems of commuter railroads, the high cost of subsidizing these railroads and the multi-county nature of their service makes it unlikely that county government by itself can resolve commuter railroad problems.

A more widespread crisis in mass transportation is the decline in use of buses, street cars, and other forms of public transit while city streets have become increasingly choked with private automobiles.(103) Privately owned transportation companies in some areas have faced increasing deficits and have been sold to cities, counties, and special districts. Dade County, Florida has acquired privately owned transit companies.(104) Allegheny County, Pennsylvania is buying and integrating the services of 31 privately owned bus companies and will pay for this with a bond issue of nearly forty million dollars.(105) In some multi-county metropolitan areas, the problems of rejuvenating public transportation is beyond the capacity of individual counties, and state agencies, such as the Massachusetts Bay Transportation Authority, or multi-county special districts, such as the San Francisco Bay Area Rapid Transit District, have been established.

Airports and Ports

A 1964 study of 1667 counties showed 389 counties owned airports and there were joint city-county airports in 108 counties.(106) Dade County, Florida owns four airports including one of the most modern jet airports in the country.(107) Suburban Westchester County, New York maintains an airport 26 miles from New York City at which more than 65 leading corporations base their aircraft. (108) Many airports, no matter how well managed, are only able to meet their operating expenses and part of their capital expenditures. In small metropolitan areas, county ownership of the major airport is a means of equitably distributing the net cost of the airport over all residents benefiting from airport services. Similarly, when a county owns lake, river, or seaport facilities, it is able to more widely distribute the cost of these facilities.

Water, Sewage Disposal, Garbage Collection, Refuse Disposal

In the 1964 survey of 1667 counties by the National Association of Counties, 231 counties reported providing a water system and 209 reported having a sewer system. Baltimore County, Maryland extended its sewer lines because of the failure of a private sewer disposal system. In Nashville-Davidson County, Tennessee, the consolidation of Nashville and Davidson County brought the metropolitan county into the water and sewage disposal functions. Larger counties, like larger cities, have the advantage of high-volume, low cost operations. Authorities on water supply systems estimate that the operation and maintenance cost per acre-foot of treated water varies from $10 per acre-foot in a plant treating 300 acre-feet of water per day to $26 per acre-foot in a plant treating 15 acre-feet per day.(109) Water conveyance costs and sewage treatment plant costs are also much less in large volume operation.(110) Counties are in a better position to operate sewage systems than smaller units of local government. Special districts and townships often have uneconomically small sewage systems and can seldom qualify for federal loans or grants for planning treatment facilities. (111)

A total of 139 counties reported providing refuse collection and 259 reported providing refuse disposal in the 1964 survey. Orange and Los Angeles Counties in California are two of a number of counties which provide and maintain landfill sites for municipalities.(112) Both counties furnish trucks to transport the refuse which is collected in municipalities. Bergen County, New Jersey provides garbage disposal sites for private collectors serving most of the towns in the county.(113)

SUMMARY

Surveys of county functions show that counties, particularly metropolitan counties, provide a surprisingly large number of services. One study, for example, listed 285 separately identifiable governmental activities performed by Milwaukee County, Wisconsin.

Many of the services provided by county government are those in which the county is acting, to some extent, as an administrative arm of the state. When the county prosecuting attorney, for example, presents the case against the defendent in a civil suit, he is a part of the state court system. Similarly, the assessment and collection of property taxes, the recording of deeds, and other traditional county services are mandated by state law and provided by counties mainly as an arm of state government.

However, many of the services performed by county governments in densely populated areas are not services that the county performs as an arm of the state but the same type of urban services provided by cities. These include: construction and maintenance of expressways; operation of airports; operation of park and recreation systems; air pollution control; establishment of fire and police departments; provision of water and sewage lines; street construction; street lighting; garbage collection; and operation of bus systems. Counties also operate zoos, boat marinas, stadiums, concert halls, botannical gardens, community colleges, libraries, and museums.

County governments have come to furnish many additional services in urban areas for two reasons. They have been asked to provide urban services to residents of densely populated, unincorporated areas around cities. They have been requested by city officials to assume functions that cities are no longer financially able to support. It is more equitable to the residents of the central city for the county to provide services such as parks which all residents of the county use, than for the central city to bear the entire cost of these facilities.

REFERENCES

1. Bureau of Government, University of Wisconsin, County Government Activities in Wisconsin (Madison: University of Wisconsin, 1961). The study was made by sending questionnaires to all Wisconsin counties. The Bureau counted each detailed activity. For example, rather than counting library services as one activity, they counted as separate activities: (1) a law library, (2) book services to schools, (3) a county library, and (4) traveling library service.

2. Ibid., p. 2.

3. Ibid., p. 6.

4. Ibid. Florence County had a 1960 population of 3,437.

5. Reported in: Advisory Commission on Intergovernmental Relations, Alternative Approaches to Governmental Reorganization in Metropolitan Areas (Washington: Advisory Commission on Intergovernmental Relations, 1962), p. 40.

6. Returns were received from all classes of counties, but there was a greater proportion of returns from the more populous counties. Special procedures were installed to secure returns from a sample number of counties who failed to return the questionnaire. The questionnaires finally received from these counties did not vary significantly from others in the same population class. The data for each population class (see Table 2) is more significant than the data for all counties (see Table 1).

7. Advisory Commission on Intergovernmental Relations, Alternative Approaches to Governmental Reorganization in Metropolitan Areas, p. 40.

8. In California, county service areas and dependent districts are widely used to finance services to unincorporated areas. See the section on "Counties as Creators of Dependent Districts and Service Areas" in chapter 6.

9. Montgomery County, Maryland is an example of a county which provides many types of municipal services for densely populated unincorporated areas. See chapter 9.

10. The urban cycle has been described by Bernard Hillenbrand, "County Government is Reborn" in Readings in State and Local Government, edited by Joseph Zimmerman (New York: Holt, Rinehart and Winston, 1964), pp. 259-262.

11. Bureau of Government, The University of Wisconsin, op. cit., p. 2. Most but not all of these activities fall under the writer's category of general government.

12. Periodic reassessment of property is a necessary but extremely time consuming task. Los Angeles County has a program of reassessing 20% of the 1,700,000 pieces of property in the county each year. The County Officer, 28:249, June, 1963. See also chapter 3 on the duties of the assessor and chapter 5 on property taxes.

13. The County Officer, 28:249, June, 1963.

14. The Milwaukee Journal, April 21, 1964, p. 18.

15. William H. Cape, Handbook for South Dakota County Officials (Vermillion: University of South Dakota, 1961), pp. 20, 21, 28.

16. In Washington, for example, the county auditor is responsible for registering voters in rural precincts; providing polling places, election equipment and supplies; publishing and posting notices of election; and keeping necessary records of elections. Barbara Byers, County Government in Washington State (Olympia: Washington State Association of County Commissioners, 1957), p. 19.

17. In New York, this court is called the Court of Appeals. In Texas, the Supreme Court is the court of last resort in civil matters, and the Court of Criminal Appeals is the highest state court for criminal appeals. In most states, the highest appellate state court is called the Supreme Court.

18. These states are Alabama, California, Florida, Georgia, Illinois, Indiana, Louisiana, Missouri, New Jersey, New York, Ohio, Pennsylvania, Tennessee, and Texas.

19. State law permits a few of the smaller counties to be combined into judicial districts. For a brief description of the Washington Superior Court system, see Barbara Byers, op. cit., pp. 121-133.

20. Wilbourn E. Benton, Texas Its Government and Politics (New York: Prentice Hall, 1961), pp. 364-392 describes the Texas court system.

21. Civil suits of $750 or less may be tried in the Idaho Probate Court as well as minor criminal offenses such as petit larceny. The District Court in Idaho tries more serious cases.

22. Wilbourn E. Benton, op. cit., pp. 384–387.

23. In Idaho, justices of the peace are appointed by the Board of County Commissioners and Probate Court judge with the approval of the senior District Court judge serving the county.

24. County governing bodies composed of judges and justices of the peace, and judge and commissioner boards are described more fully in chapter 3.

25. For a further description, see the duties of the county recorder in chapter 3.

26. See The County Officer, 28:472, December, 1963, for a description of the Spartanburg County program and The County Officer, 29:346, August, 1964, for a description of the Sullivan County program.

27. See particularly a description of the work of the Milwaukee County extension staff in chapter 11.

28. Edgar L. Morphet, Roe L. Johns, and Theodore L. Reller, Educational Administration: Concepts, Practices, and Issues (Englewood Cliffs, N. J.: Prentice-Hall, 1959), p. 221.

29. U. S. Bureau of the Census, Census of Governments, 1962, Vol. I, Governmental Organization (Washington: U. S. Government Printing Office, 1963), p. 38.

30. Committee for the White House Conference on Education, A Report to the President (Washington: U. S. Government Printing Office, 1956), p. 16. The Committee was also concerned about school districts that are too small. The Committee lists as disadvantages of these districts: the difficulty in getting good teachers, too narrow a curriculum, high per pupil costs, and problems of school location and transportation. Ibid., pp. 15, 16.

31. Advisory Commission on Intergovernmental Relations, Performance of Urban Functions: Local and Areawide, (Washington: Advisory Commission on Intergovernmental Relations, 1963), pp. 79, 80.

32. See Table 2, chapter 3.

33. For a description of the functions of the Washington County Superintendent of Schools, see Barbara Byers, op. cit., pp. 165–171.

34. Bureau of Government, University of Wisconsin, op. cit., p. 56.

35. Flora Jaquish, "A County Official's View" in: National Association of Counties, Urban County Congress (Washington: National Association of Counties, 1959), p. 95.

36. Westchester County, Westchester (an undated publication of Westchester County, New York), p. 23.

37. Rose Vainstein, "Public Library Standards — Their Development and Use," Mountain Plains Library Quarterly (Fall 1960), cited by Advisory Commission on Intergovernmental Relations, Performance of Urban Functions: Local and Areawide, p. 85.

38. Bureau of Government, University of Wisconsin, op. cit., p. 57.

39. The Municipal Yearbook, 1963 (Chicago: International City Managers' Association, 1963), p. 344.

40. Advisory Commission on Intergovernmental Relations, Performance of Urban Functions: Local and Areawide, p. 156.

41. Westchester County inspects out-of-county dairy herds to make sure that diseased milk does not come into the county. Westchester County, Westchester, p. 16.

42. The County Officer, 29:369, September, 1964. Lee County, Florida reported a 100% kill of mosquitoes in spraying its beaches.

43. Westchester County, Westchester, p. 17

44. Jean J. Schueneman, Air Pollution Problems and Control Programs in the United States, a paper presented to the 55th Annual Meeting of the Air Pollution Control Association. (Chicago: May 20-24, 1962), Table 6, cited by Advisory Commission on Intergovernmental Relations, Performance of Urban Functions: Local and Areawide, p.174.

45. United States Department of Health, Education and Welfare, Bureau of Family Services, Characteristics of State Public Assistance Plans Under the Social Security Act (Washington: United States Bureau of Family Services, 1964) describes the division of administrative responsibility between state and local welfare agencies in each state.

46. The County Officer, 30:26, February, 1965.

47. The County Officer, 29:288, June, 1964.

48. American County Government, 30:21, April, 1965.

49. Bureau of Social and Political Research, Michigan State University, The County Board of Supervisors (East Lansing: Michigan State University, 1959), p. 41.

50. Ibid., pp. 41-43.

51. William H. Cape, op. cit., pp. 138, 139.

52. County of Los Angeles, Guide to Departmental Organizations and Functions (Los Angeles: County of Los Angeles, 1963), p. 63.

53. National Association of Counties, County Action for Outdoor Recreation (Washington: National Association of Counties, 1964), p. 3.

54. Ibid., p. 5.

55. Ibid., pp. 38, 39.

56. American County Government, 30:6, July, 1965.

57. The County Officer, 29:53, January, 1964.

58. The County Officer, 28:406, November, 1963.

59. The County Officer, 28:230, June, 1963.

60. Joseph Prendergast, "The County's Role in Recreation," Recreation 55:515, December, 1962.

61. Westchester County, Westchester, p. 19.

62. Joseph Prendergast, op. cit., p. 515.

63. George D. Butler, "Recreation Administration in Metropolitan Areas," Recreation, 55:411-414, October, 1962. Large recreation parks, reservations, golf courses, camps, zoological parks, nature preserves, cultural centers, and parkways are examples of nonlocal recreational facilities, according to Mr. Butler.

64. National Association of Counties, County Action for Outdoor Recreation, p. 6.

65. In providing planning services, counties may also be meeting the requirements for federal aid.

66. Donald Webster, Urban Planning and Municipal Public Policy (New York: Harper and Brothers, 1958), p. 4.

67. Ibid., p. 7.

68. For example, scattered marginal farms in forested areas are a cause of forest fires, excessive school bus transportation costs, and high road maintenance costs. For a description of rural planning and zoning problems see Donald Webster, op. cit., pp. 372, 373.

69. Table 2 in this chapter also shows that the proportion of counties engaged in planning decreases as the population of the county decreases.

70. Harry E. Bergh, The "Diminishing County" Myth (Orange County, California: Orange County Planning Department, 1963), p. 2. Mr. Bergh points out the relatively low costs and advantages of county planning.

71. Westchester County, Westchester, p. 27. The Commissioner of Public Works and the Commissioner of Parks, Recreation and Conservation also sit on the Planning Board.

72. Frank Gibson and Edward Overman, County Government in Virginia (Charlottesville: League of Virginia Counties and Bureau of Public Administration, University of Virginia, 1961) p. 34, 35.

73. Donald Webster, op. cit., p. 362.

74. Frank Gibson and Edward Overman, op. cit., p. 36.

75. William H. Cape, op. cit., p. 80.

76. Advisory Commission on Intergovernmental Relations, Performance of Urban Functions: Local and Areawide, p. 250.

77. Housing and Home Finance Agency, Urban Renewal Administration, The Urban Renewal Program, Fact Sheet (Washington: Housing and Home Finance Agency, 1962), p. 1.

78. Victor Jones, "Local Government Organization in Metropolitan Areas: Its Relation to Urban Redevelopment," Part IV, The Future of Cities and Urban Redevelopment, ed. Coleman Woodbury (Chicago: University of Chicago Press, 1953), p. 483. Victor Jones stresses that the Balkanization of local government in metropolitan areas results in unequal services, unequal tax burdens and unequal application of controls.

79. Advisory Commission on Intergovernmental Relations, Performance of Urban Functions: Local and Areawide, p. 250.

80. Building codes may be designed to assure that new buildings have sufficient structural strength, are reasonably safe from fire, and have proper plumbing and electrical wiring. Donald Webster, op. cit., pp. 511, 512. Donald Webster lists a number of model building and construction codes which may be adopted by cities and counties.

81. Advisory Commission on Intergovernmental Relations, Performance of Urban Functions: Local and Areawide, p. 238.

82. Ibid., p. 240.

83. Tables 1 and 2 of this chapter provide further detail.

84. The Montgomery County, Maryland Department of Information and Economic Development has published much information of this type. One report contains a detailed chemical analysis of the water used in the county.

85. A few counties have issued industrial revenue bonds to finance building construction for new industries. This practice has been attacked by Bernard Hillenbrand as endangering the tax exempt status of county bonds. The County Officer, 29:415, October, 1964.

86. Max Harral, "Nine Rural Georgia Counties Organize Regional Economic Development Group," American County Government, 30:18, 19, October, 1965.

87. The County Officer, 30:12, February, 1965.

88. Ibid., p. 26.

89. Gordon E. Misner, "Recent Developments in the Metropolitan Law Enforcement," The Journal of Criminal Law, Criminology, and Police Science, 50:500, January–February, 1960.

90. The existence of many small police departments also results in high cost staff services, inadequate police training, and personnel rosters that are too small to meet emergency conditions. Ibid., pp. 499–501.

91. Advisory Commission on Intergovernmental Relations, Performance of Urban Functions: Local and Areawide, p. 130.

92. Ibid., p. 113.

93. Ibid., p. 116.

94. Clyde F. Snider, op. cit., p. 361.

95. United States Bureau of Public Roads, Highway Statistics, 1962 (Washington, D. C.: U. S. Government Printing Office, 1964, p. 136. In addition, there were 55,953 miles within municipalities under state control.

96. Ibid., p. 136. Total road and street mileage in the United States was 3,599,581 in 1962 of which 455,244 was within municipalities and 3,144,337 was rural mileage. Counties controlled 1,741,885 miles of rural roads; states, 673,139; towns and townships, 542,189; the federal government, 119,763; and other units of government such as special districts, 67,361.

97. Clyde F. Snider, op. cit., p. 366.

98. Ward S. Armstrong, "'Do it Yourself' Roads Study is Success for Oregon Counties," The County Officer, 29:478, 498, 499, November, 1964. County roads were individually analyzed, and the accumulated data on each road was valuable in itself for county road officials.

99. For further information on the commuter crisis, see Wilfred Owen, The Metropolitan Transportation Problem (Washington: The Brookings Institution, 1956), pp. 67–104; Michael N. Danielson, Federal-Metropolitan Politics and the Commuter Crisis (New York: Columbia University Press, 1965); and Lyle Fitch, "A Transit Paradox," National Civic Review, 51:181–187, April, 1962.

100. Michael N. Danielson, op. cit., p. 51 reports, for example, that the President of the Delaware, Lackawanna and Western Railroad declared in 1958 that his railroad would abandon passenger service unless it received immediate relief from all property taxes.

101. The National Association of Counties has endorsed federal transit aid since 1962. County Executive Edward Michaelian of Westchester County, New York testified on behalf of federal transit aid as did County Executive Eugene Nickerson of Nassau County, New York. Ibid., p. 176.

102. Westchester County, Westchester, p. 22.

103. In most large cities, the number of transit passengers in 1954 was less than in 1940. The reduction in transit passengers was greatest in eastern and mid-western cities. Wilfred Owen, op. cit., p. 75.

104. The County Officer, 29:118, March, 1964.

105. The County Officer, 28:302, July, 1963.

106. For a further description of the study, see pages 72 and 73.

107. The County Officer, 28:315, September, 1963.

108. Westchester County, Westchester, p. 22.

109. Advisory Commission on Intergovernmental Relations, Performance of Urban Functions: Local and Areawide, p. 200.

110. Ibid., pp. 201-203.

111. The County Officer, 28:369, October, 1963.

112. Advisory Commission on Intergovernmental Relations, Performance of Urban Functions: Local and Areawide, p. 192.

113. Ibid.

Chapter 5

County Revenues and Finances

IN MOST STATES, county financial administration affects other units of local government because property taxes are assessed and collected by county officials and distributed to cities, school districts, and other local units. Measures which strengthen the county property tax collection process benefit all local government. This chapter describes property tax and other sources of county revenue as well as county expenditure trends, debt trends, and other aspects of financial administration.

REVENUE SOURCES

The two most important revenue sources of county government are: (1) property taxes and (2) state aid and other state government sources. Counties also receive funds from non-property taxes, federal aid, charges for services, interest earnings, and other revenues.

The pattern of county government revenues differs from state to state. In some states, counties rely heavily on the property tax; in other states, the major revenue source is state aid or taxes collected at the state level and allocated to counties. In a few states, counties receive a substantial per cent of their income from non-property taxes or current charges. Nevada counties, for example, receive 15% of their income from gambling, gasoline and other non-property taxes. Table 2 shows three differing patterns of county revenue.

Table 1
COUNTY GENERAL REVENUE, 1962*

Source of Revenue	Amount of Revenue (in millions)		Per Cent of Total Revenue	
General revenue from own sources				
Taxes				
Property	3,879		45.7	
Other	271	4,149	3.2	48.9
Charges and miscellaneous				
Current charges	824		9.7	
Interest earnings	52		.6	
Special assessments	40		.5	
Sale of property	11		.1	
Other and unallocable	133	1,060	1.6	12.5
Intergovernmental general revenue				
From state government only	3,084		36.3	
From other sources	192	3,276	2.3	38.6
		8,485		100.0

*Adapted from: U.S. Bureau of the Census, *Census of Governments, 1962, Finances of County Governments* (Washington: U.S. Government Printing Office, 1964), p. 9. Due to rounding, details may not add up to totals.

Property Taxes

County property taxes are levied on three types of property:(1) real property such as land, buildings, and other improvements of a permanent nature; (2) tangible personal property such as household furnishings, livestock, farm machinery, store inventories, and automobiles; and (3) intangible personal property such as stocks, bonds, bank accounts, and other liquid assets. In some states, all property is taxed at a uniform rate. In others, property is classified into groups with intangible personal property usually taxed at the lowest rates.

Property taxes on personal property have been particularly difficult to administer. It is very difficult for the assessor to discover the amount of intangible property a taxpayer has unless he voluntarily lists it.(1) Non-listing of intangibles and some types of tangible personal property such as jewelry and household furniture is widespread. As a result, property taxes in many areas have become largely a tax on real property and certain difficult-to-hide personal property items such as store inventories, farm machinery, and livestock. In recognition of the difficulty of taxing certain property, about half the states are reported to exempt all or some intangibles, and about 34 states exempt all or part of non-income producing tangible personal property.(2) In a number of states, automobile owners pay a special excise tax in lieu of personal property taxes.(3)

Table 2
PER CENT DISTRIBUTION OF GENERAL REVENUES
OF COUNTY GOVERNMENT BY SOURCE, IN SELECTED STATES, 1962*

	Property Taxes	Non-Property Taxes	Intergovern-mental Revenue from State	Current Charges	Other	Total
Pattern 1-heavy dependence on property tax						
Vermont	91%	0%	7%	1%	1%	100%
Montana	78%	8%	3%	7%	4%	100%
South Dakota	75%	13%	7%	3%	2%	100%
West Virginia	72%	1%	5%	16%	6%	100%
North Dakota	71%	2%	18%	2%	7%	100%
Pattern 2-heavy dependence on state sources						
North Carolina	25%	1%	60%	11%	3%	100%
Hawaii	18%	13%	52%	15%	2%	100%
Colorado	43%	1%	49%	6%	1%	100%
Ohio	33%	1%	49%	12%	5%	100%
Wisconsin	40%	**	48%	7%	5%	100%
Pattern 3-balanced pattern with dependence on several sources						
Alabama	28%	18%	42%	9%	3%	100%
Kentucky	45%	13%	14%	21%	7%	100%
Nevada	32%	15%	17%	30%	6%	100%
Washington	39%	12%	35%	9%	5%	100%

*Adapted from: U. S. Bureau of the Census, Census of Governments, 1962, Finances of County Governments, p. 11.

**Less than 1%.

Real property taxes are more easily administered than personal property taxes but still pose administrative problems. Keeping an up-to-date record on all land and buildings in the county is a time-consuming task. In a number of states, county assessors use guides prepared by state tax officials in placing values on land and buildings.(4) However, judgment must be used by assessors in determining the final assessment. After real property is once assessed, it may be carried at the same assessment year after year unless the owner adds to or sells his land or buildings. In some counties, such as Latah County, Idaho, buildings are depreciated in value as they grow older so that a home owner's assessment will diminish each year as his house ages. Periodically in many states, there is a re-assessment in which assessors revisit each parcel of property and make a new assessment of its value.

State governments have provided valuable assistance to county assessors. State tax commissions commonly conduct research on property taxes, provide tax manuals, and conduct periodic meetings for discussion of assessment procedures.(5) State universities have conducted annual conferences of assessing officers which feature experts in various fields of assessment.(6) State tax commissions also make assessments on public utility property and other types of property that are difficult to assess locally.(7)

One serious problem with the property tax is underassessment. The elected county assessors are under continuing political pressure from constituents to keep property tax assessments low. As a result, assessments are usually far below true market value, and in many states the ratios of assessed to true value vary from county to county.(8) This may result in inequities where state aid computations are based on local tax rates. For example, a state may require a school district to levy a 20 mill (2%) school tax on all property before it provides state aid. Taxpayers in counties in which property is assessed at 20% of market value will pay less in taxes and may get the benefit of more state aid than taxpayers in counties whose property is assessed at 40% of market value.(9) To counteract underassessment, some states attempt to equalize assessments between counties or adjust their state aid formulas so that counties are not penalized because their ratios of assessed to true valuation are higher than other counties in the state.

A second serious problem with the property tax is the extensiveness of property tax exemptions. Publicly owned property is almost always exempt from property taxation as is property used for religious, charitable and educational purposes. Intangible property and tangible personal property are exempt in a number of states. These exemptions include: agricultural machinery, certain types of manufactured products and the "homestead exemption" which makes owner occupied houses wholly or partially exempt from taxation.(10) These exemptions considerably reduce the yield of the property tax as well as make it more difficult to administer.

Tax limits set by state constitutions and state laws present a third serious problem with the property tax. In 1962, 37 states limited the property taxing powers of counties for general governmental purposes.(11) The constitution of Alabama, for example, sets a maximum county tax rate of 23.6 mills ($23.60 per $1,000 of assessed valuation) and sets maximums on the county tax rates for general purposes, roads, bridges, public buildings and for other purposes.(12) Tax limits of this type are found in many states and have two unfortunate consequences. They tend to establish ceilings on the extensiveness of county services through their limitations on county funds. The earmarking of amounts for specified purposes is confusing and disrupts county budgeting.(13)

The property tax itself, as well as its administration, has been criticized.(14) The property tax is not levied in accord with a person's ability to pay. A farmer earning less than $3,000 a year may pay more in property taxes than a city home owner earning more than $30,000 a year. The property tax has also been criticized because the taxes a property owner pays have no necessary relationship to the services he has received from government. Furthermore, the yield of the property tax has not kept pace with prices and government costs. Despite its faults, the property tax is still the key to local government finance.(15) Cities, school districts, and townships, as well as counties, may depend upon the property tax for years to come.

In 1963, the Advisory Commission on Intergovernmental Relations made a series of recommendations designed to strengthen the property tax.(16) The Commission urged the modernization of state tax laws and the elimination of detailed state constitutional provisions which obstruct utilization and administration of the property tax. It recommended that a thorough re-evaluation of property tax exemptions be made as a means of reducing the loss in property taxes through exemptions. The Commission suggested that assessment should be on a county-wide or multi-county basis and that state supervisory agencies should be empowered to establish the professional qualifications of assessors and certify the fitness of candidates on the basis of examinations.(17) Under the recommendations of the Commission, assessors would be appointed rather than elected, and training courses would be conducted for assessors before they took office.

Non-Property Taxes

While counties in some states such as Delaware, Indiana, Maine, Minnesota, New Hampshire, New Jersey, Oklahoma, South Carolina and Vermont make little use of non-property taxes, this type of taxation is an important source of revenue in many other states.(18) More than 10% of all county revenue in Alabama, Hawaii, Kentucky, Nevada, South Dakota, Texas, and Washington comes from this source.

County sales taxes were imposed in 1964 by: 18 counties in Alabama, 58 counties in California, 68 counties in Illinois, 4 parishes in Louisiana, 5 counties in New York, 2 counties in Tennessee, and 24 counties in Utah.(19) Louisiana parishes administer the sales tax, while California and Illinois counties have the tax collected for them by the state. Counties reimburse the state for its costs in collecting the tax for them. Sales tax rates

rates vary from 1/2 to 3%. County sales taxes are most effective when they are imposed by all counties in an area; otherwise consumers on the borders of the county may shop in neighboring counties to avoid the tax.

Selective sales taxes on certain commodities are another important source of county income. In 1964, gasoline taxes were imposed by 12 Alabama counties, 4 Hawaiian counties, 3 Mississippi counties and 17 Nevada counties.(20) Alabama counties impose a tax on lubricating oil and other fuels. In 1964, six counties in Alabama and Shelby County, Tennessee imposed a cigarette tax. Garrett County, Maryland, some Alabama counties, and certain Louisiana parishes have the authority to levy a tax on beer. Most Virginia counties receive income from the issuance of auto license plates.

Business licenses and business taxes provide further sources of county income. Persons engaged in a number of types of businesses in Alabama must obtain county as well as state licenses.(21) Nevada counties received $2.6 million in 1959 from a county table tax on gambling establishments.(22) The tax was based on the number of games, and games such as poker were taxed at the rate of $300 a year. There were taxes imposed by a number of counties on mortgages and local real estate transfers.

The county income tax is a potential source of substantial revenue that has been largely untapped by county government. As of 1964, Jefferson County, Kentucky was the only county reporting an income tax.(23)

County non-property taxes are an important and largely untapped source of county revenue in many states. Removal of restrictions on the imposition of these taxes is needed in many states before counties can make fuller use of them.

Revenue from Intergovernmental Sources

In 1962, counties received $3,084,000,000 in intergovernmental revenue from state governments, $134,000,000 from other local governments, and $58,000,000 from the federal government.(24) Intergovernmental revenue from state sources includes state grants-in-aid and the county share of taxes collected by state government. Grants-in-aid generally consist of appropriations from state funds which do not fluctuate in amount in accordance with the amount of taxes collected. They are allocated to counties and other units of local government on the basis of formulas which take into account such factors as: the population of the county, number of miles of roads, school attendance, or number of welfare cases. Grants may be for specific purposes such as education, welfare, and highways or for general purposes. New York State, for example, provides per capita grants to counties that are not earmarked for any specific county purpose.

State shared taxes are taxes collected by state governments which are shared by the state and local communities on fixed formulas. The amount of these tax revenues received by counties bears a direct relationship to the amount collected by the state. Counties, for example, receive a share of state collected income taxes in Maryland, South Carolina, Tennessee, and Wisconsin.(25) In South Carolina, this tax is distributed to counties on a population basis, and in Wisconsin and Tennessee on the basis of the residence of the taxpayer. State collected sales taxes are shared with counties in Alabama, Arizona, Hawaii, and Kansas.(26) Louisiana parishes and counties in 23 other states receive a portion of state collected gasoline taxes. Counties in more than a dozen states receive a share of state collected motor vehicle and operator license fees. Louisiana parishes and counties in Kansas, Maryland, Minnesota, Nevada, New Mexico, and Wyoming receive a share of state collected cigarette taxes. In a dozen states, counties receive a share of state collected alcoholic beverage taxes. Tax sharing between states and counties has several advantages over separately imposed state and local taxes, according to the Advisory Commission on Intergovernmental Relations.(27) It eliminates the additional costs of taxation by two levels of government. It gives counties the benefit of state enforcement facilities and eliminates intercounty competition for lower tax rates. However, it does remove from the county the ability to impose or not impose the tax. The decision as to whether tax rates are to be raised or lowered is also made at the state level.

Federal grants-in-aid directly to county government amounted to $58 million in 1962 and were provided mainly for airport construction, low rent public housing, urban renewal and waste treatment construction. In states having county operated school systems, counties receive federal grants for school construction and operation in areas of federal military establishments. Even larger amounts of federal aid reach counties indirectly through state government. Federal aid for highways and welfare reaches county government in this manner. Federally shared revenues from the distribution of forest reserve funds, flood control funds, and grazing fees are another important source of federal revenue which comes to counties through state government.(28) Since 1962, additional federal grant programs have been established which will directly or indirectly increase county government revenues. Federal grants for urban mass transit will aid counties and other local governments in developing mass transit systems.(29) The grant may amount to as much as two-thirds of the project cost. Funds are available under the Economic Opportunity Act of 1964 for local health, educational, and industrial development projects.(30)

Intergovernmental revenues come to counties from cities, townships, and special districts. In most cases, this revenue is to reimburse the county for services performed for other local governmental units.

Other County Revenue Sources

Counties received more than one billion dollars from sources other than taxes and intergovernmental revenues in 1962. Current charges provided $824 million, of which $353 million were charges by county hospitals for services performed for their patients.(31) Other charges include amounts charged for rental of county auditoriums and stadiums, airport hanger rentals, and green fees on county golf courses. Investment earnings of counties on idle funds, special assessments against property owners for the construction of streets, sidewalks, and sewers, and sales of county property are other general revenue sources.

Counties have three sources of earmarked revenues not shown on Table 1 of this chapter. Counties earned $46 million in 1962 from utilities, $71 million from their liquor stores, and $92 million from their retirement systems.(32) Maryland, Minnesota, North Carolina, South Dakota, and Wisconsin have laws permitting municipalities and counties to operate liquor stores.(33) In 1964, 9 counties in Maryland and 36 counties in North Carolina operated liquor stores.

EXPENDITURE TRENDS

There has been a continuing upward trend in county government expenditures since 1913, as Table 3 shows. Rising price levels, which have been associated with increased personnel and material costs, are one reason for the increased dollar expenditures. Increasing populations which require proportional increases in governmental services are another reason for the upward trend. These two trends do not explain the entire 2,157% increase in county government expenditures. A third important factor in this increase is the expansion of existing county services and the extension of county services to new fields.

There is considerable variation in county expenditures from state to state. The average expenditure in 1962 by the median county in the United States was $52.22 per capita.(34) The highest county expenditure per capita was in Hawaii ($209 per capita), Colorado ($176), Maryland ($148), California ($134), Nevada ($127), and North Carolina ($113).(35) In all of these states, counties are providing extensive services in one or more fields. Maryland and

Table 3
EXPENDITURES FOR FUNCTIONS OF COUNTY GOVERNMENT, 1913-1962*
(in millions of dollars)

Function	1913	1932	1957	1962	Per Cent Increase 1913 to 1962
Parks and recreation	.4	8	67	123	30,650%
Libraries	.4	4	31	59	14,650%
Natural resources			126	226	
Health			132	193	
Sewage			103	92	
Health and sanitation	3.	33			
Police protection			193	303	
Protection to persons and property	15.	44			
Education (excluding capital outlay)	58.	178	764	1,176	1,928%
Highways (excluding capital outlay)	55.	236	800	990	1,700%
Public welfare			1,135	1,865	
Charities, hospitals and corrections	38.	182			
Capital outlay	90.	311	1,035	1,421	1,653%
Interest on debt	17.	119	90	159	835%
Other	108.2	297	1,424	2,083	
Total	385.	1,412	5,900	8,690	2,157%

*Sources: Bureau of the Census, *Wealth, Debt and Taxation, 1913* (Washington: Government Printing Office, 1915), pp. 210, 211.   Bureau of the Census, *Financial Statistics of State and Local Governments, 1932* (Washington: U. S. Government Printing Office, 1935), p. 28.   Bureau of the Census, *Census of Governments, 1962, Finances of County Governments* (Washington: U. S. Government Printing Office, 1964), p. 9. The expenditure categories used in 1957 and 1962 differ from the categories used in 1913 and 1932 in some instances. Percentage increases were only computed for expenditure categories which appear to contain relatively comparable cost data.

North Carolina counties operate many of the school systems in the state; California and Colorado counties have extensive public welfare programs; Hawaiian counties have an extensive hospital program. The lowest county expenditures per capita were in Vermont ($.37 per capita), Maine ($6), Massachusetts ($9), and

New Hampshire ($11). Counties in New England states tend to have low per capita costs because townships provide many services in New England that counties provide in other states.

In 1962, the greatest per cent of county funds was expended for public welfare, highways, education and hospitals. As Table 4 shows, there are significant variations among states in their expenditure patterns. North Carolina is typical of the four states in which public school education is largely a county function. Both California and New York have comprehensive public welfare programs administered largely at the county level. Texas is typical of a number of states with very extensive county highway programs. In Indiana, as in many states, no single function receives more than one-fourth of the total expenditures.

Table 4

PER CENT DISTRIBUTION OF GENERAL EXPENDITURE OF COUNTY GOVERNMENT BY FUNCTION, IN SELECTED STATES, 1962*

Function	U. S. Average	California	Indiana	New York	North Carolina	Texas
	%	%	%	%	%	%
Public welfare	21.5	36.4	24.0	30.3	15.1	2.8
Highways	18.0	8.2	21.4	15.3	0	38.0
Education	15.8	3.0	9.7	4.2	69.4	.1
Hospitals	10.8	11.6	19.0	6.9	4.6	12.5
General control	6.4	5.5	6.6	5.8	1.7	11.0
Police protection	3.5	3.8	2.3	5.9	1.0	5.4
Financial administration	3.1	3.0	7.2	1.6	1.2	6.3
General public buildings	2.8	3.6	1.5	3.2	0.6	5.4
Natural resources	2.6	7.6	1.7	0.9	0.5	3.6
Correction	2.4	3.8	0.9	2.5	0.3	3.7
Health	2.2	2.7	1.0	4.6	1.5	1.3
Interest on debt	1.8	1.0	0.6	2.6	1.8	4.1
Parks and recreation	1.4	1.6	0.2	2.3	0	1.9
Other and unallocable	7.7	8.1	3.9	13.8	2.3	3.8

*Adapted from: U. S. Bureau of the Census, *Census of Governments, 1962, Finances of County Governments*, p. 16.

Counties in many states do not have complete control over their own expenditures. Counties in Oregon, for example, must pay the cost of fees and mileage for jurors, indigent counsel fees, and other charges over which the county governing body has no control.(36) In Idaho, county officials are responsible for automobile licensing and titling, driver licensing, and other state functions. Furthermore, counties are required to raise taxes and provide funds for state and school district purposes. In Oregon, welfare is a state function, and schools are administered by independent school districts. Nevertheless, counties are required to raise funds for both schools and welfare. State-mandated county expenditures inflate county budgets and taxes and are difficult for county officials to explain to taxpayers.

COUNTY DEBT

At the end of the 1962 fiscal year, counties had an outstanding debt of $5.4 billion.(37). Long-term county debt amounted to $5.2 billion, of which $1.1 billion was for county schools and the remainder for other purposes. Partially offsetting this county debt were county holdings in cash and securities which amounted to $3.6 billion at the end of the 1962 fiscal year.

Counties, like cities, are subject to a variety of restrictions in state constitutions and laws on the incurrence of debt. Frequently there is a debt limit that a county cannot exceed. Michigan counties cannot increase their indebtedness beyond 5% of their assessed valuation.(38) Alabama counties are limited in debt to 3-1/2% of their assessed valuation.(39) According to the Advisory Commission on Intergovernmental Relations, county debt limits vary from 2% to 20% of assessed valuation.(40)

Constitutional and statutory debt limits on local government are severely criticized by the Advisory Commission on Intergovernmental Relations. The Commission recommends repeal of these limitations on the grounds that they are barriers rather than stimulants to budgeting, accounting, and reporting of local government.(41) Local government debt limits have also caused the establishment of special districts which are not bound by city and county debt limits and are thus able to finance needed public improvements.

The incurrence of county debt may be authorized in a variety of ways. In seven states, action of the county governing board is all that is required to incur debt.(42) In 20 states, a referendum is required in which all electors are eligible to vote, and in nine of these states the majority in favor of incurring debt must be 60% or more. In ten states, a similar referendum is required but only those owning property may vote. Provisions for authorization of bonds by referendum date back more than fifty years in most states to the days in which bond issues were relatively rare. The Advisory Commission on Intergovernmental Relations has criticized referenda of this type as seriously hampering effective and responsible local government.(43) It recommends that authority to issue bonds should be legally vested in the governing bodies of units of local government subject only to a referendum initiated by a petition of the voters.(44) If a petition signed by a sufficient number of voters did force a vote on the bond issue, the Commission recommends that a simple majority of all eligible voters should be enough to pass the bond issue.(45)

The issuance and retirement of county bonds is a complex process. County bonds are normally sold through a bid procedure to bond houses or security dealers who resell them to investors.(46) The bond houses make a careful review of the fiscal condition of the county before they bid on county bonds. The sale price of county bonds depends on a variety of factors such as the amount of outstanding debt, the assessed value of county property, and the amount of tax delinquencies.

Two general types of county bond issues are revenue bonds and general obligation bonds. Revenue bonds are issued to finance revenue producing county projects and are repaid from the revenues of these projects. The county is not obligated to repay these bonds from general revenue sources if the project revenues should fall short of expectations. In contrast, general obligation bonds are repaid from the general revenues of the county. Investors prefer general obligation bonds, and a county can receive lower interest rates on these bonds.

Counties and other units of local government have made effective use of financial advisers and bond consultants to secure the most favorable interest rates on their bond issues.(47) However, many smaller counties may not be able to afford bond consultants. The Advisory Commission on Intergovernmental Relations recommends that state governments extend technical and advisory assistance to counties and other units of local government to assist in the issuance of long-term debt.(48) Perhaps the most effective controls state government can extend over county debt are flexible limitations on interest rates rather than rigid limitations on the amount of debt.(49)

FINANCIAL ADMINISTRATION

Financial administration in county government includes budgeting, accounting, auditing, revenue collecting, and investment and debt management. Purchasing, data processing, and management anlysis are closely related to financial administration.

The Budget Process

The budget is the county's annual financial plan. Counties are typically required by law to adopt a budget each fiscal year, and many of the procedures of budget adoption are stipulated by state law.(50)   The   budget   process   usually   begins   within   county departments several months before the beginning of the fiscal year.(51) Each department makes its own estimate of needs for the next fiscal year, and these estimates are transmitted to a county budget official. In smaller counties, this budget official may be an elected county clerk, auditor, or treasurer who may only be responsible for compiling this budget data for presentation to the county governing body. In a number of larger counties, the budget requests of county departments are carefully analyzed by trained budget staffs. Milwaukee County, Wisconsin, for example, has a budget staff of six analysts having extensive knowledge of county departments. This budget staff spends two months reviewing in detail requests from county departments using cost and workload data to determine the need for funds. Later the elected County Executive schedules a series of budget hearings in which each department head must justify his request before the County Executive and the budget staff. At the end of this process, the Milwaukee County Executive prepares a five volume county budget which provides the County Board of Supervisors with detailed information on the plans, workload and costs of county programs. The budget document also contains estimates of revenues for the next fiscal year.

The second stage in the county budget process comes when the budget requests are presented to the county governing body. In smaller counties, the requests of county departments may not have previously been screened by a county budget staff. In this case, the county board members may review each item in the budget over a period of weeks conferring, in turn, with each department head and elective officer. Frequently, the county auditor, clerk or treasurer will sit in on all budget hearings to provide information for the county board. In its review, the board keeps in mind the total budget requests in relation to the revenue estimates for the county. In Alabama, as in many states, appropriations made by the county board must not exceed the income available for appropriations.(52) The county board is almost always faced with the problem of determining which requests must be reduced to keep appropriations within anticipated income. Towards the end of its budget review, the county board generally holds one or more public hearings to permit county citizens to express their views on the budget.(53) Finally, the county board adopts the budget and establishes tax levies for the next year.

In larger counties, the county governing body may call in the budget staff as well as department heads for questioning. The budget may first be considered by a fiscal committee of the county board and then reviewed by the county board as a whole in a manner not unlike the legislative review process in a unicameral state legislature. In Milwaukee County, as in a number of counties with an elected county executive, the budget passed by the board may be vetoed in whole or in part by the county executive.

Budget execution is the final stage in the county budget process. The amounts appropriated to each department are recorded on the appropriation accounting records of the county. Each time a department prepares a purchase order or commits the county to an expenditure of funds, a document is sent to the official who is responsible for maintaining the county's appropriation accounts. This official, usually the county auditor, records the encumbrance and reduces the unencumbered amount remaining the the appropriation. Similarly, when the goods purchased are received by the department, an accounting document (frequently called a voucher) is transmitted to the county auditor. This document is given a pre-audit by the county auditor and in some counties must be signed or approved by the county board. A warrant (or check) is then made out to the vender, and the county auditor makes an entry reducing the cash balance in the departmental appropriation. A county agency expending all of its appropriation may be able to secure a transfer of funds from another of its appropriation items or from an appropriation of another department. Where this is permitted, the approval of the county governing body is normally required.

The budget staff in larger counties sometimes exercises other controls to keep county agencies from overspending their appropriations. In Milwaukee County, the budget staff records month by month expenditures of county agencies, and an agency head whose unit is in danger of overspending its appropriation can expect to be called in for questioning.

Cash Accounting and Auditing

Besides the appropriation accounts kept usually by the county auditor, a second set of accounts is kept to record the cash balance in each county fund. As revenues are received by county agencies, they are transmitted to the county treasurer or a similar official who records this income and deposits the funds in a bank. The treasurer also records checks issued against county funds and keeps a current record of the balances in all county funds.(54) The treasurer reconciles the bank statements of county fund balances against his own records. If any county fund is in danger of being over-expended, the county board may order a cutback in spending or short-term revenue anticipation notes may be issued. Funds in excess of these currently needed by county departments, are frequently invested by the county treasurer in short-term U. S. government bonds.

Two types of county audits are made. A preaudit is made by a county official (usually the county auditor) before each expenditure is made to determine whether the expenditure is being made in accord with law and whether there are sufficient funds in the agency's appropriation. Officials making the preaudit will make sure that:

the proper purchasing procedures have been followed, the goods have been received, and the billing is correctly computed. A second or postaudit is commonly made after the end of the fiscal year. In many counties, this audit is made by a firm of certified public accountants or an auditor from a department of state government.(55) In this audit, inventories are checked, and accounting records are examined for errors or signs of fraud.

Purchasing

The purchasing practices of counties very widely. In rural counties, each elective official or department head usually makes his own purchases. State law often requires bid procedures if individual purchases exceed a specified dollar limit. It is often the practice for the county board to approve large purchases.

In a growing number of more populous counties, centralized purchasing procedures are used. Dade County (Miami, Florida), for example, has a consolidated purchasing division which saved the county $500,000 in its first year of operation.(56)

Centralized purchasing has many advantages.(57) If all purchases are made through one department (often only once a year), it is possible to buy in large quantities at a much lower price. Trained buyers in the purchasing office are able to write bid specifications in such a way that vendors know exactly what the county wants. The purchasing department examines supplies and equipment received to be sure that it meets bid specifications, thus guarding the county against shoddy purchases. Accounting controls are simplified when purchases are handled through a single department. In order to gain the maximum advantages from volume purchasing, counties have sometimes joined with cities, villages, and other units of local government to purchase jointly. Milwaukee County saved $25,000 for itself and cooperating cities and villages in the county in 1963 by purchasing rock salt in boatload lots.

Management Analysis and Data Processing

A number of more populous counties have employed management and data processing specialists to aid them in reducing costs. In Milwaukee County, four management analysts have been placed in the Management and Budget Analysis Department and have saved the county thousands of dollars by recommending improved procedures. In Frederick (a smaller county in Maryland), the Clerk to the County Board performs this function.(58) Los Angeles County has a large management staff and has also made use of management consulting firms for specialized studies.(59)

Data processing equipment has been used to reduce costs by many of the larger county governments. Computers are used to prepare county payrolls, prepare water billings, for highway design work, and for traffic control.(60) In payroll computation, the number of hours worked by each employee is fed into the computer which determines gross pay, makes appropriate deductions, prints the checks, and tabulates the total paid and the total of each type of deduction. San Mateo County, California uses electronic data processing to handle payrolls, welfare payments, traffic citations, fund accounting, and inventories.(61) San Mateo County also operates a computer service center and provides payroll, tax and other computer services for cities within the county. DeKalb County, Georgia has completely mechanized its accounting services and has been selected as a model for local government data processing services. (62)

SUMMARY - THE REVENUE SQUEEZE

Counties, like other units of local government, are caught in a revenue squeeze. Demands for county services, price levels, and populations are increasing. Counties have been hampered in expanding services to meet increased needs by limitations on the sources of county revenue.

Property tax revenues have not kept pace with increases in price levels and county populations in the last few decades. Elected county assessors have been placed under continuing political pressure from constituents to keep property tax assessments low, and assessments are far below market value in many states. Exemptions have considerably reduced the property tax base, and taxes on many categories of personal property are difficult to collect. Outmoded property tax limits are set by state constitutions and laws.

Other sources of revenue have not met county needs. County sales taxes were imposed by approximately 150 counties in 1964; the county income tax was used by only a single county. A larger number of counties used selective sales taxes, licenses, and fees as a means of finance, but none of these sources provide enough revenue to substitute for the property tax. Counties are restricted in the use of these non-property taxes by state constitutions and laws.

Other possible solutions to county fiscal problems lie in increased state aid, federal aid, and taxes collected by the state and shared with counties. There are administrative advantages in collecting a tax at the state or federal level and distributing funds back to counties. However, this process shifts important decisions on tax rates and program policies from the county to the federal or state level.

No solution is in sight for the fiscal problems that beset counties. However, measures to strengthen the property tax, removal of some of the limitations on property and non-property taxes, and increases in state collected, locally shared taxes seem to offer the greatest promise for county government.

REFERENCES

1. Clyde F. Snider, Local Government in Rural America (New York: Appleton-Century-Crofts Inc., 1957), p. 497.

2. R. A. Zubrow, R. L. Decker, E. H. Plank, Financing State and Local Government in Nevada (Carson City: Nevada State Printing Office, 1960), p. 164.

3. In Washington, car owners pay an excise tax at the same time they pay their automobile license fees. Barbara Byers, County Government in Washington State (Olympia: Washington State Association of County Commissioners, 1957), p. 45.

4. Ibid., pp. 42-44. Barbara Byers has an excellent description of the assessment process and the use of a state manual by assessors. Among the factors considered in fixing the value of a house are: the type of exterior finish of the house, number and use of rooms, types of inside walls and flooring, kind of heating system, and "extras" such as an air conditioning system.

5. R. A. Zubrow, R. L. Decker, E. H. Plank, op. cit., pp. 212-214 describe the work of the Nevada Assessment Standards Division. This Division has prepared an assessment manual and has carried out continuing research studies of the relationship of assessed to true value of property in the state.

6. At a typical South Dakota annual conference conducted by the University of South Dakota and State Department of Revenue, officials from Michigan, Illinois, Iowa, and Wisconsin spoke on their areas of specialization in assessing. University of South Dakota, Proceedings of the Sixth Annual Conference for South Dakota Assessing Officers (Vermillion: University of South Dakota, 1964).

7. In Nevada, the State Tax Commission is responsible for the appraising of interstate and intercounty utility property. These properties are difficult to assess locally because they require determination of factors such as the capitalization of the net income of utilities. R. A. Zubrow, R. L. Decker, E. H. Plank, op. cit., p. 206.

8. In Nevada in 1956, for example, assessment ratios ranged from 15.8% of true value in Douglas County to 30.4% in Lincoln County. The differences between assessment ratios in Nevada counties have since been reduced, perhaps as a result of the work of the Assessment Standards Division of the State Tax Commission. R. A. Zubrow, R. L. Decker, E. H. Plank, op. cit., p. 215 provide data on assessment ratios of Nevada counties.

9. In Illinois, Clyde Snider reports a similar situation, relative to a county levy for poor relief. Clyde F. Snider, op. cit., p. 501.

10. R. A. Zubrow, R. L. Decker, E. H. Plank, op. cit., p. 182 state that homesteads are exempt in 16 states, agricultural machinery of a specified value is exempt in one-quarter of the states, and certain types of manufactured products are exempt in five states.

11. Advisory Commission on Intergovernmental Relations, State Constitutional and Statutory Restrictions on Local Taxing Powers (Washington: Advisory Commission on Intergovernmental Relations, 1962), p. 39.

12. James D. Thomas, A Manual for Alabama County Commissioners, (University, Alabama: University of Alabama, 1963), p. 58.

13. Advisory Commission on Intergovernmental Relations, State Constitutional and Statutory Restrictions on Local Taxing Powers, pp. 46, 47 describes the problems of earmarked local taxes. The Commission states that: "In Minnesota this kind of legislative action has resulted in so many restrictions and limitations on local property taxing powers that it takes a 50 page booklet merely to list them all. Such a system is difficult to enforce, and if enforced impairs local government efficiency."

14. See, for example, the criticisms of Jewell Cass Phillips, Municipal Government and Administration in America (New York: The Macmillan Company, 1960), pp. 424-426.

15. This is the point of view taken by L. L. Ecker-Racz in The County Officer, 29:428, November, 1963.

16. Advisory Commission on Intergovernmental Relations, The Role of the States in Strengthening the Property Tax. Vol. I (Washington: U. S. Government Printing Office, 1963). The conclusions and recommendations of the Commission are summarized on pages 7-25.

17. In Kentucky, no person can have his name placed on the ballot for the office of county tax commissioner (assessor) unless he holds a certificate issued by the State Department of Revenue showing that he has been examined and found qualified for the office. Ibid., p. 104.

18. United States Bureau of the Census, Census of Governments, 1962, Finances of County Governments, p. 11.

19. Advisory Commission on Intergovernmental Relations, Tax Overlapping in the United States, 1964 (Washington: Advisory Commission on Intergovernmental Relations, 1964), p. 109.

20. Ibid., p. 173. The gasoline tax in Nevada is a state-imposed, locally shared tax but is included as a county tax by the Advisory Commission on Intergovernmental Relations because the counties have the option to refuse it.

21. James D. Thomas, op. cit., p. 60.

22. R. A. Zubrow, R. L. Decker, E. H. Plank, op. cit., p. 332.

23. Advisory Commission on Intergovernmental Relations, Tax Overlapping in the United States, 1964, p. 135.

24. U. S. Bureau of the Census, Census of Governments, 1962, Vol. 4 Compendium of Government Finances (Washington: U. S. Government Printing Office, 1964) p. 28.

25. Advisory Commission on Intergovernmental Relations, Tax Overlapping in the United States, pp. 138, 139.

26. Ibid., p. 111. Counties received almost $30 million from this source in 1962 in these four states.

27. Advisory Commission on Intergovernmental Relations, Local Nonproperty Taxes and the Coordinating Role of the State (Washington: Advisory Commission on Intergovernmental Relations, 1961), p. 49.

28. These federally distributed funds are of great importance to counties in Washington, Oregon, Idaho, California, Montana and Wyoming. In forested Clearwater County, Idaho, for example, 30% of all road fund receipts in 1964 came from the distribution of forest reserve funds.

29. The County Officer, 30:6, February, 1965.

30. Ibid., pp. 12, 13 and 26 describes the projects authorized in Craven County, North Carolina. An initial grant of $165,283 will be used to finance six projects and will be supplemented by a contribution of $40,013 by Craven County.

31. U. S. Bureau of the Census, Census of Governments, 1962, Finances of County Governments, p. 10.

32. Ibid., p. 9.

33. Advisory Commission on Intergovernmental Relations. Tax Overlapping in The United States, pp. 199-201.

34. Bureau of the Census, Census of Governments, 1962, Finances of County Governments, p. 20.

35. Ibid., pp. 21-67.

36. Kenneth C. Tollenaar, Executive Secretary, Association of Oregon Counties, letter dated January 3, 1966.

37. U. S. Bureau of the Census, Census of Governments, 1962, Finances of County Governments, p. 17.

38. Bureau of Social and Political Research, Michigan State University, The County Board of Supervisors (East Lansing: Michigan State University, 1959), p. 127. Counties with an assessed valuation of $5 million or less have a debt limit of 3%; other counties have a debt limit of 5%. This limitation does not apply to highway or drain bonds.

39. James D. Thomas, op. cit., p. 74. Certain debt is excluded from the constitutional debt limitation.

40. Advisory Commission on Intergovernmental Relations, State Constitutional and Statutory Restrictions on Local Government Debt (Washington: Advisory Commission on Intergovernmental Relations, 1961), p. 89.

41. Ibid., p. 75.

42. Ibid., p. 88.

43. Ibid., p. 73.

44. Ibid., p. 72.

45. Ibid. A simple majority is one vote more than 50% of the votes cast.

46. For a description of the process of selling county bond issues, see John Whitbeck, "Selling Bond Issues," The Urban County Congress of the National Association of County Officials (Washington: National Association of County Officials, 1959), pp. 102-104.

47. Middlesex County (New Jersey), Fairfax County (Virginia), and Dallas County (Texas) are examples of counties using New York bond consultants. The County Officer, 30:53, March, 1965.

48. Advisory Commission on Intergovernmental Relations, State Constitutional and Statutory Restrictions on Local Government Debt, p. 82.

49. Ibid., pp. 77-83. For example, state law might provide that no local government shall issue bonds at a net interest cost that is more than 1.4 times the current yield rate of the highest grade municipal securities.

50. For a description of the requirements of New Jersey law on county budget procedures, see James M. Collier, County Government in New Jersey (New Brunswick, N. J.: Rutgers University Press, 1952), pp. 56, 57.

51. The fiscal year in some states begins on January first and corresponds to a calendar year. In other counties, the fiscal year begins the second Monday in January, the first of April, the first of July, or some other date.

52. James D. Thomas, op. cit., p. 67.

53. Before the County Board may adopt a budget in final form in New Jersey, state law requires that a public hearing be held. James M. Collier, op. cit., p. 57.

54. The county treasurer may share with the county board key decisions about the selection of banks for county funds. See William H. Cape, Handbook for South Dakota County Officials (Vermillion: University of South Dakota, 1961), pp. 52, 53 for a description of the South Dakota procedures for selecting banks for county funds.

55. New Jersey counties may employ a registered municipal accountant to conduct their postaudit. If a county fails to have a postaudit completed and filed within four months of the close of the fiscal year, the New Jersey

Division of Local Government is empowered to conduct the postaudit with its own staff and bill the county for the costs. James M. Collier, op. cit., p. 59.

56. The County Officer, 28:115, March, 1963.

57. For an extensive description of the procedures and advantages of centralized purchasing, see Maurice G. Postley, The Case for Cooperative or Centralized Purchasing, Information and Education Service Report No. 17 (Washington: National Association of Counties, n.d.).

58. The County Officer, 29:356, August, 1964.

59. The County Officer, 29:440, October, 1964.

60. James S. Baker, Using Computers in County Government, Information and Education Service Report No. 30 (Washington: National Association of Counties, 1964). This description of county use of data processing systems may also be found in The County Officer, 29 (May, 1964).

61. The County Officer, 28:288, July, 1963.

62. The County Officer, 30:13, July, 1965.

Chapter 6

County Intergovernmental Relationships

COUNTY GOVERNMENT IS PART OF A NETWORK of inter-governmental relationships that connects federal, state, and local governments in the United States. Counties were established primarily by state governments and there are important legal, fiscal, and other links between the state capital and the county seat. Fiscal, program, and informational links with the federal government are growing more numerous, although they are much less important today than county-state relationships. Gaining importance also are intergovernmental relationships between counties and other units of local government. In many areas, county governments are spearheading efforts at intergovernmental cooperation at the local level.

COUNTY-STATE RELATIONSHIPS

Legal relationships between state and local governments differ from the legal relationship between the national government and state governments. The Constitution of the United States provides a federal form of government with the nation and the states having independent sources of power. Congress cannot invalidate a law passed by a state legislature. Amendments to the United States Constitution must be ratified by either the legislatures of three-fourths of the states or conventions called in three-fourths of the states.

Within each state, however, state government and local governments do not have independent, equal sources of power. Counties, cities, and other units of local government have few, if any, powers which are not derived from state constitutions and state laws and which cannot be taken away through changes in state constitutions or state laws. Local units of government have no means of formally blocking state constitutional amendments inimical to their interests since these amendments are ratified by the state legislators and/or state voters rather than through action of local legislative bodies or conventions.

In a number of states, counties are given specific constitutional recognition as legal subdivisions of the state.(1) County government, in these states, cannot be abolished without amendment of the state constitution.(2) State constitutions frequently prescribe the manner in which counties may be formed or consolidated, often establish county elective offices, and sometimes list the terms and manner of election of county officials. By requiring county boards and independently elected county offices, many state constitutions are permitting only one form of county government. In some states, however, optional forms of government are permitted by the constitution.(3)

Within the framework of the state constitution, state laws control county government. These laws commonly prescribe in detail the duties of county officials. They limit the functions that counties can perform, set county tax limits, establish a system of county funds, and may prescribe detailed county procedures and forms.(4) To secure additional powers and funds, county officials are largely dependent upon the state legislature.

State legislation has taken several forms.(5) In former years, state legislatures passed much special legislation — each law dealing with a specific county. This type of legislation enabled the legislature to be flexible in providing individually for the needs of each county. However, it greatly increased the number of bills before the state legislature, facilitated discrimination against some counties, and resulted in legislators from the entire state acting on matters of concern to only one county. Reaction against abuses of special legislation resulted in the passage of constitutional amendments in many states which prohibited this type of legislation.

General laws are a second, and more common, form of state laws affecting counties. These laws reduce favoritism and discrimination by treating all counties alike. However, they are inflexible and provide the same functions for large urban counties as for small rural counties. In attempting to overcome this, some states have taken a third approach and have established a classification of counties based on county population. Washington, for example, has 11 population classes which vary from class AA counties having a population of 500,000 or more to class 9 counties having a population of 3,300 or less. Thus, some state laws apply to counties in the larger population classes, and others apply to counties with less population. Since urban and rural counties frequently have different problems, this is a more flexible type of state law. However, the system of county classification has been expanded in California to the point where there are 58 classifications of counties for salary purposes — one for each county. Thus, the legislature can establish salaries for each California county just as easily as if special legislation was permitted in that state.(6)

No matter what form state legislative control over counties takes, there are inherent disadvantages. One means of reducing these disadvantages is to permit counties greater freedom in framing their own rules and regulations. Optional charter laws in Montana, New York and a few other states have permitted counties to choose among several forms of county government organization. County home rule charters, framed in accord with a home rule constitutional amendment, have provided even greater flexibility to counties. The county home rule movement is described in greater detail in chapter 12.

State constitutions and laws are not the only form of state influence on county government. State courts can invalidate the ordinances and administrative actions of county officials and may, in some states, remove county officers for cause. State governors and administrative officers also have an extensive influence on county officials. The most drastic, and least used, forms of state control are appointment, removal, and substitute administration. A few county officials, such as county prosecutors in New Jersey, are appointed by the Governor.(7) It is more common for the Governor to be able to remove local officials for cause. The Governor of Minnesota, for example, may remove a county officer for malfeasance or nonfeasance in the performance of official duties.(8) Substitute administration, another form of state control, occurs when state agencies assume temporary control over some local government function. Many states have statutes which permit local health activities to be administered by the state if local health officers fail to perform their duties satisfactorily.(9) Drastic forms of state control may occasionally be justified but can have a serious effect on the administration of county government if used too frequently.

Administrative regulations, inspection, and review of plans are other means of state influence over county government. In a number of states, state health and welfare agencies exercise extensive control over county administration through voluminous regulations. In New Jersey, local health officers have been required to pass an examination by the State Board of Health before they can be licensed.(10) States frequently require counties to prepare and submit financial reports and prescribe county budgeting and accounting forms. In a number of states, including Washington, officials of the State Auditor's Office audit county records. Plans for county roads may require approval of the State Highway Department in some states.

State aid is another means of state influence over counties.(11) To receive state aid, in most instances, counties must meet state standards or comply with certain state regulations. While many of these requirements have helped raise standards in county administration, others have unduly restricted county discretion. State aid has been invaluable to counties in meeting rising costs. However, it can distort expenditure patterns by encouraging counties to expand funds in one administrative area to match state grants while reducing expenditures for other needed functions which do not receive state grants.(12)

State influence on county government may come also from the provision of information, advice, training programs and technical assistance. State Tax Commissions frequently furnish information to assessors and may hold institutes or schools for them. State health departments supply publications on a variety of subjects to local health officials and may hold annual conferences to help bring these officials up-to-date on new developments in their fields. New York State agencies provide technical assistance in personnel administration and management techniques to local government. In New York, the Office for Local Government was established in 1959 in the Executive Department to: serve as a clearinghouse for information about local government affairs, assist cooperative local efforts to solve common problems, and to help the Governor coordinate the activities of state agencies working with local government.(13) The New York Office for Local Government prepares local government studies and provides advice to local officials upon request.(14) Washington and Tennessee have established somewhat similar state agencies to aid local government.(15) The information, advice, training and technical assistance provided by state offices of local government and other state agencies help counties without unduly reducing county discretion.

Counties have benefited from information, advice, training, and technical assistance programs, but many state controls have tended to block rather than facilitate, progress in county government. Rigid state constitutional provisions which establish county tax and debt limits and set certain forms of county government organization are serious impediments to improvements in county government. Overly detailed state laws which set county salaries or limit the services that counties can provide also hamper county progress.

State, county, and municipal governments have a common interest in maintaining the financial strength and vigor of the nation's federal form of government. Governor Smylie of Idaho, speaking at the 1965 Congress of the National Association of Counties, stressed the common interests of state and local government in solving their serious revenue problems.(16) In recommending that a portion of the federal income tax revenues be returned to the states, he suggested that part of this money should be earmarked for local government.(17) The sincere interest of many recent governors in helping local units of government solve their financial problems is an important sign of improved state-local cooperation.

COUNTY-FEDERAL RELATIONSHIPS

Counties and other units of local government are not mentioned in the United States Constitution, and laws passed by Congress cover national-state relationships much more extensively than national-local relationships. One writer states that contacts between national and local government should legally take place through state government, since local units of government are the creations of the states.(18) In practice, there are many federal-local relationships which bypass state agencies as well as many relationships which involve state agencies.

Federal agencies provide counties with a variety of research reports, statistics, studies, and other publications. The U. S. Bureau of the Census has published Finances of County Governments, Governmental Organization, and other studies of importance to counties. The Uniform Crime Reports of the Federal Bureau of Investigation are used by county sheriffs. The quality standards of materials developed by the National Bureau of Standards are available to counties as is the model ordinance on smoke abatement prepared by the Bureau of Mines. Counties can get information on records management from the General Services Administration and information on zoo administration from the National Zoological Gardens.(19) Counties administering school systems can receive many types of statistics and research studies from the United States Office of Education.

Federal agencies also provide counties with advisory, consulting, and training services. The Federal Bureau of Investigation maintains a fingerprint file which county sheriffs contribute to and make use of in criminal investigations. County police officers also make use of the F.B.I. training schools and laboratory facilities. The Civil Aeronautics Administration provides advice and consulting services on airport construction and operation.(20) Federal civil defense agencies have undertaken the training of many local civil defense officials.(21)

Extensive contact between federal and county officials occurs in the administration of federal grants-in-aid. Most federal aid is channeled through state government, and state officials interpret and expand federal regulations in administering these aid programs. However, there are a number of occasions in which federal, state and county officials are jointly involved in the approval of funds for the construction of a specific highway or in the interpretation of welfare regulations. Federal public assistance officials make periodic reviews of public assistance case records in county offices to determine whether recipients on county assistance rolls are eligible for federal grants. Contact between federal and local officials is even more extensive in the case of federal grants which go directly to counties such as grants for urban renewal, waste treatment construction, low rent public housing, and airport construction. (22) There are also many contacts between county officials and federal agencies such as the Forest Service and Bureau of Land Management which have extensive land holdings in the West.

In certain fields, such as agricultural extension and environmental sanitation, federal-state-local relationships are so extensive that federal-state-local cooperation is taken for granted by county officials. The agriculture extension agents and sanitarians in many areas have part of their salaries paid by all three levels of government. Sanitarians employed by the county may be enforcing federal, state, and local laws. County agriculture agents may be as much at home explaining new federal farm surplus programs as administering the county fair or working with state agricultural experiment station employees on pest control measures.

In establishing aid programs and field organizations, federal agencies have sometimes weakened rather than strengthened county government. The federal reclamation program, for example, encourages the establishment of independent irrigation or water user districts rather than the establishment of county irrigation agencies. (23) The area redevelopment program has established a network of special purpose regional and local area programs which are often independent of county and city government. The Advisory Commission on Intergovernmental Relations is concerned about these practices and recommends that Congress favor general purpose units of government (such as cities, towns, and counties) rather than special purpose units of government (such as public authorities and special districts) in the distribution of federal aid. (24)

The relationship between national and county government is vastly different today than in the early 1920's. Direct contact between federal and county officials has become much more frequent as federal grants which go directly to counties have increased in number and scope. County officials have taken a much greater interest in national legislation and programs and are making their views known in Washington, D. C. through the National Association of Counties. Vice President Hubert Humphrey has been designated by President Johnson as White House Liaison with county officials. He held an important policy discussion with county officials in the

White House in March, 1965.(25) Federal, state, county, and city officials have become increasingly concerned about the same metropolitan problems. One result has been a greater emphasis on intergovernmental partnership and cooperation. The county viewpoint on this cooperation is best expressed by the following quotation from the National Association of Counties.

"We are now in the age of partnership and governmental togetherness. In modern America, we are increasingly aware that the concept of separate levels of government, operating with exclusive responsibilities and exclusive sources of revenue, is now obsolete. We have embarked on bold national partnership programs designed to bring the combined resources of the federal, state and local governments to bear in solving basic problems.

Our 3,043 counties and their nearly one million employees are deeply involved in the local administration of these national partnership programs. We believe that these programs could become vastly more effective if county and other local representatives were given a wider policy-making role."(26)

COUNTY RELATIONSHIPS WITH OTHER UNITS OF LOCAL GOVERNMENT

Counties, cities, towns, villages, townships, school districts, special districts and public authorities are separate legal entities, but they do not exist in complete isolation from each other. Within most counties there are almost daily contacts between local government officials, and within many counties a variety of forms in intergovernmental cooperation exist. Counties are involved in these intergovernmental relationships in many ways: (1) as a legal and fiscal arm of the state in relationships with townships and special districts, (2) as a vendor of services to other local governmental units, (3) as a purchaser of governmental services, (4) as creator of dependent districts and service areas, (5) as a participant in informal cooperative arrangements, (6) as a partner in joint city-county agencies, (7) as a partner in intercounty agencies, and (8) as a participant in voluntary regional conferences.

Counties as a Legal and Fiscal Arm of the State in Relationships with Townships and Special Districts

State legislatures in some states have given counties significant legal and fiscal powers with respect to townships and special districts. Action taken by the county board is frequently required

during the process of creating a special district. A drainage district
is created in South Dakota by a petition of property owners which
must be approved both by the state engineer and the county board.
(27) More frequently, the county board is asked to call a public
hearing on the proposal to establish a special district, to give proponents and opponents of the district an opportunity to be heard.
The county board may also be required to check petitions for the
creation of a special district to insure that they contain the requisite
number of signatures or to supervise an election held to vote on the
creation of a special district.

The boundaries of townships and special districts in some states
may be altered only with the approval of the county board. In
Michigan, a petition is generally filed by persons in townships
wishing changes in township boundaries.(28) A hearing is called by
the county board after due notice and, if three-fifths of the members
of the county board approve, the boundary changes are made. In
each California county, city and county officials are appointed to a
commission which has the power to decide whether new cities or
special districts are created within the county.(29)

County boards may play a significant role in the financial affairs
of townships, school districts, and special districts. In Michigan,
townships, school districts and other units of local government must
prepare budgets and file them with the County Tax Allocation Board.
(30) This Board (composed of three county officials, a school district official, and a municipal official) examines these budgets and
determines the tax rates required to meet the proposed budgets. The
Board has the power to reduce the tax rates of local units of government within the county to keep these rates within constitutional
limits.

Counties as Vendors of Services

In many areas of the country, cities, townships, special districts
and other units of local government have found it advantageous to
rent equipment or purchase service from county governments. In
Kansas, for example, cities which cannot afford expensive road
machinery may rent this equipment from counties.(31) Seven counties in Colorado reported maintaining town roads and charging towns
either on a cost or fee basis.(32) Townships in Wisconsin, Minnesota, Kansas, Nebraska and other states have also contracted with
counties to maintain township roads.(33) Through economies of large
scale operation, counties have maintained township roads at lower
cost than townships have been able to maintain their own roads.

While many sales of county services are made on the basis of
telephone conversations, letters, and memoranda, formal service
agreements and contracts are signed in other instances. Service

contracts may stipulate that the county provide a specified level of services at a specified rate. The city or other local government unit agrees to pay the rate specified in the contract and has the option of renewing or not renewing the contract. Roscoe Martin reports that "there are literally thousands of local service contracts in effect throughout the county" and that "cities and counties are the units most actively engaged in this practice."(34) Services frequently furnished by contract are: water, sewage disposal, library service, health services, fire protection, building inspection, and planning. In Los Angeles County, the county government provides nearly all the services for Lakewood and 27 other suburban cities through service contracts.

Counties as Purchasers of Services

Counties purchase services less frequently than they sell them. A few cities and metropolitan special districts sell water, sewage disposal and other services to counties which in turn supply unincorporated areas and small cities.

Counties as Creators of Dependent Districts and Service Areas

Dependent special districts are described by Bollens as lacking fiscal independence, adequate administrative autonomy, or both.(35) In California, there are hundreds of dependent districts governed by the Boards of Supervisors of California counties.(36) They are most often used to provide fire protection, flood control, sanitation, sewer maintenance, and water supply. The Los Angeles Flood Control District is an example of a dependent district.(37) It was created after a 1914 flood caused serious damage to the Los Angeles area. The governing body of the district is the Los Angeles County Board of Supervisors, and county officers such as the county counsel and purchasing agent provide services for the district. In two important respects, it is distinct from county government . It covers slightly less than three-fifths of the county and taxes property only within the area of the district. Its employees are directed by the district's own chief engineer and are not county employees. Through the dependent Los Angeles Flood Control District, the County Board is able to provide services for and tax those citizens needing flood control, storm drainage and similar services.

A county service area is a type of dependent district which has no governmental structure of its own. The County Board serves as its governing body, and it uses county employees as staff. Under California law, these service areas may be initiated by request of two of the five members of the county board of supervisors or a petition signed by 10% or more of the voters in the area.(38) The county board establishes the county service area by resolution and sets the boundaries of the area and the services provided.(39) The county government is reimbursed for the costs of providing services by taxes levied by the county service area on its residents. County service areas may be established for police service, fire protection, parks and other services. They are one means of providing urban services to unincorporated areas and taxing the residents of these areas for the services. San Diego County has created a Department of Special District Services as part of the county regular administrative organization to provide services for dependent districts of this type.

The County as a Participant in Informal Cooperative Arrangements

Counties enter into a number of cooperative arrangements with cities and other units of local government that do not involve the sale of county services. Many cooperative arrangements are informal agreements to exchange information and services. The county sheriff and city police departments commonly exchange many types of information and cooperate in establishing roadblocks to capture fleeing criminals. In Los Angeles County, for example, the Sheriff's Department keeps extensive criminal records of persons booked at the county jail and makes them available to law enforcement officials in cities within the county. The County of Los Angeles has an agreement to provide mutual aid in suppressing fires with 45 cities in the county which maintain their own fire departments. (40) The Los Angeles County Purchasing Department has one of the largest cooperative purchasing programs in the nation and buys gasoline and other items for 34 cities, 71 school districts, and 3 special districts within the county.(41) The Milwaukee County Purchasing Department is one of a number of other county purchasing agencies which works cooperatively with cities to purchase commodities in bulk thus reducing the cost to each cooperating local government.

Counties also enter into informal agreements and relationships with other counties. Colorado counties cooperate on snow removal and sometimes exchange equipment.(42) There is extensive inter-county cooperation in the six county area around Detroit in studies of airport and other area needs.

Provisions of state constitutions and state laws have facilitated cooperative agreements between counties and other units of local government in many states.(43) Alaska, California, Hawaii, and Missouri have constitutional provisions which provide broad authorization for these agreements. Minnesota, Nebraska, New York, Pennsylvania, Wisconsin, and other states have laws facilitating these agreements.

The County as a Partner in Joint City-County Agencies

An important form of city-county cooperation in some areas is the establishment of a joint city-county agency. Forsyth County, North Carolina and the City of Winston-Salem have formed a joint city-county tax collecting department.(44) The department is operated by the county, but the city pays a proportionate share of the cost. Forsyth County and Winston-Salem also have a joint city-county planning department, civil defense office, board of elections and library system. The 1964 survey by the National Association of Counties showed that there were joint city-county civil defense agencies in 6% of the reporting counties, joint city-county airports in 7%, and joint city-county health departments in 5% of these counties.(45) Joint city-county agencies are also found extensively in the fields of assessing, fire protection, industrial development, libraries, planning, sewage disposal, tax collecting, water supply, and zoning.

The County as a Participant in Inter-County Agencies

Inter-county agencies are used in areas in which a governmental problem extends beyond county boundaries or one county has insufficient financial resources to adequately support a governmental function. In the 1964 study by the National Association of Counties, 5% of all reporting counties stated that they furnished mental health services jointly with another county. Inter-county cooperation in providing services was also used by more than 1% of the reporting counties in the fields of child guidance, health, and libraries. The Washington Suburban Sanitary Commission, established in 1918, is one example of an agency spanning two counties.(46) Its governing body is a six member commission appointed by the Governor of Maryland. Two commission members are nominated by the Prince George's County Commissioners, two are nominated by the Montgomery County Commissioners, and two are selected by the Governor. The Commission provides water, sewage disposal and refuse collection.

The County as a Participant in Voluntary Regional Conferences

Counties participate in voluntary regional conferences which bring together, at regular intervals, the chief elected officials of counties, cities, and other units of local government. These officials discuss common problems, exchange information, and arrive at agreements on policy questions. The decisions made by the conference are not binding on their members; and members are not even required to participate in the decision-making processes. However, participation has been high, and the conferences have provided an excellent means for local officials to get together to discuss common problems.

The oldest of the active voluntary regional conferences is the Supervisors Inter-County Committee of the Detroit area. Each county is represented on the Committee by its Chairman of the Board of Supervisors and six other representatives.(47) There are no regular dues or assessments, but the Committee can recommend that member counties contribute to the cost of the Committee. The Committee elects a Chairman annually and has an Executive Director appointed by the Chairman. Much of the work of the Committee is done through standing committees such as the Legislative Committee, Taxation Committee, General Public Services Committee, and the Water, Sewage and Drainage Committee. The Supervisors Inter-County Committee of the Detroit area meets to adopt a state legislative program and has been successful in getting many of its bills passed by the Michigan Legislature. It helped secure passage of a bill establishing an Inter-County Highway Commission with power to develop a metropolitan area-wide plan for major expressways and thoroughfares. It has been instrumental in the initiation of badly needed studies of airport facilities, sewerage, and drainage. The Committee, with the cooperation of Wayne State University, established an experimental course in executive development for key administrators of the city of Detroit and six county governments.

A slightly different type of voluntary regional conference was established in the Washington, D. C. area.(48) The Metropolitan Washington Council of Governments was created in 1957 and has two governing bodies. It has a 68 member committee which meets semi-annually and includes the members of the governing bodies of six counties and representatives of the District of Columbia, Congress, five cities and the General Assemblies of Maryland and Virginia. It also has a smaller 19 member executive committee which meets monthly and makes decisions in the name of the larger body. The Council has a paid staff and has been active in making studies of transportation, sewage disposal, and health services. It has promoted the use of air-pollution control devices for automobiles. It has no power to require compliance with its decisions by member governments.

Four other large, voluntary regional conferences are: the Metropolitan Regional Council (New York, New Jersey and Connecticut), the Association of Bay Area Governments (San Francisco area), the Mid-Willamette Valley Intergovernmental Cooperation Council (Salem, Oregon area), and the Regional Conference of Elected Officials (Philadelphia area).(49) None of these agencies has the power to coerce its members, but all have contributed to the resolving of governmental problems in their areas.

ILLUSTRATIONS OF COUNTY RELATIONSHIPS WITH OTHER UNITS OF LOCAL GOVERNMENT

The relationships between county governments, cities, and other units of local government vary significantly among counties. The following illustrations show three of the many types of relationships at the local level.

City-Parish Relationships in East Baton Rouge Parish

On January 1, 1949, the governments of the city of Baton Rouge and East Baton Rouge Parish were reorganized, and significant changes in city-parish relationships resulted.(50) Prior to reorganization, Baton Rouge was governed by a three member City Commission, and the governing body of the parish was a seventeen member Police Jury which had powers similar to county governing boards in many states. Baton Rouge, in 1948, had an area of almost 6 square miles and a population of nearly 35,000. East Baton Rouge Parish had an area of 462 square miles and a population of nearly 148,000 in 1948. Densely populated urban areas extended beyond the city limits of Baton Rouge, and the parish government could not effectively provide urban services in these areas.

After reorganization, an extensive merger of city and parish governments took place.(51) The City of Baton Rouge is governed by a seven member City Council, and the governing body of East Baton Rouge Parish consists of the seven city councilmen and three other persons elected from the rural area of the parish.(52) City and parish councils operate separately, each adopting its own budget and ordinances, but improved coordination of city and parish activities have resulted. City and parish shared the same chief executive, a Mayor-President, elected for a term of four years by the voters of the entire parish. In many staff and functional areas, such as finance, personnel, purchasing, planning, and public works, the separate city and parish staffs were consolidated.(53) In other functional areas, such as in police administration, city and parish remain separate.(54) The merger of staffs, particularly in the planning and public works fields, has brought planning and subdivision controls to the entire parish and facilitated the development of much needed improvements in highway, sewage, and other services.

The 1949 reorganization established three general taxing areas in the parish. The City of Baton Rouge was expanded to more than six times its former size to include most of the densely populated urban area of the parish.(55) City residents pay parish taxes plus an additional city levy to meet the costs of urban services such as garbage collection, street lighting, sidewalks, and fire protection. Areas reserved for industry have been established in the parish and are assessed only parish taxes on the stipulation that they must furnish their own municipal services.(56) The remainder of the parish is subject only to parish taxes and receives the predominantly non-urban services of parish government. Thus, the tax rates paid by citizens of the parish vary in relation to the services they receive.

The city-parish reorganization served to discourage the proliferation of units of local government at a time when the pressing urban needs of the area surrounding Baton Rouge might have encouraged the establishment of many special districts or satellite municipalities. Baker and Zachary, two small municipalities which were incorporated prior to 1949, continued without change after the reorganization. The new city-parish charter, however, prohibits the incorporation of any new city, town or village within the parish. (57) Existing special districts were continued but brought within the parish government. Street lighting, garbage, fire protection, and other districts provide services to parish residents who pay the cost of these services as they did before. However, much of the overhead costs have been eliminated, and the work of these parish districts is coordinated with each other and the city-parish governments.

In evaluating the success of the merger of Baton Rouge and East Baton Rouge Parish, William Havard and Floyd Corty conclude:

> "The Baton Rouge experiment has to be regarded as a success because the city and parish were finally consolidated whereas the history of such attempts is mainly a record of failures. What is more, the system has survived and demonstrates some capacity for the self-correction of weaknesses and possible adaptability to further consolidation. If the success is tempered by certain limitations, it is no more than may be expected, and it is unquestionably a major improvement over the condition of governmental paralysis that seems to afflict so many of the nation's areas of prodigious growth."(58)

City-County Relationships in Dade County Florida

During the 1940's and early 1950's, three attempts were made to merge municipalities in Dade County with the county government. After the voters of Miami, in 1953, nearly approved the abolition of the city government and the transfer of its functions to county government, the Miami City Commission appropriated $50,000 for a study of the metropolitan area problem.(59) The Public Administration Service of Chicago was chosen for the study. It submitted recommendations in 1955 calling for the creation of an area-wide government to provide services that were regional in nature and the retention of municipal governments for purely local functions.(60) This two level approach to metropolitan government was authorized by an amendment to the Florida Constitution passed in 1956, and embodied in a home rule charter for Dade County approved by the voters in May 1957.

The new charter for Dade County, which took effect in July, 1957, made no change in the organization of city government but completely reorganized county government. The number of members of the Board of Commissioners of Dade County was increased and the Board was given the power to appoint (and remove) a County Manager.(61) Most administrative operations were brought under the county Manager's supervision, and the assessor, tax collector, sheriff, surveyor, purchasing agent, and supervisor of voter registration were made appointees of the manager rather than elective officials. The powers of the County Manager have been subsequently somewhat reduced by a charter amendment in 1962 requiring the Board of County Commissioners to approve the manager's appointments of department heads and his administrative orders to create, merge or combine departments.(62) The County Manager-Council form of government has survived repeated attacks by opponents of the plan and has succeeded in consolidating departments, standardizing procedures, and establishing up-to-date data processing, records management, and other staff services.

The Dade County Charter greatly altered the relationship between county and city government. The Charter preserved existing cities, but prohibited the incorporation of new cities without authorization of the County Board of Commissioners.(63) Municipalities may not annex land without approval of the County Board of Commissioners, and the Board is granted power to establish and govern special districts. The county government was given the power to provide major streets and highways, mass transit, water and sewage systems, hospitals, welfare services, air and marine ports, uniform traffic regulations, uniform building codes, planning, housing, urban renewal, parks and recreation, industrial development, the assessment and collection of property taxes and other regional functions. The county government was also empowered to "set reasonable minimum standards for all governmental units in the county for the performance of any service of function."(64) If any city fails to comply with these standards and does not make corrections within a reasonable time after notice, the county government is empowered to take over the municipal function.

The Dade County Charter has faced strong opposition from city officials who oppose the transfer of city functions to the county, and from other persons who favor abolishing or changing the manager–council form of county government.(65) Despite this opposition, the government of Dade County has been successful in completing a land use plan, establishing a uniform traffic code, adopting stringent regulations to prevent air and water pollution, undertaking countywide traffic engineering, and making significant improvements in many governmental services in the county area. Relationships between county and city governments, however, have not been as harmonious as in many other counties.(66)

Intergovernmental Relationships and the Lakewood Plan in Los Angeles County

The government of Los Angeles County and its relationships with other units of local government within the county have evolved over a sixty year period. In 1912, the county adopted a home rule county charter which strengthened county administration by providing a merit system and reducing the number of county elected officials.(67) The voters elect a five member Board of Supervisors, an Assessor, District Attorney, Sheriff, and judicial officials. County administration was further strengthened by the establishment of the position of Chief Administrative Officer in 1938, and by the growth of a professional, career civil service within the county. The Chief Administrative Officer was assigned "the duties of supervising administration and assisting the board to obtain information upon which it could determine policy.(68) Chief Administrative Officers have had "a strong influence upon county administration through budget control, coupled with pressure and advice concerning departmental procedures and organization."(69) The staff of the Chief Administrative Officer includes not only budget, management, and personnel units, but also a county–city services section which coordinates the activities of county departments which furnish contract services to cities.

Los Angeles County has been described as "probably the best known example of a county performing a multiplicity of municipal functions."(70) Soon after Los Angeles County adopted its home rule charter in 1912, the city of Los Angeles transferred the inspection of weights and measures and the administration of charities to county government.(71) From time to time, Los Angeles County has received new county-wide functions by action of the state legislature or has expanded an existing program such as regional parks until it covers the entire county. Los Angeles County also provides flood control, police protection, street lighting, water, fire protection, and a variety of other municipal services to unincorporated areas of the county through county departments or special districts administered by the county.

The Lakewood Plan is one of the best known aspects of intergovernmental relationships within Los Angeles County. The county government has been contracting to provide services to cities within the county since 1907.(72) In 1954, Los Angeles County extended its contractual services by offering to provide almost all municipal services to any city within the county.(73) Lakewood, a rapidly growing suburban community, incorporated in 1954 and chose to have the county provide its services. Initially Lakewood had a staff of only a city manager, clerk, city attorney and a few secretarial aides.(74) Many of the services which Lakewood received as a city were the same services that it had received as an unincorporated community. Both police and fire protection, for example, were provided by the county before incorporation.(75) After incorporation, the county agreed to have some of the Sheriff's patrol cars assigned exclusively to Lakewood and agreed to have them marked with the city's seal as well as the Sheriff's.

In 1965, every one of the 76 cities in Los Angeles County contracted for at least one county service.(76) Twenty-nine cities operated under the Lakewood Plan in 1965 and received virtually all of their municipal services from the county.(77) The county provides more than three dozen separate governmental services by contract, including: assessment and collection of taxes, health services, engineering, fire protection, law enforcement, library services, parks, personnel services, planning, zoning, recreation, sewer maintenance, street construction and maintenance, and street lighting. Some of the contract services, such as the building inspection service, are paid for from fees at no cost to the city receiving the service. In some cases, a state law sets the charge made by the county. In many cases, the county charges cities a rate based on the actual cost of performing the service. There are other cases in which the county provides services to cities through fire, library, street lighting or other special districts.

The Lakewood Plan has made it possible for newly incorporated cities to receive the services of a competent, trained organization immediately after incorporation, and to avoid large initial outlays for equipment and buildings.(78) Since cities determine the differing levels of services to be provided by the county and have the option of cancelling such service contracts, the local autonomy and home rule of the city is protected. The Lakewood Plan is reported to have increased the efficiency of many county departments, because they now have a clientele who can cancel their contracts if their services or costs are not acceptable. Opponents of the plan claim that it is government by remote control and that it encourages suburban areas to incorporate and receive services from the county rather than be annexed to surrounding communities.(79) Proponents of the plan emphasize its voluntary nature, the low cost of county services, and the general satisfaction of citizens in cities using the Lakewood Plan. Roscoe Martin states that the Lakewood Plan "is not 'the' solution to the metropolitan problem, but it is one of several solutions which offer promise."(80)

SUMMARY

Relationships between state and county governments take two main forms. The state, through its constitution and laws, establishes many restrictions on the organization, powers, and finances of county government. A second relationship is between counties and state administrative agencies which provide information, advice, technical assistance, training, grants, and the enforcement of state regulations. Action by state administrative agencies is usually more flexible and adapted to county needs than rigid constitutional provisions and state laws.

Federal administrative agencies provide information, advice, technical assistance and, in some cases, grants-in-aid directly to county governments. As direct contacts between federal and county officials have increased, county officials have taken an increasing interest in national programs and have made their views known in Washington, D. C. through the National Association of Counties.

County governments have a wide variety of relationships with cities, villages, townships, school districts, and special districts. They purchase and sell services to other local government units, create dependent districts, and serve as a legal and fiscal arm of the state in relationships with townships and special districts. They are participants or partners in city-county agencies, inter-county agencies, voluntary regional conferences, and a variety of cooperative arrangements. In many of these relationships, counties are providing leadership in resolving governmental problems in their local areas.

REFERENCES

1. Article 18, Section 1 of The Idaho Constitution states that: "the several counties of the territory of Idaho, as they now exist, are hereby recognized as legal subdivisions of this state."

2. This point was made by Clyde F. Snider, Local Government in Rural America (New York: Appleton-Century-Crofts, Inc., 1957), pp. 64, 65.

3. The county-manager, county administrator, or county executive forms are permitted in more than a dozen states including California, Georgia, Florida, Maryland, Montana, North Carolina, New York, Tennessee, Virginia, and Wisconsin.

4. In Idaho, one section of state law (section 31-2404) even specifies the column headings on certain records kept by the County Recorder.

5. The writer is particularly indebted to Clyde F. Snider, op. cit., pp. 57–83 for his description of local government law.

6. The California Legislature sets the salaries of some county officials such as auditors, district attorneys, and members of the boards of supervisors. The salaries of many other county officials are set by the county boards of supervisors.

7. James M. Collier, County Government in New Jersey (New Brunswick, N. J.: Rutgers University Press, 1953), p. 26.

8. Clyde F. Snider, op. cit., p. 95.

9. Ibid., p. 99.

10. Lane Lancaster, Government in Rural America (New York: D. Van Nostrand Company, 1952), p. 325.

11. Counties received $3,084,000,000 from state government in 1962 or 36.3% of their total revenue. For further information on state aid, see chapter 5.

12. Concern over this impact on local government was expressed by Robert Morlan, Capitol, Courthouse and City Hall (Cambridge, Mass.: Riverside Press Co., 1960), p. 37. Robert Morlan was also concerned about the effect of state aid in unduly restricting the scope of local discretion.

13. John C. Bollens and Henry J. Schmandt, The Metropolis (New York: Harper and Row, 1965), p. 543.

14. The Office for Local Government has published, for example, an excellent report comparing the provisions of seven county charters in New York State. Office for Local Government, County Charters in New York State (Albany, N. Y.: Office for Local Government, 1963).

15. John C. Bollens and Henry J. Schmandt, op. cit., p. 543.

16. The text of Governor Robert E. Smylie's address may be found in American County Government, 30:18, 19, September, 1965.

17. Ibid. Governor Smylie also recommended coordinating state and local expenditure of these funds.

18. Lane Lancaster, op. cit., p. 331.

19. Jewell Cass Phillips, Municipal Government and Administration in America (New York: The Macmillan Company, 1960), p. 126.

20. Ibid.

21. For a brief description of federal–local relationships in civil defense see: Arthur Bromage, Introduction to Municipal Government and Administration (New York: Appleton-Century-Crofts, Inc., 1957), pp. 155–157.

22. A list of federal grants which go directly to localities may be found in: Advisory Commission on Intergovernmental Relations, The Role of Equalization in Federal Grants (Washington: Advisory Commission on Intergovernmental Relations, 1964), p. 26. A further description of federal grants and their impact on local government may be found in: Advisory Commission on Intergovernmental Relations, Impact of Federal Urban Development Programs on Local Government Organization and Planning (Washington: U. S. Government Printing Office, 1964). For a list of new grant programs enacted by the 89th Congress, see American County Government, 31:11, January, 1966.

23. Advisory Commission on Intergovernmental Relations, Impact of Federal Urban Development Programs on Local Government Organization and Planning, p. 24. This is an example of what the Commission calls federal encouragement of special purpose organizations.

24. Ibid., p. 23.

25. The important meeting of the Vice President with county officials is described in Bernard Hillenbrand, "Creative Federalism and Counties," American County Government, 30:9, May, 1965.

26. The White Paper of the National Association of Counties on the Role of Counties makes a number of specific recommendations designed to strengthen federal-state-local relations. One suggestion would strengthen the Advisory Commission on Intergovernmental Relations. A second suggestion calls for the establishment of a national advisory board for each federal partnership program with state and local officials represented. American County Government, 30:15-17, May, 1965.

27. William H. Cape, Handbook for South Dakota County Officials (Vermillion: University of South Dakota, 1961), pp. 76, 77.

28. Bureau of Social and Political Research, Michigan State University, The County Board of Supervisors (East Lansing: Michigan State University, 1959), pp. 25, 26.

29. These Local Agencies Formation and Annexation Commissions in California are described by Robert G. Smith, Public Authorities, Special Districts and Local Government (Washington: National Association of Counties, Research Foundation, 1964), pp. 200, 201. The commission in each county is composed of two county officials appointed by the County Board of Supervisors, two city councilmen, and a fifth member appointed to represent the public by the other four members.

30. Bureau of Social and Political Research, Michigan State University, op. cit., pp. 122-124.

31. William H. Cape, County Government in Kansas (Lawrence: University of Kansas, 1958), p. 23.

32. Conrad McBride, County Road Administration in Colorado (Boulder: University of Colorado, 1958), p. 29. Nine Colorado counties maintain some township roads without charges.

33. Clyde F. Snider, op. cit., p. 369.

34. Roscoe C. Martin, Metropolis in Transition (Washington: Housing and Home Finance Agency, 1963), p. 6.

35. John Bollens, Special District Governments in the United States (Los Angeles: University of California Press, 1957), p. 228.

36. Ibid., pp. 232, 233.

37. This district is more fully described by John Bollens, op. cit., pp. 233-235. The district does not cover the desert areas and offshore islands of Los Angeles County.

38. Ibid., p. 239.

39. Ibid. The creation of a county service district may be blocked by a written protest signed by at least 50% of the registered voters in the proposed area or the owners of at least 50% of the property value in the area.

40. L. S. Hollinger, Chief Administrative Officer, County of Los Angeles, letter dated January 25, 1966.

41. Ibid.

42. Conrad McBride, op. cit., p. 29.

43. These constitutional provisions and laws are described in detail by W. Brooke Graves, "Interlocal Cooperation," The County Officer, 28:17-28, January, 1963. W. Brooke Graves provides numerous illustrations of the agreements entered into under the authorization of these constitutional provisions and laws.

44. Wally Dunham, "Informal City-County Agreements" in Urban County Congress (Washington: National Association of Counties, 1959), p. 50.

45. The results of the study are more fully described in Table 1 of chapter 4.

46. Washington Suburban Sanitary Commission, Annual Report (Hyattsville, Maryland: Washington Suburban Sanitary Commission, 1963), p. 37.

47. American Municipal Association and National Association of Counties, Voluntary City-County Regional Cooperation (Washington: American Municipal Association and National Association of Counties, 1963), and Edward Connor, "The Detroit Area Inter-County Plan" in Urban County Congress, pp. 40-46 were used as sources on the Supervisors Inter-County Committee of the Detroit area.

48. Roscoe Martin, op. cit., pp. 39-50 has an extensive description of the Metropolitan Washington Council of Governments.

49. Advisory Commission on Intergovernmental Relations, Alternative Approaches to Governmental Reorganization in Metropolitan Areas (Washington: Advisory Commission on Intergovernmental Relations, 1962), p. 35.

50. Louisiana parishes are similar to counties in other states. The reorganization of the governments of the City of Baton Rouge and East Baton Rouge Parish has been referred to as a "modified consolidation" by William Havard and Floyd Corty and as a "partial consolidation" by John Bollens and Henry Schmandt. William Havard and Floyd Corty, Rural-Urban Consolidation, The Merger of Governments in the Baton Rouge Area (Baton Rouge: Louisiana State University Press, 1964), p. 139 and John C. Bollens and Henry J. Schmandt, op. cit., p. 431.

51. The history of the reorganization plan and the first few years of reorganization are described by Gordon Kean, "The Plan of Government for the Parish of East Baton Rouge and City of Baton Rouge, Louisiana" in Urban County Congress, pp. 35-39. The city-parish government faced a serious lack of funds in its early years which was met by the enactment of a sales tax in 1951.

52. In 1964, the voters of the parish approved an increase in the number of rural representatives in the Parish Council from two to three so as to reflect the large population increase in the rural area.

53. William Havard and Floyd Corty, op. cit., pp. 36-39. The offices of attorney, clerk, and treasurer were also made city-parish offices.

54. The constitutional office of sheriff could not be abolished without amending the state constitution, and this was one reason that the city police staff was not merged with the staff of the sheriff in the parish.

55. Nearly ninety thousand people were brought into the City of Baton Rouge as a result of the reorganization. William Havard and Floyd Corty, op. cit., p. 51.

56. Residences were excluded from industrial areas. If industries fail to maintain services within the industrial zone, all or part of the zone will become part of the area which is subject to both city and parish taxes. Ibid., pp. 33, 34.

57. Ibid., p. 32.

58. Ibid., p. 147.

59. Gustave Serino, Miami's Metropolitan Experiment (Gainesville: Public Administration Clearing Service, University of Florida, 1958), p. 9.

60. The Public Administration Service report also recommended that the areawide government provide local services to the unincorporated areas on a cost or special district basis. Ibid., p. 11.

61. The number of county commissioners was increased from 5 in 1957 to 11 in 1958 and 13 in 1960. John C. Bollens and Henry J. Schmandt, op. cit., pp. 462, 463 describe the Dade County election district system. In 1966, Dade County had a nine member legislative body composed of a mayor and eight commissioners. All are elected on a county-wide basis. Porter W. Homer, County Manager, Dade County, Florida, letter dated January 18, 1966.

62. John C. Bollens and Henry J. Schmandt, op. cit., p. 466. The County Manager was further weakened in 1963 by making the Office of Sheriff elective.

63. Ibid., p. 462.

64. O. W. Campbell, "The Dade County Approach — Administrative Aspects" in Urban County Congress, p. 24.

65. Two county managers resigned or were dismissed during the 1957-1965 period. For a description of the problems faced by these two managers see John C. Bollens and Henry J. Schmandt, op. cit., pp. 466, 467.

66. An excellent description of county-city relationships may be found in John C. Bollens and Henry J. Schmandt, op. cit., pp. 463-470.

67. Winston W. Crouch and Beatrice Dinerman, Southern California Metropolis, (Los Angeles: University of California Press, 1963), p. 181 contend that "in spite of the fact that the county possesses an advantage over local units in territory, it would not have been a contender for metropolitan leadership if it had continued to employ the traditional form of county government it had prior to 1912."

68. Ibid., pp. 186, 187.

69. Ibid., p. 187.

70. Daniel R. Grant and H. C. Nixon, State and Local Government in America (Boston: Allyn and Bacon, Inc., 1963), p. 347. Professors Grant and Nixon point out that Los Angeles County government performs more functions than the City of Los Angeles and has a budget that exceeds that of the city.

71. Winston W. Crouch and Beatrice Dinerman, op. cit., p. 189.

72. Roscoe C. Martin, op. cit., p. 15.

73. Los Angeles County will provide almost all, but not all, types of services. Legal, fiscal, auditing and administrative services will not be provided by contract. L. S. Hollinger, Chief Administrative Officer, County of Los Angeles, letter dated January 25, 1966.

74. Roscoe C. Martin, op. cit., p. 16.

75. Before incorporation, the County Sheriff provided law enforcement services and the county fire protection district provided fire protection.

76. City-County Services Section, Chief Administrative Office, County of Los Angeles, Los Angeles County's Contract Services Program (Los Angeles: County of Los Angeles, 1965), pp. 1, 4. There were 1,550 separate county service agreements with cities.

77. All except two cities which have been incorporated in the county since the Lakewood Plan developed have used the Lakewood Plan after incorporation. Ibid., p. 4.

78. Samuel Gove, The Lakewood Plan, (Urbana: University of Illinois, 1961), p. 9, quotes an official in one of the contracting cities as follows: "The contract plan is designed to provide effective public services at the lowest possible cost to the taxpayers under local control. To a new city like Pico Rivera, this plan is particularly advantageous because it reduces the need for large outlays of money for equipment and facilities; permits the operation of city government with a minimum of full time employees, and has the advantage of making available to the city, at cost, the full resources of county government and equipment."

79. The City of Long Beach was reported to have opposed the plan because the incorporation of Lakewood thwarted its expansion plans. The Mayor of Downey referred to the Lakewood Plan as "government by remote control" and withdrew from his police and fire service contracts with the county. Samuel Gove, op. cit., p. 11.

80. Roscoe C. Martin, op. cit., p. 25.

3/ COUNTY CASE STUDIES

The variation in the patterns of county government through-out the nation may be pictured most vividly by case studies of the environment and operation of a number of differing county governments. The following chapters are case studies of five, very different counties. These counties are not typical in the sense that they represent five major types of counties. The variations among counties are so great that it is doubtful whether any five counties could ever be selected to typify all 3,049 American counties. The counties are geographically distributed to include counties in the East, Mid-West, South and West. The counties range in size from Petroleum County with less than a thousand persons to Milwaukee County with slightly over a million people. The counties used have the plural executive, county manager, and county executive forms of government with the plural executive form under-represented in the sample. The case studies are not intended to be statistically representative of all counties but are intended to enable the reader to better visualize the environment, organization, services, finances, and intergovernmental relations of specific county governments in action.

Chapter 7

Petroleum County

PETROLEUM IS A CATTLE RAISING COUNTY in central Montana with a 1960 population of 894. It was formed in 1924 from the eastern part of Fergus County and named for the booming Cat Creek oil fields. Some of the wells in this field are still producing, but oil no longer provides a major county payroll.

Most of Petroleum County is a rolling, treeless prairie with areas of sagebrush interspersed with areas of range and pastureland. The rainfall averages only 12 inches a year. The county has a population of one-half person per square mile, and one can drive along a main highway for ten miles without seeing a house. Along the Musselshell River and several of the larger creeks, the land is irrigated, alfalfa is grown, and the farms are closer together. The larger farms in the county have several thousand acres, and the large farm houses and latest farm equipment attest to their prosperity.

Winnett, the county seat, was platted in 1914 and had a population of 360 in 1960. One of its streets, state highway 244, is paved; most of the remaining streets are gravel or dirt. Winnett has a weekly newspaper, two small hotels, four churches, and several gas stations, stores and bars. An occasional boarded up store and vacant lot near the city center indicate that Winnett has declined in population.

Petroleum County faced a crisis in the early 1940's. The county went heavily into debt in the 1920's for the expansion of roads and other services. During the 1930's, drought, depression, diminishing farm income, and decreased oil production brought economic problems and reduced property tax revenues. Assessed valuation declined by more than 50% from 1926 to 1942. Montana law, in the early 1940's, permitted a maximum tax rate of 16 mills for general administrative purposes limiting Petroleum County revenues for this purpose to $12,028.(1) Petroleum County's general fund appropriations amounted to $22,882, and its cash balance was nearly exhausted.(2) The county first tried consolidating elective offices and then, failing to sufficiently reduce costs, adopted the county manager plan. In the first year of operation under the county manager plan, personnel costs were drastically reduced resulting in substantial savings. Roland R. Renne reports that under the old form of government Petroleum County "employed 13 individuals to operate county government, in addition to electing three county commissioners."(3) After adoption of the county manager plan, there were five county employees and three county commissioners. Total salaries for regular employees amounted to $7,960 in 1946 as compared to $14,283 shortly before the adoption of the plan.(4) The county manager plan has been credited with reducing debt as well as expenditures. In 1942, the county had $20,706 in outstanding warrants and a $40,000 bonded indebtedness. Four years later, it had retired all of its bonds and had only $131 in outstanding warrants.(5) Petroleum has retained its county manager form and has kept expenditures remarkably low.

There are twelve units of local government within the county. These include: the county government, the municipal government of Winnett, a soil conservation district, a high school district, and eight elementary school districts. The two-story sandstone county courthouse is the hub of government activity within the county. The soil conservation district supervisors meet in the courthouse, and the federal soil conservation agent, Agricultural Stabilization and Conservation Service and Selective Service Board have offices there. School district officials have frequent contact with the county manager on school business since he is also county superintendent of schools. The state district court and welfare caseworker have offices in the courthouse. A large courtroom on the first floor of the courthouse is used by many groups as a meeting room.

FORM OF GOVERNMENT

Petroleum County has a county manager form of government. The voters of the county elect three commissioners and a county attorney. The County Commissioners appoint the County Manager who appoints four other county employees: the Deputy Director of Finance, the Deputy Sheriff, the Clerk and Recorder, and the Deputy Clerk and Recorder. The County Commissioners also appoint two full-time and one part-time county road employees.

One of the advantages of the county manager form of government in a small county is that the county manager and his staff can do the work of many elective and appointive county officials. The County Manager of Petroleum County, for example, does the work of the county treasurer, director of finance, assessor, public administrator, sheriff, coroner, and county superintendent of schools. The Deputy Sheriff serves also as courthouse janitor and land reclassifier. The Clerk and Recorder serves as clerk, recorder, and clerk of the district court. Before Petroleum had a county manager form of government, it was common for some elected officials to appoint deputies. The job of the treasurer's office was sufficiently complex so that it was necessary for the treasurer to retain an assistant with prior experience in the office. About the time the treasurer learned enough to be able to handle the work of his office without an assistant, his four year term would be over and he would be ineligible to succeed himself.

Table 1
STRUCTURE OF PETROLEUM COUNTY GOVERNMENT

1. Form of county government	County manager
2. Legislative body	Three member Board of County Commissioners elected by the voters
3. Chief administrative officer	County Manager, appointed by the County Commissioners, who also serves as Director of Finance, Treasurer, Assessor, Public Administrator, Sheriff, Coroner, and County Superintendent of Schools
4. Officials appointed by the County Manager	Deputy Director of Finance (who serves as deputy treasurer) Deputy Sheriff (who serves as courthouse janitor and land reclassifier for the County Manager in his role as Assessor)* Clerk (who serves as recorder and clerk of the district court) Deputy Clerk and Recorder
5. Other officials appointed by the County Commissioners	County road employees Election judges
6. Other county elected officials	County Attorney

*The town marshall of Winnett is a second Deputy Sheriff and receives a small monthly salary from the county.

The present County Manager has lived in the county 46 years and was a county commissioner in 1942 when the county manager form of government was adopted. He is the sixth county manager and has held this position for nine years. He receives a salary of $5,400: $1,200 as sheriff, $1,500 as county manager, $1,200 as county superintendent of schools, and $1,500 as assessor.

COUNTY FINANCES

Petroleum County depends heavily upon the property tax: 72% of county revenue for county government purposes comes from this source. The other major sources of county revenue include automobile registration fees and charges for the rental of office space in the county courthouse to government agencies. The county has no bonded indebtedness.

STAFF AND AUXILIARY SERVICES

The County Manager and his staff provide nearly all staff and auxiliary services. The County Manager is responsible for appointing his assistants and for providing policy information to the County Commissioners. The County Clerk and Recorder attends the County Board meetings, takes notes for the Commissioners, prepares warrants, maintains expenditure records, and compiles the budget. Legal services are provided by the independently elected County Attorney.

The budget process in Petroleum County is less elaborate than in larger counties. The budget requests are submitted to the Clerk and Recorder by the first Monday in July. After review by the Clerk and Recorder and County Manager, they are submitted to the County Commissioners on or before the second Monday in July. The commissioners review the budget at a public hearing held on the second Monday in July and prepare the final budget by the first Wednesday in August. The fiscal year begins July first, so the final budget is adopted a month after the beginning of the fiscal year.

COUNTY SERVICES

Residents of a sparsely populated, rural county such as Petroleum have less need for county services than residents of a more urban county. Petroleum County government provides ten services as Appendix A shows.

General Government

In Montana, court administration is more a state than a county function. Montana has a Supreme Court and a number of state district courts. One district court serves Petroleum County and nearby Fergus and Judith Basin Counties. This court has a judge, clerk, juvenile officer, and part time court reporter. Petroleum County pays part of the salaries of the juvenile officer and the court reporter. The Petroleum County Clerk of Court takes notes when the court reporter is not present and collects court fees. The district court has criminal jurisdiction and handles civil, probate, and juvenile cases. Petroleum County also has a justice of the peace who resides in Winnett and is paid entirely from fees.

The County Attorney, who is elected for a term of four years, is paid partly from state funds and partly from county funds. He serves as prosecuting attorney and provides legal advice for the County Commissioners. He has a private law practice as well.

Election administration is also a county function. The County Commissioners appoint three election judges for each of the County's six election precincts. They supervise the conduct of elections and help tabulate the ballots. The County Commissioners add up the precinct totals after each election and may recount all the ballots after a close election.

Assessment and collection of property taxes is another important general governmental function. The County Manager serves as Assessor and the Deputy Director of Finance collects property taxes for all units of government within the county.

Agriculture

Petroleum County does not have a county agricultural extension agent, a weed control supervisor, or a county fair. However, there is a very active Soil Conservation Service and Agricultural Stabilization and Conservation Service. The Soil Conservation District in the county receives the services of a technician supplied by the federal government. He provides advice on the building of stock ponds and other conservation projects. In some of these projects, farmers can receive matching funds from the federal government through the Agricultural Stabilization and Conservation Service. The county collects one-half mill which goes to pay postage, office expense and other expenses of the Soil Conservation District. The District is governed by a five member board elected for three year terms.

Some of the work normally handled by the agricultural extension agent is handled through other offices. Agricultural extension bulletins are available to farmers at the offices of the Agricultural Stabilization and Conservation Service and the Soil Conservation Service. There is a 4-H club in the county whose leaders drive fifty miles to Lewistown to work with the Fergus County Agent.

Farmers in Petroleum County sometimes join classes in Lewistown taught by the Fergus County Agent.

Education and Libraries

Schools are the function of the eight elementary school districts and one high school district which serve the county. The County Manager acts as County Superintendent of Schools and prepares a number of financial and statistical reports for the State Department of Education. He also reviews the budget requests submitted by the school districts. These budgets are brought before the County Commissioners who have the power to make reductions. In practice the commissioners never do.

Winnett has a public library which is used by county residents. A one-half mill levy on all county residents helps support the library.

Health and Welfare

There is no physician in Petroleum County, and county residents who are ill usually go to a doctor in Roundup (45 miles to the south), Lewistown (54 miles to the west) or Billings (78 miles to the southwest) for treatment. The county employs a physician from Roundup at $25 per month to serve as county physician. He prepares the reports required by the state on births, deaths, communicable diseases and other health matters. He is also responsible for inspecting Winnett's water supply and the restaurants in the county to see that proper sanitary standards are maintained.

Welfare is a combined state and county function in Petroleum County. One caseworker, employed by the State of Montana to handle cases in both Petroleum County and Musselshell County to the south, spends several days a month in Petroleum County. The county pays part of the cost of welfare administration and part of the cost of welfare grants and medical care. The caseworker determines the eligibility of persons for assistance and brings each new case to the County Commissioners at their monthly meeting. The commissioners have a right to disapprove each assistance case but rarely do. However, commissioners have extensive knowledge of the persons in their home districts and are often able to supply valuable information to the caseworker about the income and assets of applicants for assistance.

Parks and Recreation

Petroleum County does not have any parks or recreation programs. However, Winnett does have a swimming pool financed through private sources. There is a large irrigation lake twelve miles from Winnett, constructed by the Montana State Water Board, which provides boating, water skiing and fishing.

Physical Planning and Development

Petroleum is a sparsely populated rural county and there is no county planning.

Public Safety

The County Manager serves as County Sheriff and is responsible for police administration in the unincorporated area of the county. He is assisted by a Deputy Sheriff who has had training at several schools conducted by the Federal Bureau of Investigation. This Deputy Sheriff also serves as land reclassifier and court house janitor.

Petroleum County and Winnett have cooperative arrangements in both police and fire administration. The town marshall of Winnett serves as a second Deputy Sheriff. The county owns a fire truck, and Winnett furnishes a place to store the truck and pays a man to maintain the equipment. The remaining firemen are volunteers.

Public Works and Transportation

County roads are the most important public works service provided by Petroleum County. The state maintains the two paved roads in the county, and the county maintains the many miles of gravel farm roads. The county road foreman usually is present at the monthly meetings of the Board of County Commissioners and receives his work assignment for the next month. The Board of County Commissioners sometimes tours the roads to see how work is progressing.

There is no county airport, but there is a small private airstrip. Water and sewage are municipal functions in Winnett and not county functions. In the rest of the county, each property owner provides his own water and septic tank.

SUMMARY

Petroleum County, Montana faced a crisis in the early 1940's. It is a small rural county, and its assessed valuation declined during the drought and depression of the 1930's to a point where the county government could not raise sufficient revenue to pay all the independently elected officials. Petroleum adopted a county manager form of government in 1942 and substantially reduced its operating costs. The voters of Petroleum County now elect three County Commissioners and a County Attorney. The Commissioners appoint a County Manager who, in turn, selects four other full time county employees. In a small county, the county manager form of government provides much flexibility since one appointed official can do the work of several elected officials. The County Manager, for example, also serves as Sheriff, Assessor, Treasurer, Director of Finance, Coroner and County Superintendent of Schools. With the county manager form of government, Petroleum County has been able to keep its operating costs low at a time of rising governmental costs.

REFERENCES

1. Roland R. Renne, "Rural County Can be Efficient," National Municipal Review, 33:448, October, 1944. The writer is heavily indebted to Dr. Renne for the history of Petroleum County and its adoption of the county manager plan.

2. Ibid.

3. Roland R. Renne, "Too Small to be Efficient," National Municipal Review, 36:80-81, February, 1947.

4. Ibid., p. 81.

5. Ibid.

Chapter 8

Latah
County

LATAH COUNTY, IDAHO, with an area of 1,084 square miles and a 1960 population of 21,170, is more densely populated than Petroleum County but contains many sparsely settled areas. There are areas of pine-covered hills and mountain slopes in northern and eastern Latah County that are uninhabited except for logging crews and a few subsistence farms. The valleys of this mountainous area contain cattle ranches, dairy farms, small logging towns and farm communities. Westward and southward in the county, the rainfall is less, pines are found mainly on hilltops, and the land slopes downward into a rolling area of rich dark soil that is ideally suited to the raising of wheat and seed peas. Fields are contour plowed, crops rotated scientifically, and stately farm homes indicate the general prosperity of the area. Farming is a mainstay of the county economy, and most county commissioners in the past decade have been farmers or retired farmers.

Latah County is dependent not only upon its farms but also upon its largest urban center, Moscow, a city of fourteen thousand located in the wheat growing section of the county. The University of Idaho, with an enrollment of six thousand, is the city's largest employer. The grain elevators and pea processing plants along the railroad tracks and the stores along the city's broad main street provide other important sources of employment. The city is growing slowly, and the many residential areas with substantial houses, tree shaded streets, neatly cut lawns, and flower gardens give the city a middle income, college town appearance.

There are eight other municipalities in the county ranging in size from 191 to 880 people. The largest, Potlatch, contains one of the large lumber mills in the state. Latah County is not required to provide urban services for the unincorporated areas, as in many metropolitan counties, because almost all the residential subdivisions lie within the incorporated cities and villages. The municipalities of Latah County do not presently have the serious urban problems of large metropolitan areas. However, there are some areas of substandard housing and undesirable mixtures of commercial, residential and industrial uses that may become more serious in future years as the county becomes more urban.

There are forty units of local government for Latah County's twenty-one thousand people — almost as many as in Milwaukee County which has a population of more than one million. These units of local government include: the county government, nine cities and villages, nine county highway and rural road districts, six fire protection districts providing fire fighting forces mainly for unincorporated areas, eight cemetery maintenance districts, five school districts, a soil conservation district, and a rural library district. Special districts, such as highway and fire protection districts, have a more important role in providing services for unincorporated areas in Latah County than they do in many counties, since Latah County government does not provide these services.

Latah County was established by Congressional Act in 1888 shortly before Idaho became a state. The present county courthouse is a modern, brick two-story building located on the crest of a small hill overlooking the Moscow business district. To the rear of the courthouse is an older building housing the Sheriff's offices and jail. Located in the courthouse are the county offices as well as the District Court and a number of state and federal offices. Farmers find it particularly convenient to have the federal offices which are responsible for soil conservation, farm forestry, and crop insurance in the same building with the county weed control supervisor and county extension agents. Similar benefits result from having the state public assistance and health offices in the same building with county officials providing emergency assistance and medical care.

Latah County, like other Idaho counties, does not have a home rule charter, and its structure and functions are specified in detail by the state constitution and state law. The state constitution requires the election of three county commissioners, a prosecuting attorney, auditor, assessor, coroner, sheriff and treasurer. The state constitution establishes the elective position of probate judge until otherwise provided by the state legislature. The establishment of other elective offices is prohibited by the constitution. State law sets the salaries of county commissioners and the prosecuting attorney and establishes salary ranges for other elected county officials. Idaho law not only lists the functions of each elective official but even specifies some administrative details such as the column heading on indexes of marriage certificates kept by the county clerk.

FORM OF GOVERNMENT

Latah has the traditional form of county government with a Board of County Commissioners and seven other elective officials. The county is divided into three commissioner districts. Each commissioner must reside within the district which he represents but is elected by the voters of the entire county. Two commissioners are elected each biennium — one for a two year term and one for a four year term. County commissioners are paid $3,000 a year and are not expected to devote full-time to county work. They meet as a legislative body the second and fourth Mondays of each month and meet more frequently while reviewing the budget, when sitting as a Board of Equalization and when emergencies arise. In addition to their legislative duties, they may spend a day or two each week on administrative matters such as the interviewing of applicants for emergency assistance and medical care.

Acting as a body, the Board of County Commissioners approves the county budget, enacts ordinances, establishes new county agencies, approves all bills presented for payment, and takes many other official actions. The County Clerk prepares the agenda for the County Board's meetings and takes the official minutes. During the course of a typical meeting, the County Board may: approve an application for a beer and liquor license, discuss an application for a welfare grant, appoint a new member to the County Fair Board, approve a change in plans for a new wing of the Latah County Nursing Home, and discuss relationships between the Moscow Planning Commission and the County Planning Commission. The County Board also acts as a Board of Equalization to consider tax assessment appeals and may consider, at such a hearing, the appeal of a rancher for reduced assessments because his cattle spend part of the year at summer pasture in a neighboring county where he is taxed for that period.

The County Commissioners appoint the members of five boards and commissions but appoint relatively few other employees as Table 1 shows. They appoint the Weed Eradication Supervisor, the Courthouse Janitor, and several part-time employees including the County Physician and Civil Defense Director.(1) The County Board has no administrative staff of its own and receives the assistance of the elected County Clerk to prepare the budget and handle many administrative and fiscal matters.

Independently elected officials have more extensive responsibilities in Latah County than in the other four counties studied.

Table 1
STRUCTURE OF LATAH COUNTY GOVERNMENT*

1. Form of county government	Traditional, plural executive
2. Legislative body	Three member Board of County Commissioners elected by the voters
3. Chief administrative officer	None although County Clerk provides staff and budget services for the County Commissioners
4. Officials appointed by the Board of County Commissioners	Civil Defense Coordinator (part-time) Weed Eradication Supervisor County Physician (part-time) Janitor Election Judges and Registrars (part-time) Justices of the Peace appointed by the County Commissioners and Probate Judge with the approval of the senior District Court Judge
5. Unpaid boards whose members are appointed by the County Commissioners	County Planning Commission County Advisory Board Board of Health County Fair Board County Nursing Home Board Agriculture Extension Advisory Committee Predator Board
6. Other county elected officials	County Auditor Assessor Treasurer Sheriff Coroner Prosecuting Attorney Probate Judge

*Excluded from this table are the Agricultural Extension Agents and the employees of the Idaho Department of Health who work in Latah County. Although Latah County pays part of the costs of these employees, they are primarily state employees.

These seven independently elected officials are: the County Auditor (who serves also as County Clerk, Recorder, and Clerk of the District Court), the County Treasurer, the County Assessor, the Sheriff, the Prosecuting Attorney, the Coroner, and the Probate Judge. These seven officials, whose functions are described later in the chapter, appoint many more full-time employees than the County Commissioners do. The commissioners are, however, charged by law with the general supervision of those county officials — responsibility which they exercise mainly through the budget process.

COUNTY FINANCES

Latah County government depends heavily upon the property tax for its revenues. Property was assessed at 16.1% of market value in Latah County in 1964, and the total tax rate for county purposes in 1964 was $2.55-1/2 per $100 of assessed valuation. Other important sources of county revenues are: the allocation of state liquor store profits to counties, business licenses, fees, and fines.

The largest county government expenditures are for general government, health and welfare, and agriculture. Little or no county funds are spent for libraries, parks and recreation, or public works. These are primarily municipal and special district functions in Latah County.

STAFF AND AUXILIARY SERVICES

Responsibility for staff and auxiliary services is decentralized in Latah County. The county does not have a civil service system, and each of the independently elected officials selects his own staff. However, the turnover of county employees after each election is not large, and a number of employees have served through several different administrations. The county has a decentralized purchasing system with each elective official making his own purchases. As a matter of practice, the independently elected officials discuss their larger purchases with the County Commissioners since they must get the Commissioners' approval for the payment of all bills. Responsibility for treasury management and the investment of idle treasury funds rests with the elected County Treasurer. Responsibility for accounting is divided between the County Clerk, who maintains the appropriation accounts, and the County Treasurer, who maintains records of county bank balances and cash.

Budgeting is the most important staff function in Latah County government. The County Commissioners do not appoint a budget officer to assist them in their budget review, but the County Clerk acts in this capacity. The elected County Clerk compiles the budget requests submitted by county officials and transmits them to the County Commissioners along with his estimates of revenue. He acts as staff to the County Commissioners as they review in detail the budget requests of each agency. After this review is completed, a public hearing is held the second Monday in February to give citizens an opportunity to express their views. At the conclusion of the hearing, the Commissioners take final action on the budget. During the fiscal year, the County Clerk checks to see that officials do not spend more than their appropriations. Approval of the County

Commissioners is required for an official to spend more than his appropriation or to raise the salary of any employee during the fiscal year. The County Clerk acts in an advisory capacity to the County Commissioners during this expenditure control period.

COUNTY SERVICES

Latah County has a larger population than Petroleum County, and county government provides its citizens with a greater variety of services. Most of the twenty types of services provided by Latah County government are the traditional general government, agriculture, health and welfare, and public safety functions in which the county is acting mainly as an arm of the state.(2) Municipal type services are primarily provided by cities and villages as most residential subdivisions are within the incorporated municipalities.

General Government

The administration of justice, the recording of legal documents, property tax assessment and collection are among the general governmental functions of Latah County government. The functions of the seven independently elected officials, who play a major role in providing these services, are described below.

Assessor. The County Assessor and his staff of seven make all property tax assessments in the county to provide the tax base for school districts, municipalities, special districts, as well as for the county. The Assessor's office has up-to-date maps and records of property ownership in the county. Two of the deputy assessors have a continuing program of contacting property owners to update their assessment records. In determining the value of land, consideration is given to the amount of land, its location, its topography, its crop potential, and other factors. In determining the value of a home, they use a valuation book prepared by the State Tax Commission to determine the basic valuation per square foot. Houses are classified and extra features beyond the classification, such as a finished basement, extra plumbing, or extra built-ins add to the valuation.

On the second Monday in January each year, the Assessor's staff begins to prepare the Property Tax Roll. In June, a valuation summary is sent to each taxpayer(3) and the taxpayer has a right to complain to the County Assessor if he believes his property has been improperly valued. If he is not satisfied with the Assessor's action, he has the right to appeal to the County Commissioners who meet as a Board of Equalization from the fourth Monday of June to the second Monday in July.

The Assessor is responsible for selling motor vehicle license plates and submitting vehicle title applications to the state. As a service, the Assessor's office permits mail registration of motor vehicles. For the license fee plus a 50¢ handling charge, the Assessor will mail county residents the same auto license number they had in the previous year. This service was started by a former county assessor who felt that it would help make the Assessor's office more popular with the taxpayers.

County Auditor. The County Auditor has four titles: County Clerk, County Auditor, County Recorder, and Clerk of the District Court. As County Clerk, he acts as staff for the County Commissioners, compiles a preliminary budget for the commissioners, signs and files certain accounting documents, and maintains a number of official records such as the book listing all warrants drawn from the Treasury. As County Auditor, he is responsible for: reviewing all vouchers before they are presented to the County Commissioners for approval, preparing warrants in payment for these vouchers, maintaining an appropriation accounting system, and preparing an annual financial report. As County Recorder, he is responsible for recording deeds, mortgages, wills, marriage certificates, and many other important legal documents. He is also responsible for preparing indexes to these documents and providing Photostats of them for a fee. As Clerk of the District Court, he assigns to the court the part-time services of two legal stenographers. The County Auditor is the only county official, aside from the County Commissioners, whose work regularly brings him into contact with all county business. He has a staff of four.

County Treasurer. The County Treasurer, with a staff of two deputies, collects county property taxes and assesses penalties for failure to pay on time. The Treasurer's office receives funds paid into the Treasury, invests funds not immediately needed by the county, and pays out funds on warrants prepared by the County Auditor. The Treasurer administers the estates of persons who die without an heir and the estates of indigents.

Coroner. The Latah County Coroner is a physician who serves on a part-time basis and is paid $1,080 a year. He ascertains the cause of death where a physician was not in attendance at death or where the cause of death is not known. If the Coroner cannot ascertain the cause of death, he may order an autopsy performed by a pathologist or may get a toxological report. He works closely with the County Prosecuting Attorney and the Sheriff in investigating deaths of suspicious origin and may call a Coroner's inquest.

Probate Judge. The Probate Court Judge resolves cases involving wills and testaments, grants letters of administration and guardianship, appoints persons as appraisers of estates, and handles many other probate functions. In addition, he hears and decides civil cases where damage or debt does not exceed $750 and decides many types of juvenile cases. The Probate Court employs a part-time secretary and pays half the salary of the Deputy Sheriff who serves as Probation Officer for the Court.

Prosecuting Attorney. The County Prosecuting Attorney provides legal advice for the County Commissioners and other county officials and serves as the attorney in any case in which the county is a party. He also prosecutes violations of county ordinances or violations of state law occurring within the county and presents the case against the defendant. In the case of violations of state law, the Prosecuting Attorney may share responsibility for prosecution with the Idaho Attorney General or other state officials. The Prosecuting Attorney is not paid a sufficiently high salary to devote full time to the office and maintains a private law practice as well as serving the county.

Sheriff. The Sheriff performs a number of civil functions in addition to the public safety functions described later in the chapter. These civil functions include serving eviction notices, subpoenas, and divorce papers. The Sheriff or his deputies also spend time in handling some of the legal and administrative work for Sheriff's sales, in inspecting out-of-state cars before they are registered, and in acting as bailiff for the District Court. The Sheriff has the responsibility for issuing drivers' licenses but has deputized a Moscow travel agent to perform this work for him for a fee.

Other functions. Other county services classified as general government include the work of the County Commissioners, the services of maintaining the County Courthouse, and the supervision of elections. The County Commissioners have the power to establish, abolish and change election precincts and to appoint election judges and registrars.

Agriculture

The three extension agents of the Latah County Agriculture Extension Service provide services not only for farmers in the county but for many other county residents. One agent teaches evening classes for farmers on wheat production techniques and other subjects. On request, he identifies injurious insects and weeds for farmers and gardeners and prescribes means for controlling them. He arranges for the testing of farmers' soils through the University of Idaho and gives recommendations on the types of fertilizers needed. He does much to raise the level of agricultural practices and production in the county by keeping farmers abreast of new research developments. A second agricultural agent is a specialist in livestock production and 4-H work. He provides training for the more than 100 4-H club leaders in the county, judges livestock at county fairs, and helps farmers and ranchers to improve their live-stock raising practices. The third agent, a home economist, in-structs the leaders of women's groups and 4-H clubs in the best methods of food preparation, food preservation, sewing, and other skills. These leaders, in turn teach these skills to other groups. Home demonstration and 4-H clubs are very active in the county, and participation is extensive by nonfarm as well as farm families. The agricultural agents are members of the staff of the University of Idaho assigned to Latah County for extension work. The County Commissioners contract with the University for extension work, pay about a third of the costs, furnish office space for the extension agents, and usually interview the persons assigned to the county before they sign a contract with the University. The Commissioners also appoint the members of the Agriculture Extension Advisory Committee which provide a valuable link between county govern-ment and county residents.

The county fair is an important county agricultural event. The Board of County Commissioners appoint the nine members of the County Fair Board who have overall responsibility for conducting the fair and maintaining the fairgrounds. A county agriculture ex-tension agent acts as Secretary of the County Fair Board and general manager of the fair. All three extension agents spend much of their time shortly before and during the fair helping to make it a success. The fair encourages the development of better livestock and crops by rewarding youngsters for excellence in 4-H, FFA and other youth group projects. The fair gives farmers an opportunity to compare ideas on farming practices and see livestock exhibits. Hobby and homemaking exhibits, livestock judging contests, and a talent show are also part of the fair.

Weed eradication is another important county agricultural pro-gram. The county employs a County Weed Supervisor to spray the weeds along the rights-of-way of many county roads. He is supplied by the county with chemicals and part-time labor. Noxious weeds, particularly Canadian thistle and morning glory, cost county farmers more than one million dollars a year. If a farmer is allowing weeds to spread unchecked over his land, his neighbors can complain to the weed supervisor who will inspect the farm and try to persuade the farmer to take corrective action. If the farmer fails to comply after warnings, the weed supervisor may be empowered to spray the weeds and bill the farmer for the service. If the bill remains unpaid, it may be entered as a lien against the farmer's property. The county agriculture extension agents and the Weed Eradication Supervisor work closely with a county weed committee and 19 community weed committees to encourage farmers to keep their weeds under control.

Education and Libraries

County government is not responsible for the administration of schools or libraries. There is no County Superintendent of Schools, and five school districts provide public school education for county children. Latah County does not have a county supported community college, but the state supported University of Idaho, located in Moscow, provides county residents with an excellent opportunity for higher education.

Library services are provided by the City of Moscow and the Latah County Free Library District rather than by county government. The Latah County Free Library District maintains a library in the basement of the courthouse and has a bookmobile serving the county area outside the city of Moscow. While the county government does not provide school or library services, it does assess and collect the property taxes which largely finance these services.

Health and Welfare

Public health is a combined state and county program in Latah County. The North Central District of the Idaho Department of Health assigns three public health nurses, a sanitarian, two clerical workers, and the half-time services of a clinical social worker to the county. Latah County provides office space for these employees, carefully reviews their budget, and pays most of their costs. The public health nurses teach classes for expectant mothers, provide literature and information on child care, provide rehabilitative care for older persons to enable them to continue to live in their own homes, conduct immunization clinics, and make regular visits to schools to check the sight, hearing, and other health problems of school children. The sanitarian inspects the sanitary facilities of restaurants, food processing plants and dairy farms and assists communities and individuals in constructing and maintaining water treatment, sewage disposal, and refuse treatment plants. The clinical social worker divides his time between Latah and Nez Perce Counties, providing both counties with child guidance clinics for the treatment of emotionally disturbed children and assistance in casework for adults. The social worker calls upon a consulting psychiatrist and clinical psychologist for assistance when needed, and advises psychiatric treatment or hospital committment for the most severely disturbed children or adults.

The County Commissioners appoint a three member Board of Health which meets monthly and prepares local health regulations in accord with state law and Health Department rules. Two of the members of the County Board of Health serve without pay; the third, the County Physician, receives compensation for his medical care of county nursing home patients.

Public welfare is also a combined state and county program. The Idaho Department of Public Assistance has an office in the Latah County Courthouse and furnishes grants and medical care for recipients of: old age assistance, aid to the blind, disability assistance, aid to families with dependent children and medical assistance for the aged. It also provides a child welfare program. The Latah County welfare program furnishes emergency assistance, drugs, and medical care for needy persons who do not qualify for state assistance programs. Emergency aid is provided by means of disbursement orders rather than cash. The County Commissioners personally interview applicants seeking aid, ascertain whether help should be granted, and determine the amount and type of aid needed. They also determine which applicants should receive free drugs and free medical services from a doctor of their own choice. The County Commissioners receive clerical assistance from the County Clerk's office but spend many hours a month on this type of casework.

An outstanding feature of the Latah County health and welfare program is the Latah County Nursing Home. The nursing home was built in 1957 from federal and county funds and took the place of a drafty, antiquated county poor farm. The Moscow Council of Church Women publicized the plight of the county's senior citizens at the poor farm, and, as a result, a bright, attractive, one-story building was constructed on the outskirts of the city of Moscow. After the nursing home was built, many county organizations donated television sets, pictures, wheel chairs, and other equipment for the health and comfort of the patients.

The County Nursing Home is run by a nonprofit corporation and receives appropriations for operating expenses from the county, fees from private patients, and medical payments from the Idaho Department of Public Assistance for those who qualify. An unsalaried Nursing Home Board of seven members, appointed by the County Commissioners, is responsible for the operation of the Nursing Home and appoints the manager of the home. The manager and sixty member staff of the home give much personal attention to the patients. Solariums have been provided at the end of each wing for patients to use to watch television or to look out at the rolling wheat fields and distant mountains. Occupational therapy is furnished and patients are given religious, holiday, and recreation programs by county residents. Many groups, including the Moscow beauty schools, provide free services for those who live in the home. The Nursing Home is a source of pride to the entire county.

Parks and Recreation

The county owns a small lake which is stocked by the State Department of Fish and Game. There are several other stocked lakes in the county, a large United States Forest Service park, and several municipal parks. Organized recreation programs are provided by the city of Moscow and several smaller communities.

Physical Planning and Development

Latah County does not have the serious land use problems of metropolitan areas, but these problems are growing, particularly in the unincorporated area just outside the city of Moscow. Because Moscow has a zoning ordinance and Planning Commission, there has been a tendency for auto junk yards and other unsightly land uses to locate in the unincorporated county area rather than in the city. The Latah County Commissioners appointed a County Planning Commission in 1963, and Latah County voters gave the County Commissioners approval to enact a zoning ordinance in 1964. The Latah County Planning Commission has not as yet developed a comprehensive plan or enacted a zoning ordinance.

Public Safety

Public protection is largely a municipal and county function in Latah County. Moscow has more than ten policemen; some of the other municipalities of the county have one or two police officials. The County Sheriff provides police protection in the unincorporated areas of the county and in those municipalities without a police force. The Sheriff's Office also assists the smaller police forces of the county in handling more serious cases. The Sheriff is assisted by three full-time deputies in his patrol of the county and his criminal detection work. The Sheriff and his deputies are also responsible for picking up accused persons and holding them for other law enforcement agencies, issuing tickets for traffic violations, inspecting to see that taverns are closed on time, handling juvenile cases, and investigating crimes. The County Sheriff maintains the only jail in the county and hires several part-time employees as jailers. A high proportion of the time of the Sheriff's Office is spent on civil rather than criminal matters. His functions in serving process papers and issuing drivers licenses have been described earlier in this chapter.

Fire protection is provided by the municipalities of Latah County and by six fire protection districts.

Civil defense is a county function, and the County Commissioners appoint a part-time civil defense coordinator. He assists in marking and stocking fallout shelters, furnishes literature to interested citizens, and helps train personnel to man civil defense posts in the event of a crisis.

Public Works and Transportation

Latah County government does not provide public works services. The major highways are maintained by the State Highway

Department, forest service roads by the United States Government, and street systems by the municipalities of the county. The rural roads of the county are the responsibility of nine highway and roads districts.

Municipalities and special districts also provide other types of public works. The larger municipalities have their own water and sewage systems. The Moscow–Pullman Airport, which serves most of the county, is maintained by taxes raised by the city of Moscow and the nearby city of Pullman, Washington.

SUMMARY

Latah is an agricultural county containing a university city of 14,000 population. It does not have extensive unincorporated areas requiring municipal type services. It has the traditional plural executive form of county government with a three member Board of County Commissioners and seven independently elected county officials. It provides its citizens with the traditional state mandated, general government, agricultural, health and welfare, and public safety services. Up to this time, municipal type services have been adequately provided by the cities and villages of the county. However, as Latah County grows, it may have new functions thrust upon it.(4) There are criticisms of the costly and inadequate road services provided by highway districts, and Latah County, like some nearby counties, may find it necessary to make road construction and maintenance a county government function. There is growing concern about the lack of planning and zoning particularly in the area just outside the city of Moscow. The County Planning Commission may need to hire consultants or staff to work cooperatively with the Moscow Planning Commmission in preparing a comprehensive plan and zoning ordinance for the county. As Latah County grows, it will face more of the problems of urban counties and will undoubtedly need to adjust its services to meet the changing needs of county residents.

REFERENCES

1. The County Commissioners also have some discretion in the appointment of the County Agricultural Agent and his staff. They are staff members of the University of Idaho assigned to Latah County for extension work, but the County Commissioners do interview them before they contract with the university to have them assigned to the county.

2. See Appendix A.

3. Widows with income and property of less than a certain amount are exempt from property taxes on the first $1,000 of assessed valuation.

4. Additional flexibility was provided Idaho counties by H. B. 236 passed at the 1963 session of the Idaho legislature. This bill permits the provision of a number of joint city-county services, the transfer of city services to the county, or the transfer of county services to the city. Services listed by the bill include: sewage disposal, fire protection, library service, planning, zoning, inspection and enforcement of sanitation and health regulations, regulation of garbage and trash collection, airport facilities, jails, and detention homes. Rev. Stat. Idaho, 1965, Sec. 50-904 through 59-911.

Chapter 9

Montgomery County

MONTGOMERY COUNTY, MARYLAND in 1920 was similar in many respects to Latah County of the same period. It was a placid farm county whose main town and county seat, Rockville, had a population of just 2,845. Unlike Latah County, Montgomery has faced a population explosion which has seen successive waves of Washington residents cross the borders from the adjacent District of Columbia. Dairy farms have been transformed into housing subdivisions and cornfields into shopping centers. The population of Montgomery County grew from 34,921 in 1920 to 83,912 in 1940, to 340,928 in 1960, and to 453,000 in 1966. Montgomery County is the northwest sector of the rapidly growing Washington metropolitan area which had a 1960 population of approximately 2.4 million.

Lower Montgomery County, near Washington, is today an expanding suburban area dotted with a growing number of towering government and corporate offices and gleaming, smokeless research and industrial plants. Just over the Washington border in Montgomery County, there are twelve story ultra-modern apartment and office buildings, busy shopping arteries, the spacious lawns and buildings of the Bethesda Naval Hospital and National Institute of Health, and tree lined streets of stately brick homes built in the 1930's. Farther north and west, there are huge shopping centers and more recent subdivisions with neatly mowed lawns, patios and outdoor barbeques. This suburban area has reached Rockville near the center of the county and transformed the once sleepy, farm market town into a bustling shopping and governmental center of nearly 50,000. This densely populated third of the county

179

contains more than 90% of the county population and requires municipal police, fire, street, water, recreation and other services.

Upper Montgomery County, which begins a few miles west and north of Rockville, is a gently rolling, fertile area of dairy, live-stock and general farms, suburban estates, and a few small towns. Largely untouched by the population explosion, as yet, it can anti-cipate being gradually engulfed by the westward march of subdivi-sions and the location of governmental installations and industrial research complexes along super–highways radiating north and northwest from Washington. The governmental needs of this area are changing from those for traditional county services to needs for greater police protection and other municipal services.

In 1966, there were 27 units of local government in Mont-gomery County.(1) These included: the county government, the cities of Rockville and Takoma Park, ten towns, ten special taxing areas, the Maryland–National Capital Park and Planning Commis-sion, the Washington Suburban Sanitary District, a soil conserva-tion district and a housing authority. The cities and towns of the county contain only 16% of the county population. The smaller towns of the county provide few services except street maintenance, street lighting, drainage, traffic control and refuse collection. The largest city, Rockville, provides additional services such as planning, zoning, police protection, and parks. Rebates are given some cities and towns for maintaining their own recreation, library and police services, but this practice was criticized by a management report as being less efficient than county provision of these serv-ices.(2)

Eighty–four per cent of the people of Montgomery County live in unincorporated areas and most live in suburban, lower Montgomery County. County government and two bi–county agencies provide most municipal services to these people. The Maryland–National Capital Park and Planning Commission furnishes parks, planning, and some park roads. The Washington Suburban Sanitary Commission, with headquarters in Prince Georges County, supplies water, sewage, and refuse collection. The ten special taxing districts, one serving just over 100 persons, also furnish some services such as street cleaning, lighting, and trash removal. There are sixteen fire dis-tricts and two rescue districts which are not classified by the Bureau of Census as having full district status. One fire company operates on a subscription basis as do the two rescue companies. The remaining fifteen fire companies are financed by taxes levied by the County Council. All fire and rescue companies have been integrated through a modern communications system operated by the county. The county has taken the lead in providing, or participating in the provision of, municipal services to the unincorporated areas of the county.

Montgomery became a county in 1776 and served primarily as an arm of state administration for much of its early history. For more than 100 years, it was governed by a Board of County Commissioners similar to those in most Maryland counties today. The voters of Maryland, in 1915, approved a constitutional amendment which permitted counties to determine their own form of government and prohibited the state legislature from passing laws dealing with individual counties which had adopted home rule charters. Montgomery County voters approved a home rule charter in 1948 when it became increasingly apparent that the plural-executive form of county government was not meeting the needs of a rapidly expanding suburban area. The home rule charter provided for a council-manager form of county government and extended the powers of the county government to determine its own functions. However, the Maryland Constitution makes clear that the state legislature can extend, modify, amend or repeal the powers of home rule counties by general law.

FORM OF GOVERNMENT

Montgomery County has a council-manager form of government as shown by Table 1. The voters of the entire county elect seven councilmen, five of whom must reside in council districts. The councilmen are elected on a partisan ballot for four year terms and are paid $30 for each meeting day. Each year, the Council elects a President (to preside over council meetings and act as ceremonial head of the county), a President Pro-Tem (to act in the President's absence), and a Secretary (to sign certain county documents). Each councilman has one vote, and council officers have no more power than the other councilmen.

The County Council has the power to pass laws, ordinances and resolutions. It adopts an annual budget and may also propose amendments to the county charter which are then placed before the voters for approval or rejection. In its executive role, the County Council appoints a County Manager, approves or rejects certain appointments made by the County Manager, selects the personnel of some boards and commissions, creates and changes zoning classifications, and acts to establish rates which property owners are assessed for curbs, sidewalks, and other improvement projects. The Council met more than 230 times in 1965 and held over 500 public hearings.

The County Manager serves as chief administrative officer of the county and is responsible for carrying out Council policies. He serves at the pleasure of the Council and is paid an annual salary of $27,000. The present County Manager is a professional engineer and previously was Director of Public Works for ten years. He selects the heads of six staff agencies and twelve departments, is responsible for the preparation of the annual budget, and supervises or coordinates nearly all county government agencies.

Table 1

STRUCTURE OF MONTGOMERY COUNTY GOVERNMENT

1. Form of county government	Council-manager
2. Legislative body	County Council of 7 members elected by the voters
3. Chief administrative officer	County Manager appointed by the County Council
4. Agencies headed by appointees of the County Manager	Manager's Office Clerk to the County Council Personnel Office Purchasing Office Community Development Office Central Duplicating Services Buildings and Grounds Department Finance Department Information and Economic Development Department Inspection and Licenses Department Liquor Control Department Police Department Public Health Department Public Libraries Department Public Safety Department Public Welfare Department Public Works Department Recreation Department
5. Agencies headed by appointees of the County Council	Appeal Tax Court Board of License Commissioners County Attorney County Personnel Board Juvenile Court Montgomery County Planning Board People's Court Revenue Authority Washington Suburban Sanitary Commission (appoint 2 of 6 members) Welfare Board
6. Other county elected officials	Circuit Court Judges Clerk of Circuit Court Board of Education County Surveyor Register of Wills Sheriff State's Attorney

Independently elected executive officials, required by state law or constitution, play a much less important role in Montgomery County than in plural executive counties such as Latah. The County Surveyor is unpaid and has no important public duty. The Register of Wills and a small staff record wills and other matters concerning estates and guardianships. His staff also collects court costs and inheritance taxes. The State's Attorney prosecutes cases involving the violation of state criminal laws, traffic regulations, and some county and municipal laws and ordinances. The County Sheriff has been stripped of his police powers and serves only to transport prisoners and to serve summons, subpoenas and other court papers. The voters of Montgomery County also elect a Board of Education, the judges of the Circuit Court, and the Clerk of the Circuit Court. It is only in the administration of justice and in education that independently elected officials play a leading role in Montgomery County Government.

COUNTY FINANCES

Montgomery County receives most of its revenue from property taxes. Other large sources of county income are: state grants; the county's share of state collected income, gasoline, cigarette and other taxes; federal grants; and county revenues from licenses, fees, service charges and other sources. Property is assessed at approximately 55% of market value in the county, and the County Department of Finance is responsible for property tax assessment and collection.

The total county administered non-education tax rate declined in Montgomery County from $1.10 per $100 of assessed valuation in 1940 to 33-1/2¢ per $100 in 1965. This decrease is due, in part, to the efficient operation of the council-manager form of county government and, in part, to the rise in property tax values in the county as new suburban areas have developed. This county administered tax rate includes a 3-1/2¢ per $100 recreation tax levied on all county residents except residents of Rockville and two villages which have their own recreation programs. It also includes a 6¢ per $100 suburban district tax, paid by residents of the more suburban area of the county, for street cleaning, tree planting and maintenance. In addition, residents of all parts of the county pay a tax of $2.57 per $100 to operate the county-wide school system.

STAFF AND AUXILIARY SERVICES

Staff and auxiliary services are more fully developed in Montgomery County than in less populous Latah County. Montgomery County has a comprehensive civil service system which covers more than 95% of all county employees exclusive of those in the school system. Personnel regulations and policies are adopted by a three member bi-partisan Personnel Board appointed by the County Council for three year overlapping terms. The Personnel Board also hears and decides appeals on disciplinary matters or on employee complaints. The county has a Central Personnel Office of eleven specialists, headed by a Personnel Officer, which serves the Personnel Board and the County Manager. This staff prepares and administers competitive examinations, reviews job classifications, makes wage and salary surveys, conducts training and safety programs, and provides many other types of personnel services. Particularly outstanding is their training program. More than 140 policemen participate in a college level training program which provides courses in criminology, abnormal psychology, sociology, and other subjects taught by staff members of the University of Maryland. The county pays the cost of this training, and policemen are encouraged to take these courses to keep themselves professionally up-to-date. The County Manager takes an active interest in personnel matters and appoints the head of the Central Personnel Office and its staff.

The Department of Finance provides many staff and auxiliary services. Personnel of this Department assess the county property, collect county and other taxes, and perform accounting, auditing and budget functions. A modern data processing center in the Finance Department computes property taxes owed by county residents, bills these taxes, prepares the county payroll, and performs other machine work. Centralization of many of the large clerical and computing functions in the Department of Finance has facilitated the use of data processing equipment.

Budgeting is the responsibility of the County Manager and a six man professional staff in the Department of Finance. The budgets of county agencies are received in November of each year and intensively reviewed. In March, the County Manager presents a modern budget document containing workload, costs, and personnel data to the County Council. The budget is passed in April after the Council has made a thorough review of each item. The County Manager spends over half his time in budget work during the budget making period and considers budgeting an extremely important staff function.

The county has centralized purchasing and duplicating units. The Central Purchasing Office buys in large quantity through competitive bidding and saves the county thousands of dollars a year. The Central Duplicating Service operates an automatic addressing system and machines for duplicating, collating, and photocopying.

Two other staff services are provided by the County Attorney and the Department of Information and Economic Development. The County Attorney, with a staff of eight, represents the county in all legal proceedings and acts as legal adviser to the County Council, County Manager and other county officials. The Department of Information and Economic Development handles information given to the public and news media as well as providing information useful to prospective industries which may wish to locate in the county.

COUNTY SERVICES

Montgomery County provides its citizens with a much greater number of services than Petroleum or Latah Counties. The cities and towns contain only 16% of the county population, and the county has stepped in to furnish needed municipal-type services for the more than two hundred thousand county residents who live in unincorporated, suburban areas. Montgomery County government provides 35 general types of services.

General Government

Montgomery County furnishes all the traditional general governmental services but does not directly administer election supervision. A bipartisan state Board of Supervisors of Elections supervises elections and receives appropriations for this purpose from the Montgomery County Council. County government provides a court system, a prosecuting attorney, the recording of legal documents, the serving of legal papers, and property tax assessment and collection. In addition, the county operates a liquor warehouse and 14 retail liquor sales outlets. The county nets more then $1-3/4 million a year in liquor and beer sales.

As previously mentioned independently elected county officials play a less important role in the provision of general government services in Montgomery County than in the more traditional Latah County. Tax assessment and collection is a function of the Department of Finance, not an independently elected County Assessor and a County Treasurer. Instead of having an independently elected County Coroner, two County Medical Examiners are appointed by the State Post Mortem Examiners Commission to investigate all violent deaths, or deaths unattended by a licensed physician. Montgomery County does have an elected prosecuting attorney, (called the State's Attorney), an elected Register of Wills, an elected Clerk of the Circuit Court, an elected County Surveyor, and an elected Sheriff.

Montgomery County has a more specialized court system than do smaller, more traditional counties. Three courts serve the county: the Circuit Court serving Montgomery and Frederick

Counties, the People's Court, and the People's Court for Juvenile Causes. The Circuit Court, similar in many ways to the District Court serving Latah County, has jurisdiction over civil suits involving $1,000 or more and serious criminal cases. The People's Court hears traffic cases, less serious criminal cases, and civil suits involving less than $1,000. The People's Court for Juvenile Causes exercises jurisdiction over dependent, delinquent and neglected children under 18. It also hears cases arising from non-support, questions of paternity, and charges of contributing to the delinquency of a minor. These courts have their own professional staffs with the Juvenile Court staff including a Supervisor of Social Work, a Psychologist, and several probation officiers.

Agriculture

Montgomery County has an active extension service with a staff of sixteen. Approximately 40% of the cost of this service comes from county funds; the remainder from state and federal funds. For the 2,400 persons employed on farms, mainly in the northern part of the county, the extension service provides information and assistance similar to that provided farmers in more rural Latah County. For the 98% of the people of the county who do not work on farms, the extension service provides information on lawns, gardens, nutrition and a variety of other subjects. During the 1965 calendar year to meet the needs of gardeners and homemakers, more than 65,000 bulletins were distributed, 38,000 telephone calls were answered, nearly 400 newspapers articles were written, and almost 600 radio broadcasts were prepared. The extension agents also work with hundreds of 4-H and home demonstration clubs.

Education and Libraries

The public school system of Montgomery County is a single, unified system governed by a seven member Board of Education. The board members are elected for staggered four year terms, serve without pay, and receive a small monthly expense allowance. The Board of Education makes decisions on general educational policy, appoints the professional County Superintendent of Schools, and adopts an annual budget request. The County Council has some power to approve and make changes in the budget request adopted by the Board of Education. Over 70% of the cost of operating the county educational system comes from county taxes; the remainder comes from state aid, federal aid, and miscellaneous local revenues.

The county school system includes: kindergarten, the first twelve grades, two junior colleges and an adult educational program. There are more than 140 schools and 105,000 children in the Montgomery County school system. The junior colleges have two year programs for students who will transfer to four year colleges and terminal programs to equip students for full-time employment in a number of vocational fields. Characteristic of the many modern features of the county educational program is the use of team teaching, educational television, and the employment of trained persons outside the school system to help English teachers read and correct papers. The school system has an outstanding research unit which makes studies such as one made to determine the best methods of foreign language teaching. Also outstanding is an evening high school where drop-outs may complete their high school education.

The library system of Montgomery County is administered by a Department of Public Libraries whose director is appointed by the County Manager. There are fourteen public libraries and three bookmobiles which make stops at elementary schools and 28 small communities. In 1965, there were over three and one-half million volumes borrowed from libraries in the county. This was twelve times the number borrowed 13 years earlier just before all public libraries in the county were incorporated into one county system. Besides loaning books, the libraries loan informational and cultural films and 16-millimeter sound projectors. The Department has microfilm editions of the New York Times, collections of foreign books, and Braille books for the blind. The only other library system in the county is that of the small city of Takoma Park.

Health and Welfare

The Public Health Department of Montgomery County is under the direction of a physician appointed by the County Manager with the approval of the County Council and the State Board of Health. The more than 220 employees of the Department provide the public health education, nursing, school health, and environmental health services described in the chapter on Latah County. In addition, the Department, through its eleven health centers, provides adult health services such as administering drugs to certain tuberculin patients being treated at home, and providing physical therapy to elderly patients in their own homes or in nursing homes. The Health Department has a child guidance clinic, an alcoholic clinic, a mobile dental unit, and a comprehensive mental health out-patient program staffed with psychiatrists and social workers. About two-thirds of the cost of the health program comes from county sources; the remainder from state and federal aid.

The Public Welfare Department is under the direction of a seven member board composed of one member of the County Council and six members selected by the County Council from a list of non-partisan county citizens prepared by the State Department of Public

Welfare. The Board of Public Welfare appoints a Directof Welfare from a state civil service list of qualified persons and employs more than forty social workers. The Department has a full range of welfare services for adults and children. Grants are provided for recipients of old age assistance, aid to the blind, aid to the permanently and totally disabled, aid to families with dependent children and general assistance. Medical care is given to persons 65 and over and to other medical indigents. Casework services are provided for all recipients including protective casework services for children who are being neglected or abused by recipient or non-recipient families. In neglect and abuse cases, caseworkers work closely with the People's Court for Juvenile Causes to give parents help in caring for their children or to give evidence to the Court so that it can take appropriate action. The Department provides an adoption service and foster care for children committed by the courts as neglected or voluntarily relinquished by their parents. Being a growing suburban county with a relatively young population with a high average income, Montgomery County has fewer old age assistance cases per thousand people than usual. However, it does have a number of cases of aid to families with dependent children and cases of neglect or mistreatment of children.

Parks and Recreation

The Montgomery County Recreation Department has a wide range of programs. During the summer, it operates over 100 playgrounds and furnishes equipment and supervision for the many children who make use of them. The Department also has a full summer program of arts and crafts, swimming, track meets, and many athletic events for adults as well as children. On a year round basis, the Department maintains and staffs two recreation centers which provide meeting places for senior citizens, teen-agers, and many other groups. Self-supporting classes are conducted for school age children in painting, sketching, dancing, and drama, and similar fee-supported classes are conducted for adults in bridge, dancing, flower arranging, and ceramics. Teen-age clubs use the recreation centers for dances and club meetings under adult supervision. The 22 full-time and 400 seasonal Recreation Department employees are paid from a special property tax. Rockville and the smaller communities of Gaithersburg and Washington Grove provide some recreation programs of their own and are exempted from this tax.

The park system of Montgomery County is administered by the bi-county Maryland-National Capital Park and Planning Commission (MNCPPC). The governing body of this agency is composed of ten members — five appointed by the County Council of Montgomery County and five appointed by the Board of County Commissioners of adjoining Prince Georges County. This intercounty cooperation has produced a park system of 15,000 acres most of which is in Montgomery County. This system is financed through a special property tax against most Montgomery County(3) and Prince Georges County residents.

Physical Planning and Development

Physical planning is largely the responsibility of the bi-county Maryland-National Capital Park and Planning Commission. The Commission has a Planning Department of more than 80 persons and is continually engaged in preparing new master plans for areas of Montgomery and Prince Georges Counties. These master plans, which now cover about a third of Montgomery County, describe the location of proposed future schools, highways, parks, and recreation centers as well as proposed zoning areas. Five National Capital Park and Planning Commissioners from each county constitute the Local Planning Board of that county.

The Montgomery County Council and other agencies of county government are involved in the implementation of the master plan within the county. The County Council adopts and may amend the county zoning ordinance. It also may adopt and amend the subdivision regulations proposed by the Commission. The County Council's action on the capital budget of various county agencies affects decisions on the building of schools, highways, and recreation centers. The Board of Appeals, whose five members are appointed by the County Council, grants special exceptions or variances in the application of zoning regulations.

The County Department of Information and Industrial Development supplies information helpful to organizations interested in locating new businesses in the county.

Public Safety

The Montgomery County Police Department covers the entire county and furnishes the only full patrol force for 99% of the county.(4) The county police have a reputation for competence and integrity and provide the same types of services as large city police agencies. A patrol and traffic force of 350 uniformed men maintains a continuing motorized patrol of the county. A staff of more than 40 detectives succeeded in closing 76% of all cases investigated within the county in 1965. The Department has a criminal identification staff, a complete records division, and a juvenile aid staff which patrols places where juveniles gather and works with parents and the Juvenile Court to help prevent delinquency. The Police Department maintains a force of more than 170 part-time employees to safeguard school crossings and has three officers with trained dogs who have been particularly effective in tracking lost children and criminal suspects. The entire Police Department is under a civil service merit system and is directed by a professional police officer appointed by the County Manager.

Wealthy homes in the county are naturally attractive to house-breakers. Burglary, traffic violations, and accidents rank high as police problems. The large motorized patrol force and a new police communications system are helping to resolve these problems. The hub of the police communications system for the county is ten feet underground in the county civil defense shelter. Calls received from police anywhere in the county are taken by message takers working in shifts on a 24 hour a day basis. A message taker, who receives a call on an accident, will quickly note the time and place of the accident on a punched card. The card is conveyed by a moving belt within 35 seconds to one of two radio dispatchers, each of whom covers half the county. Each dispatcher has before him a huge lighted map of his part of the county with the beats of all patrol cars indicated on it by colored lights. The dispatcher glances upward to see a green light on for car 200, whose beat is nearest the accident. He radios this car to proceed to the scene of the accident, and then places the punched card in one of the numbered slots beside him. The card is time stamped, and the light on the board under car 200 turns from green to orange to indicate that the car is responding to a call and cannot, under ordinary circumstances, accept another call. Within a few minutes after the center receives notification of the accident, a patrol car is on the scene. During his investigation and work in rerouting traffic, the patrolman may be in touch with the radio dispatcher to report the situation and secure assistance. When he completes his work, he again calls the dispatcher who notes this on the punched card. The card is again placed in the slot, time stamped, and the light on the board for the patrol car turns from orange back to green. The punched card is then placed on a conveyer belt to be reviewed by the supervisor, filed, and used later for statistical purposes.

Unlike many counties, the elected Sheriff of Montgomery County has a minor role in police protection. The Sheriff and his deputies are responsible for serving civil summonses, subpoenas and other papers issued by the courts and transporting prisoners between the courtrooms, the county detention center and penal institutions.

The Department of Public Safety maintains the county's communications, operates the county jail, administers the civil defense program, and provides important fire prevention and inspection services. There are 16 fire districts which cover the county. Full-time fire departments are maintained in some of the more densely populated areas, and volunteers are used to man or partially man fire equipment in other areas. County government assists these fire companies by investigating the causes of fires, inspecting for violation of the fire code, and maintaining a modern fire communications system for all fire and rescue companies in the county.

The hub of the fire communications system is located in the civil defense shelter near the police communications system. Calls coming from anywhere in the county are received by message takers who record the type of fire and location. The radio dispatcher uses a card system to show what fire companies should be dispatched to the scene and has quick reference to a lighted board showing the equipment that is in action (red light) or being repaired (yellow light). Therefore, he is quickly able to dispatch alternate companies. The dispatcher is able to radio the fire companies needed and, not only sound the alarm in the fire station, but also turn on the lights of the station and open the station doors. If volunteer firemen are on duty in their homes, he can rouse them from sleep with an alarm that sounds in their homes. About the only thing the remote control system doesn't do, one county employee stated, is to open the cage of the Dalmation, which usually rides on the fire truck.

During the course of the fire, the radio communications system is used to keep continuing contact with radio equipped fire trucks and to call in additional equipment. The radio dispatcher keeps track of the equipment used in the fire through the lighted board and is thus able to shift the equipment of several fire districts to the scene of a serious blaze. He is also able to dispatch ambulances and rescue cars to where they are needed. Through its radio communications system, the county is able to coordinate the work of fire fighting crews in the 16 fire districts.

The county has provided facilities for a complete civil defense center in a shelter adjacent to the county building under ten feet of earth and concrete. It is designed to protect not only against fallout but against a blast ten to fifteen miles away in Washington which might shatter county buildings and send tons of rubble down on top of the shelter. All of the major equipment in the center is mounted on shock absorbers to minimize blast damage, and the center contains provisions for thirty days, its own power system, three wells, and radiation detection devices. This center contains the present police and fire communications systems, an emergency public works communications system, and a school communications system that can quickly communicate with each county school. Several radio transmitters and receivers are in the civil defense center to be manned by ham operators in case of attack. The civil defense warning system, manned 24 hours a day, can instantly blow warning sirens in 46 parts of the county.

The Civil Defense Unit has stocked shelter spaces for over 100 thousand county residents for a 14 day period and has marked spaces for 180 thousand more residents. Scattered about the county are five 200 bed emergency hospitals ready to be put to use in case of emergency. As public buildings are constructed, consideration is given to the need for more fallout shelter space. One elementary school has been built entirely underground with a view to defense needs.

Public Works and Transportation

The County Department of Public Works, headed by a director appointed by the County Manager, is responsible for the traditional county road function and many urban functions as well. The Department constructs and maintains roads and streets and provides street lighting, signs, sidewalks, gutters, curbs, storm drainage, traffic control, street cleaning, roadside tree care, and parking lots. The Department also operates a huge incinerator to serve the entire county. Forty-five parking lots with 5300 spaces and 3 garages with 1200 spaces are operated by county administered subordinate taxing districts.

The 1,400 mile county road system does not include all roads and streets in the county. The State Highway Department maintains about 500 miles of roads, and some municipalities of the county (containing about 16% of the county population) maintain their own streets and provide some other services such as street lighting and street cleaning. Many new roads are built by land developers with the county approving the plans. The county Department does, however, provide a remarkably large variety of public works services for most county residents.

County public works are financed by a variety of means. The cost of new streets, sidewalks, curbs, and gutters is usually assessed against the abutting property owners. A small tax is assessed against residents of the more densely populated areas of the county who receive street cleaning and roadside tree care services. A tax is levied against commercial property owners in four areas to pay the cost of parking lots and garages. Federal funds, state funds, and general county funds are also used.

Water supply, sewage disposal, and some storm drainage is provided for most of the densely populated southern and eastern parts of the county by the bi-county Washington Suburban Sanitary District. The six members of the governing commission of this District serve four years terms and are appointed by the Governor of Maryland. Two are chosen from nominees submitted by the Montgomery County Council, two from nominees submitted by the Prince Georges County Council, and two are chosen by the Governor. The District secures its water principally from the Potomac River and from reservoirs on the Pautuxent River and has its own filtration and sewage disposal plants. The city of Rockville has its own water and sewage system. In the more rural areas of the county, water is provided from wells and sewage is disposed of through septic tanks.

Neither the county nor any other governmental unit within the county provides bus transportation or a rapid transit system. One large private bus corporation serves most of the county area. The Revenue Authority of Montgomery County does maintain, under lease, an airport for private planes. This Authority, which is supported wholly from fees and other charges, also operates a county golf course.

SUMMARY

Montgomery is a rapidly growing county in the Washington metropolitan area. Most county residents live outside municipal limits in the suburban area adjacent to the District of Columbia. County government and two bi-county districts(5) provide municipal services for the residents of these unincorporated areas as well as for some municipal residents. In a 1962 study, the Public Administration Service found significant efficiencies in the large scale county operations and warned the county against tax rebates which would encourage municipalities to establish their own library, police, and recreation programs.(6) Montgomery County has shown that counties can provide efficient, low cost municipal services for an expanding suburban area, and that there is little need for municipal services for an expanding suburban area, and that there is little need for municipal government in such an area.

Important factors in the success of Montgomery County government have been the county manager plan and the career civil service system. The county manager system has provided stable, professional administration. The civil service system, which encompasses more than 95% of all non-school employees of the county, has helped furnish a well trained career civil service.

REFERENCES

1. Letter from the County Manager of Montgomery County, dated January 17, 1966. In 1962, the Bureau of the Census reported 28 units of government within the county.

2. Public Administration Service. The Government of Montgomery County, Maryland (Chicago: Public Administration Service, 1962), p. 22.

3. Seven cities and towns of Montgomery County, containing less than 10% of the county population, are excluded from this tax.

4. The city of Takoma Park has a small police force, and the city of Rockville has several policemen. In addition, the state police patrol some of the main roads to catch traffic violators, and park police patrol certain parks.

5. The Washington Suburban Sanitary District and the Maryland–National Capital Park and Planning Commission.

6. Public Administration Service. op. cit., p. 22.

Chapter 10

Davidson County

DAVIDSON COUNTY, IN CENTRAL TENNESSEE, is the center of a metropolitan area in itself rather than being part of a larger metropolitan area as is Montgomery County, Maryland.(1) The county has a land area of 532 square miles and in 1960 had a population of 399,743.(2) Nashville, the county seat, is the capital of Tennessee, an important educational and religious center, the site of the home of Andrew Jackson, and the county music capital of the nation.(3) It is a banking, insurance, and printing center for the region and an industrial center specializing in glass, metal products, chemicals, and shoes. In 1962, the governments of the city of Nashville and of Davidson County were consolidated leaving six small municipalities and seven special districts as the only other governmental units in the county.

The State Capitol is built on a hill overlooking the Cumberland River. Located within a few blocks of the State Capitol are state and federal office buildings, several large hotels, and many banks and office buildings of the city. Between the State Capitol Building and the Cumberland River, the former slum district has been cleared through urban renewal, and this area has been used for new government buildings, new offices, park-like terraces, and off-street parking for state employees.

Surrounding the governmental and financial district of Nashville is an area of older stores, warehouses and offices. Beyond this, are areas of older homes and commercial centers along the main streets. It is in these areas of older homes that most of Nashville's seventy thousand Negroes live.

The main middle and upper class residential sections begin two to three miles from the State Capitol and continue as far as twelve miles from the city center. There are areas of tree lined streets, stately old homes, parks, and college campuses. Farther out along the main roads leading from the city, there are newer subdivisions of moderate priced ranch homes, huge new shopping centers, and several of the newer industrial plants. Still farther out are scattered estates and suburban homes with their large lawns, gardens, and fish ponds. The suburban area reaches to the county line on the south and close to the county line in places on the east and west. Beyond the suburbs, lies a gently rolling dairy and livestock region and a hilly wooded area that partially surrounds the county.

In the early 1950's, Davidson County was faced with serious governmental problems.(4) The city of Nashville was providing a full range of municipal services to an area of 22 square miles with a population of 170,000. The city boundaries encompassed only part of the residential area, and more than one hundred thousand suburban residents lacked full scale urban services. Some municipal services were provided by six small satellite cities, but most of the suburban area was unincorporated. Water was supplied to fringe communities by Nashville and sold by public utility districts and private companies at rates as high as three times the rates charged Nashville residents. Some utility districts and private companies laid water lines which were too small to allow sufficient water pressure for fire hydrants. More remote suburban districts had to depend upon very costly deep wells or cisterns. The suburban areas outside Nashville had to depend largely upon septic tanks in an area where limestone near the surface made absorption of sewage into the ground difficult. Police services were supplied by a patronage-ridden county sheriff's office, constables, and private police companies serving residents who paid their subscription fees. Fire protection was provided mainly by subscription fire departments that sometimes stood by and watched a nonsubscriber's house burn to the ground.

The city of Nashville was having its problems as well. It was paying for a comprehensive park system, but many of its parks were located in suburban areas where they were patronized primarily by suburbanites. City residents were paying large school taxes which partially went to support the county school system.

Concern about metropolitan problems mounted, and a 1952 study commission recommended city and county home rule, county wide administration of certain functions, and annexation of a 69 square mile area by Nashville.(5) A year later, the Tennessee Constitution was amended to permit consolidation of any or all city and county functions if approved by a majority of persons living in the city and a majority living in the county outside the city.(6) Two years later, County Judge Beverly Briley suggested the possibility of one government for Nashville and Davidson County in a speech in Nashville, and the following year the Nashville City and Davidson County Planning Commissions prepared a report favoring consolidation. In 1957, the state legislature passed enabling legislation permitting consolidation. However in 1958, a consolidation charter was defeated because it failed to secure a majority vote in the suburbs.(7)

After consolidation failed, Nashville decided to annex suburban areas. By 1961, the city succeeded in annexing, largely against their wishes, 49 square miles with a population of 87,000. The city was unable to provide sewers immediately for most of this newly annexed area, and these residents found themselves taxed more heavily for what they considered insufficient additional services. In 1962, the second try for consolidation was successful partly because of better organized grass roots support for consolidation and partly because of opposition to the annexation and tax policies of the Mayor of Nashville who was against consolidation. A suit was filed challenging the legality of the new metropolitan government, but it was resolved favorably and the new government came into effect on April 1, 1963.

The merger of the governments of Davidson County and the City of Nashville eliminated much duplication of functions within the county, but it did not eliminate all other agencies providing local government services. The six satellite cities continue to provide zoning and street maintenance services, and some of them furnish police protection. The private police forces have been discontinued. Private fire companies continue to exist but are expected to discontinue service in the next few years. As the county extends its water and sewer lines, the public utility districts and private companies which provide water and sewer services should gradually disappear. The Nashville Suburban District was acquired by Metro in February, 1964, and others will gradually be acquired. Within ten years, it is possible that most of the satellite cities will either disincorporate or wither into inactivity, and most of the public utility districts and private water, and fire companies will have discontinued operation.

FORM OF GOVERNMENT

The metropolitan government of Nashville and Davidson County has a strong executive form of government which is similar to the strong mayor-council form of city government. The executive head of government is the Mayor, elected for a term of four years at a salary of $25,000 a year. The legislative body is a 40 member Metropolitan County Council whose members are elected for four year terms and paid $300 a month. Relationships between the Mayor and Council are similar in many ways to relationships between the President and Congress. The Mayor prepares recommended legislation, submits an executive budget and has overall responsibility for the conduct of the executive branch of government. The Metropolitan County Council enacts ordinances, reviews the executive budget, and has general oversight of administration. The Mayor

Table 1
STRUCTURE OF NASHVILLE-DAVIDSON COUNTY GOVERNMENT

1. Form of county government	Strong executive
2. Legislative body	Metropolitan County Council of 40 members elected by the voters.
3. Chief administrative officer	Metropolitan County Mayor elected by the voters
4. Agencies headed by a director appointed by the Mayor	Mayor's Office Code Enforcement Civil Defense Finance includes budget, accounts, purchasing, treasury, collections, data processing, public property Fire Law Metropolitan clerk Police Public works Water and sewage
5. Agencies headed by a board or commission whose members are appointed by the Mayor	Agriculture Extension Board Board of Tax Equalization Board of Zoning Appeals Civil Service Commission Electric Power Board Employees Benefit Board Farmers Market Board Metropolitan Board of Education Metropolitan Board of Fair Commissioners Metropolitan Board of Health Metropolitan Board of Hospitals Metropolitan Board of Parks and Recreation Metropolitan Planning Commission Metropolitan Traffic and Parking Commission Metropolitan Welfare Commission Nashville Housing Authority Nashville Transit Authority
6. Agencies headed by appointees of the Council	Audit Board
7. Other county elected officials	Chancery Court Circuit Court County Court Clerk Criminal Court County Judge and Probate Court District Attorney General General Sessions Court Metropolitan Court Juvenile Court and Detention Home Public Defender Quarterly County Court County Trustee Metropolitan tax assessor Sheriff

may veto a county ordinance; the Council may override the Mayor's veto by a 2/3 majority.

The Mayor of Nashville-Davidson County has greater authority and responsibility than any executive official in Petroleum, Latah or Montgomery counties. As Table 1 shows, he appoints the heads of almost all important departments, boards, authorities and commissions. He has the responsibility for leadership in planning, organization, personnel management, financial management, and law enforcement.(8) As political and policy leader, he is responsible for preparing a legislative program for the metropolitan council and encouraging citizen support and knowledge of the goals of metropolitan government. He serves also as ceremonial head of the county-wide metropolitan government, welcoming influential visitors, making speeches on important occasions, and representing the interests of the county-wide area before national and state government. Metropolitan County Mayor Beverly Briley is a strong individual who has worked tirelessly to build up an able, efficient staff and to implement sweeping program changes. Not everyone would agree with all his policies, but few would deny that he has provided dynamic leadership — the type of leadership that generates great citizen interest in county government — the type of leadership that voters can understand and hold responsible at the polls.

The Metropolitan County Council is composed of five members elected at large and 35 elected from single-member districts. The presiding officer of the Council is a Vice-Mayor elected for a term of four years and paid $4,200 a year. The Vice-Mayor cannot vote in the Council except to break a tie. He does select the members of all Council committees, assigns proposed ordinances to committees, and exercises a significant degree of leadership in the Council.

The Council holds regular meetings twice a month, but council members meet frequently at special council meetings and committee meetings during the month. An ordinance is normally given its first reading by the Council and then assigned by the Vice-Mayor to one of 14 standing committees. These committees review the proposed ordinance carefully, often revise it, and may return it to the Council. The ordinance is read for the second and third times and, if passed, is sent to the Mayor. The Mayor has ten days in which to approve or veto the bill. If he does not take action before ten days elapse, the ordinance becomes law without his signature. The Council is authorized to conduct, or have its committees conduct, investigations of county government by a 3/4 vote of its entire membership, and the Mayor cannot veto such an authorization. No authorization for investigation of county government has been passed by the Council to date, but the standing committees are exercising continuing oversight of administration through day to day contacts with the Mayor, department heads, and other executive officials in the metropolitan government.

Independently elected officials play a less influential role in Nashville–Davidson County than they do in Montgomery County. Aside from judges and officials whose duties are closely related to the court system, the only other independently elected officials in Davidson County are: the County Trustee, the Metropolitan Tax Assessor, and the Sheriff. The County Trustee collects real and personal property taxes, and the Metropolitan Tax Assessor is responsible for assessment of all properties in the county. The Sheriff has been stripped of his law enforcement duties but is responsible for process serving and maintenance of the Metropolitan Jail and Workhouse. The Sheriff is elected for a two year term, and the County Trustee and Metropolitan Tax Assessor are elected for terms of four years.

An important feature of the Metropolitan Government of Nashville and Davidson County is the division of the county into two service districts. The General Services District covers the entire area of Davidson County, and the Urban Services District encompasses the area of Nashville at the time the Metropolitan Charter was adopted. The area of the Urban Services District may be expanded by annexation whenever particular areas of the General Services District come to need urban services. However, the Metropolitan Government cannot expand the Urban Services District unless it can provide urban services to the areas annexed within a year. The Metropolitan Government is authorized to provide an extensive list of services to residents of the General Services District including police, courts, jails, assessment, health, welfare, hospitals, schools, parks and recreation. It is authorized to provide additional services such as fire protection, water, sanitary sewers, storm sewers, street lighting, street cleaning, and refuse collection for the Urban Services District. All county residents pay taxes for the General Services District; county residents living in the Urban Services District pay an additional tax for the additional services which they receive.

COUNTY FINANCES

More than half the revenue of the Metropolitan Government of Nashville–Davidson County comes from property taxes and payments made in lieu of property taxes by the Electric Power Board, Nashville Housing Authority and Tennessee Valley Authority. Other large sources of county income are: state aid, state shared taxes, federal aid, licenses, permits, fines, charges for services, and revenues from municipal enterprises. The Metropolitan Government anticipates, for example, receiving $642,000 from the operation of the airport, $190,000 in golf fees from municipal courses, and $836,000 from the operation of the general hospital.

Property tax assessment is the responsibility of an assessor elected for a term of four years. The collection of property taxes is administered by a second elected official, the County Trustee. Thus, two important areas of fiscal administration are not under the control of the County Mayor.

STAFF AND AUXILIARY SERVICES

The Mayor has a staff office which was established in accord with recommendations made by the Nashville City and Davidson County Planning Commissions before he assumed office.(9) An experienced newspaperman and his assistant are responsible for the Metropolitan Government's relationship with news media. They prepare press releases for the Mayor and prepare material for the Mayor to use on radio and television shows. The Metropolitan Government has increased citizen interest in the community, and the two large newspapers have assigned their experienced reporters to cover local government news. As a convenience for reporters who check the Mayor's Office periodically for news, the public relations staff places the latest metropolitan news on tape which is played over a telephone answering service when the public relations staff is out of the office.

The Information and Complaint Section is another unique staff service of the Mayor's Office. The two member staff of this section answers telephone calls and letters requesting information about the Metropolitan Government or registering complaints. Many complaints result from misunderstandings or from lack of knowledge as to the proper person to contact. Each letter receives an answer prepared by the Section and signed by the Mayor. The staff members follow-up to see that departmental officials take remedial action on justifiable complaints and keep records on the number of communications they receive on each type of governmental service.

The Mayor also has staff assistants in his office to handle relationships with metropolitan departments on personnel and other matters, relationships with the County Council, and urban development and budgeting.

The Department of Finance also serves as an important staff arm to the Mayor. The budget staff of this Department, with the Mayor's Assistant on Budgets and Urban Renewal, are responsible for budget preparation. The Department also has divisions of Internal Audit, Data Processing, Accounts, Payroll, Treasurer, Purchases, and Collection. Unification of most of the important fiscal and data handling services under one department has many advantages. It provides a high-level fiscal advisory staff for use by the Mayor, permits day to day control over expenditures, and encourages reduction in large volume paperwork operations. The accounting and budgeting divisions cooperate in administering a system of expenditure controls. The Data Processing Division has implemented the recommendations of a management study by Ernst and Ernst to streamline procedures for the preparation of payrolls, voter registration and the property tax record keeping, billing and collection.(10) The Purchasing Division saves thousands of dollars through mass purchasing. The Department of Finance is supervised by a Director appointed by the Mayor.

The Metropolitan Planning Commission has an important staff role. The capital budget of Nashville-Davidson County is reviewed first by the staff of this Commission and then by the staff of the Department of Finance and by the Mayor. The Metropolitan Planning Commission has made a number of important studies having management as well as physical planning implications. The advice of the Commission and its staff is sought by the Mayor's Office on many matters.

Nashville-Davidson County has a comprehensive civil service system which covers more than 95% of all employees exclusive of teachers employed by the Board of Education and professional personnel employed by the Board of Health and Board of Hospitals. Responsibility for administering the civil service system rests with a five member Civil Service Commission. The Commission appoints a Personnel Director who supervises the Commission staff. This staff administers the pay and classification plan, conducts examinations, and is responsible for many other personnel functions. The County Mayor and his staff have taken a personal interest in securing highly qualified personnel for top positions. For example, the man appointed by the Mayor as Acting Fire Chief was brought into Nashville from another state and has a national reputation in his field.

The heads of the major departments (Finance, Law, Aviation, Fire, Police, Public Works and Water and Sewerage Services) act informally as a cabinet for the Mayor. These are men appointed by the Mayor and are important advisers to him.

COUNTY SERVICES

The functions of the Metropolitan Government of Nashville and Davidson County include all the services formerly provided by the City of Nashville and by Davidson County. With the exception of the services furnished by some private utilities and utility districts and by six small cities containing 4% of the population of the county, the Metropolitan Government is responsible for all local government services in the county. As Appendix A shows, the Metropolitan Government provides 50 general types of services and has exclusive responsibility with respect to nearly all of these functions.

General Government

The Metropolitan Government of Nashville and Davidson County supplies all of the traditional, general gove.. tal services. Assessment and collection of property taxes, electioi. administration, and judicial administration are county functions. Independently elected officials play a less important role in providing general governmental services than in a more traditional county government such as Latah. However, assessment and collection of property taxes are under two independently elected officials, the Metropolitan Tax Assessor and the County Trustee.

The Metropolitan Charter for Nashville and Davidson County made important changes in the court systems within the county. A Metropolitan Court was created with two judges elected by the voters of the county for eight year terms. One judge has responsibility for hearing cases involving violations of traffic ordinances. A second judge hears cases involving other violations of metropolitan ordinances. The charter also established the position of Public Defender to provide legal counsel for persons unable to pay for this service. The Metropolitan Charter changed the powers of the County Judge. Formerly, the County Judge presided over the Quarterly County Court which had power to levy taxes and had many specific administrative responsibilities.(11) The County Judge and Quarterly County Court remain, but they have been stripped of administrative and fiscal responsibilities.(12) The County Judge retains his judicial responsibilities in probate and other matters. The Chancery Court, Circuit Courts, Juvenile Court and other specialized courts serving Davidson County were not affected by the creation of the Metropolitan Government.

Agriculture

The agricultural extension office of Davidson County has a staff of ten and provides many of the same types of services described in the chapters on Latah and Montgomery counties. Dairy products, soybeans, hogs, cattle, and poultry are the main farm products in the county, and the extension agents conduct a farm management school for these farmers. As the suburban area surrounding Nashville has expanded toward the county borders, the extension agents have found themselves answering an increasing number of inquiries from suburban gardeners. Nashville–Davidson County owns and has the major responsibility for operating the Tennessee State Fair which is held in the county. Extension agents work with 4-H club leaders and home demonstration club leaders who prepare exhibits for the fair. The Metropolitan Government operates a farmers market so that farm families can bring their produce into the Urban Services District (Nashville) and sell it.

Education and Libraries

Since July 1, 1964, there has been only one school system in Nashville-Davidson County. This school system is administered by a nine member Board of Education appointed by the Mayor for staggered six year terms, subject to confirmation by two-thirds of the Council. The Board appoints the personnel of the school district, fixes salaries, acquires school sites, and has other functions similar to those of the boards of most school systems. The budget approved by the School Board is reviewed, and may be changed, by the County Mayor. The Mayor's education budget may be changed by the County Council. If two-thirds or more of the members of the Metropolitan Board of Education believe that the funds appropriated by the Council for education are insufficient, they may call for a referendum election to determine whether an additional tax should be levied and the proceeds added to the school budget.

There are several important advantages to consolidating the former city and county school systems. Equalization of teachers' salaries within the county is facilitated by the consolidation. More equitable distribution of financial support of schools also results. Savings estimated at one million dollars resulted in the interim transitional period due to the transfer of 1,000 students from over-crowded county schools to city schools where vacant rooms existed.

Library services for the entire county area are provided by a seven member Library Board appointed by the Metropolitan County Mayor with confirmation by a majority of the Metropolitan County Council. The Library Board appoints a Chief Librarian and may enter into a five year contract with a qualified person. The Library Board has a staff of more than 100 employees and provides adult, children's and extension services.

Health and Welfare

The Metropolitan Government of Nashville and Davidson County is responsible for the health and welfare services for the entire county. Health services are under the supervision of a five member Metropolitan Board of Health, each member serving a five year term without compensation. The Board selects a Chief Medical Director who must be a physician. Some of the main functions of the

Board of Health are the investigation and control of communicable diseases, collection and tabulation of vital statistics, provision of health services for school children, anti-rabies vaccinations, tuberculosis case finding, and operation of child guidance centers and mental health clinics. The hearing and speech center, partially supported by a foundation grant, is another important Board of Health project.

The Metropolitan Hospital Board of seven members, appointed by the Mayor, provides the only local government institutional care in the county. The Board appoints a Director of Hospitals who is responsible for the operation of the General Hospital, a tuberculosis hospital, a psychiatric hospital and home, and a convalescent hospital having mainly older patients. Many psychiatric patients are cared for by the state administered Central State Hospital.

The only local government welfare services in Nashville and Davidson County are administered by the Metropolitan Welfare Commission of seven members, appointed by the Mayor. The state of Tennessee administers the grant programs for old age assistance, aid to the blind, aid to the permanently and totally disabled, and aid to families with dependent children, but the Metropolitan Government pays part of the cost. The Metropolitan Welfare Commission is responsible for administering general assistance, child welfare, foster care, and certain medical programs for the indigent. It also supervises two small children's homes and two homes for the aged.

Parks and Recreation

Prior to the consolidation of Nashville and Davidson County government, the city of Nashville had the only extensive park system in the county. Most of the larger parks were outside the city, and more than 70% of the patrons of these parks were not Nashville residents. Thus, Nashville residents were paying for parks that were primarily used by nonresidents, and there was some opposition to extending the park system by the development of new land outside the city. Consolidation of Nashville and Davidson County has brought a larger, county-wide tax base to support the park system. Furthermore, in planning new parks, metropolitan officials can disregard city boundaries to place parks where they are currently most needed.

Responsibility for metropolitan parks is placed in a seven member Metropolitan Board of Parks and Recreation. It is responsible for formulating park policies and selecting a Director who is required to have at least five years experience in park or recreation administration. The park system has one huge regional park of 2,800 acres, two large urban parks of more than 100 acres, ten playfield parks of about 20 to 30 acres, and 95 playfields of less than ten acres. Included in the park system are four golf courses (one of 27 holes) and three putting greens. There are also tennis courts, a boat launching ramp, fishing areas, many picnic areas, lodges for group picnics, hiking and bicycle trails, croquet grounds, swimming pools, a steeplechase course, and even a model airplane flying field complete with a simulated scaled down carrier flight deck. The Board of Parks and Recreation has constructed a number of recreation center buildings and has full scale summer and winter recreation programs.

Centennial Park is typical of one of the larger parks. Named in honor of the hundredth anniversary of the city, it is located near both white and colored residential areas and has fully integrated facilities. Its community center building is used by more than a thousand persons a week. It has a large basketball court which is used by church and industrial leagues and a smaller gym with bar bells and other weight lifting and exercising apparatus. Two television rooms are used extensively by senior citizens. There are several conference and class rooms that are used for adult and children's classes in art, ceramics, flower arrangement and other subjects. Across the grassy park mall from the community center is a large concert stage used by the Nashville Symphony Orchestra for summer outdoor concerts. Other facilities in the park include five ball diamonds, seven tennis courts, several covered shelters, a large picnic area under the trees, a rose arbor, croquet courts, sand boxes and play equipment for small children, a large pond with fishing for children under 16, and a locomotive with a ramp for children to climb into the cab.

Physical Planning and Development

Physical planning is a long established and very important function in the Davidson County area. Nashville established a City Planning Commission in 1931, and during the 1930's the city adopted a comprehensive plan, a zoning ordinance, subdivision regulations, and a major thoroughfare plan.(13) As early as the 1930's, it was clear to Nashville Planning Commission officials that planning in Nashville could not be effective unless there was also planning in the suburban area outside the city limits. From 1935 until the establishment of the Davidson County Planning Commission in 1939, the Nashville City Planning Commission was designated as the Nashville Regional Planning Commission and had jurisdiction in the city of Nashville and in an area up to five miles beyond the city limits. The nationally recognized staff of the Nashville City Planning Commission participated in a number of studies of the economy and governmental services in the Nashville area during the 1940's and 1950's. During the 1950's the Nashville City and Davidson County Planning Commissions shared the same professional staff. It was this staff that formed the backbone of the present Metropolitan Planning Commission after consolidation of Nashville and Davidson County governments.

The Metropolitan Planning Commission of Nashville and Davidson County has ten members: the Mayor, a member of the Metropolitan County Council, and eight members selected by the Mayor and confirmed by the Council. It has a staff of more than forty persons. The Planning Commission has adopted a comprehensive plan for Davidson County including land use, recreation, and major thoroughfare plans. The planning staff has also made studies of the economy of the area, a housing study, a market analysis, a plan for the location of schools and public buildings, and a plan to alleviate flooding and problems of poor surface drainage. Armed with an act of the 1959 State Legislature, the staff has implemented an official map plan.(14) Under this act, no building can be constructed on the bed of any proposed street or highway. Thus, the Metropolitan Government is protected against higher acquisition costs when it purchases this land for highway or street purposes.

Zoning is another important function of the Metropolitan Planning Commission. The planning staff prepares a zoning plan and presents it to the Planning Commission. A majority of the Planning Commission and Metropolitan County Council must approve the plan before it becomes a zoning ordinance. The Metropolitan Planning Commission is in a strong position to block attempts to destroy the comprehensive plan through piecemeal changes in zoning. All proposed changes in the zoning ordinance must be submitted to the Planning Commission before they are received by the Council, and a 2/3 vote of the Council is necessary to override an adverse vote of the Planning Commission. If the Mayor vetoes the Council action in changing the zoning ordinance against the recommendation of the Planning Commission, a 3/4 vote of the Council is necessary to override the Mayor's veto. During the transition period to Metropolitan Government, the Board of Zoning Appeals of the City of Nashville and the Board of Zoning Appeals of Davidson County continued in existence. After zoning regulations are adopted for the entire metropolitan area, a Metropolitan Board of Zoning Appeals will be established.

The Metropolitan Planning Commission also prepares subdivision regulations for the entire county area. An architect, realtor, or subdivider who is planning a new subdivision, contacts the Planning Commission staff to receive assistance and information about subdivision regulations. After a preliminary plat for the subdivision is prepared, it is reviewed and approved by the Metropolitan Planning Commission. Prior to approval, the Planning Commission staff checks with the Board of Health, the Department of Public Works, and the Department of Water and Sewerage Services to see that the requirements of these agencies are met by the proposed subdivision. The Planning Commission also approves the final plat of the subdivision. The subdivision regulations tend to assure a more orderly development of subdivisions than would otherwise occur.

The Metropolitan Planning Commission plays a prominent part in capital improvements budgeting in the metropolitan area. The Metropolitan Charter provides that no street, park, or public building shall be constructed or authorized in the metropolitan area unless it has the approval of the Planning Commission. Departments submit their capital budget requests to the Planning Commission. They are reviewed both by the Planning Commission staff and Finance Department staff, and priorities are established. The Planning Commission reviews the capital improvements budget and then submits it to the Mayor. After action by the Mayor, it is submitted to the Metropolitan County Council, and the Council makes the final decision on the budget.

The Planning Commission also actively participates in urban renewal projects in cooperation with the Nashville Housing Authority. The Planning Commission identifies areas in need of urban renewal and prepares a workable program to secure federal funds. The Nashville Housing Authority, headed by a Board of Commissioners whose members are appointed by the Metropolitan County Mayor, is responsible for clearing the land, construction of streets and other facilities, and reselling the land for private development or transferring it to state or metropolitan agencies for public use. One urban renewal project is completed; others are underway. The Capitol Hill Redevelopment Project cleared 96 acres of slums in the heart of the city near the State Capitol. Prior to redevelopment, the estimated property tax return on this area was only $47,000. After the slums had been cleared, part of the land was resold for two modern apartment buildings each having about 200 units, and part was resold to several corporations to construct attractive new office buildings. This property now returns $158,000 in property taxes. Part of this land has been used to build a large municipal auditorium and part to provide attractive walks and parking areas for state employees. The Capitol Hill Redevelopment Project cost $11.7 million of which the federal share was $5.2 million.

Three other urban renewal projects are underway and will provide space for a new industrial site, new public housing, and new private housing developments.

Public Safety

Consolidation of Nashville and Davidson County has brought important changes in police services in the county area. Before consolidation, there were two large police forces: the city police department and the county Sheriff's office. Now, the Sheriff's Office is limited to serving process papers and responsibility for the Metropolitan Jail and Workhouse. Police protection throughout the entire county is provided by the Department of Metropolitan Police whose director is appointed by the County Mayor. Three satellite cities still have small police forces which range in size from one to six persons.

Combining police protection in Davidson County under one major police force has brought many benefits. There is much more uniformity in enforcement throughout the area. Unification of records into a centralized system has resulted in more efficient record keeping, more accurate studies of police problems, and better utilization of records in tracking criminals. The Department of Metropolitan Police has instituted a six weeks' training program which it hopes to expand to 12 weeks. Training is particularly important in increasing the effectiveness of former deputy sheriffs who have joined the new Department. Formation of a Vice Squad with a select group of officers assigned to juvenile vice problems, improvement of the Homicide Division, and the use of radar equipment are other improvements. The New Department of Metropolitan Police has a traffic unit which uses three wheeled vehicles in downtown areas to check illegal parking and moving violations. One squad of this unit specializes in tracing hit and run cases and has been able to track down 94% of these cases. The other main units of the Department are patrol, school mothers patrol, detectives, records, communication, training, and intelligence and internal security. The latter unit checks out police applicants before they are hired and tries to get advanced intelligence on racketeers moving to Nashville and Davidson County. A comprehensive survey of the Department of Metropolitan Police is being made by the International Chiefs of Police, and the recommendations of that agency are expected to further increase police efficiency.

Consolidation of Nashville and Davidson County has brought improved fire protection services, but these services have not been extended to the entire county. The Metropolitan Fire Department serves primarily the Urban Services District (the former city of Nashville) but also provides fire protection for the airport, the large parks, schools, institutions and buildings operated by the Metropolitan Government throughout the county area. Improvements since consolidation have included more extensive training programs, increased fire prevention inspections, and prefire planning for possible industrial and commercial fires. Particular problems for fire fighting that require advanced planning are the petroleum tanks and chemical plants of the industrial area and the narrow streets in parts of downtown Nashville. At the recommendation of the National Board of Fire Underwriters, the Metropolitan Government hired, as Acting Fire Commissioner and consultant, a man who has had much experience in supervising and reorganizing fire departments and who left an important post at the University of Illinois to take the position.

The Metropolitan Government has a civil defense unit of 6 persons. It has organized 16 active civil defense units which meet to drill once a week. Seventy-five shelters accommodating 83,000 people have been stocked.

Public Works and Transportation

Consolidation of Nashville and Davidson County governments resulted in the merger of the Nashville Department of Public Works and the Davidson County Highway Department. The amalgamation has made possible major improvements in staff services and a savings of $30,000 through the consolidation of accounting, budgeting, requisition, and other services. Engineering functions of the two departments were combined making it possible to employ specialized personnel and to buy equipment that neither the county nor city department could previously have afforded. The Metropolitan Department of Public Works is responsible for construction and maintenance of highways, county roads, and city streets. The six satellite cities are responsible for maintaining their own streets and usually contract with private companies for this purpose. The Director of the Department of Public Works must be a licensed engineer and is appointed by the mayor.

Consolidation of Nashville and Davidson County is making possible a comprehensive water and sewer system for the urban parts of the county under one county wide agency, the Metropolitan Department of Water and Sewerage Services. One of the first results of this consolidation was the rejection of county plans for a sewerage treatment plant at the junction of Mill Creek and the Cumberland River. This plant was to have been located so close to the intake of the city water system that the intake pipes would have had to be relocated. Instead, the Mill Creek Sewerage system is to be merged with the existing central metropolitan sewerage system eliminating an estimated $1 million in construction costs plus $50,000 per year in maintenance costs.

Both the water and sewerage divisions of the Department are embarking upon major programs to expand services. The water division is undertaking a $5-1/2 million expansion program to increase water intake and treatment from 60 million to 90 million gallons a day. It is replacing the small pipelines laid by some private utilities with larger pipes which can carry sufficient pressure to be adequate in fire fighting. The sewerage division is undertaking an $11 million expansion program to extend sewers to the entire Urban Services District. After this is completed, sewers will be extended to other urbanized portions of the county.

Until the Department extends service to all urban parts of the county, some of the private and public utility districts will continue to provide service. However, as water and sewers are extended, many of these districts will be merged with the metropolitan water and sewer systems. The Department of Water and Sewerage Services has taken over service to the former customers of the Suburban Water District and has reduced water rates to 12,000 families.

Other public works functions of the Metropolitan Government are maintenance of the Nashville Airport, traffic, and parking. The Department of Aviation operates the airport, and the Metropolitan Traffic and Parking Commission builds and operates parking lots and parking garages.

SUMMARY

In 1960, Davidson County, a metropolitan area with a population of nearly four hundred thousand, was faced with serious urban problems. Nashville, the main population center, had been unable to expand very much through annexation, and the city was ringed with large unincorporated suburban areas that lacked important municipal services. Water was sold to suburbanites by public utilities and private companies at several times the rates charged Nashville residents. Most suburban dwellers lacked a sewerage system in areas where seepage and overflow of septic tanks caused health problems. Police and fire protection was inadequate. The city of Nashville had its problems too. With an inadequate tax base, it was supporting services, such as parks, which were used by many suburban residents. Nashville's attempts to resolve its problems through annexation and through a tax on county residents working in Nashville were unpopular.

The answer to these metropolitan problems came through consolidation of the governments of Davidson County and the City of Nashville. This has brought economies through consolidation of staff services, school systems, and purchasing. It has also enabled metropolitan officials to disregard city boundaries in planning expansions of park, water, sewerage, and other facilities to meet the needs of the entire densely populated area of the county. Consolidation of Nashville and Davidson County has not immediately resolved all the water, sewer and other problems of suburban dwellers, but it has resulted in a long term plan for solving these problems and important immediate steps in accomplishing these plans.

The form of government of Nashville-Davidson County seems well adapted to an aggressive resolution of the metropolitan problems of the area. The Metropolitan County Mayor is elected for a term of four years by the voters of the county, and he appoints (with

Council approval) the heads of most departments, boards, and com- missions. The forty member Metropolitan County Council enacts ordinances, reviews the Mayor's budget, and exercises general oversight of administration. The responsibility for the resolution of the metropolitan problems of the area has been placed squarely in the hands of the Mayor and Council instead of being diffused among officials of many units of local government.

A public opinion survey, conducted in the spring of 1964, indi- cated that the Metropolitan Government of Nashville and Davidson County had increased in popularity since its establishment.(15) In 1962, 57% of the voters favored the new government and 43% opposed it; in 1964, 71% of those polled were favorable and 29% were un- favorable. The new metropolitan government gained most in popu- larity in the old city of Nashville and lost popularity only in the six small cities outside Nashville. As Daniel Grant has pointed out, the real test of Metro is yet to come, but thus far voters seem to be favorably inclined toward the new government.(16)

REFERENCES

1. In 1962, Davidson County, Tennessee was a metropolitan area in itself. Since 1962, Wilson and Sumner Counties, with a 1960 population of nearly 64,000, have been added to the Nashville metropolitan area.

2. U. S. Bureau of the Census. Census of Governments: 1962, Vol. I, Governmental Organization (Washington: U. S. Government Printing Office, 1963), p. 233. This report lists seven municipalities and seven special districts in Davidson County in 1962. The government of the city of Nash- ville passed out of existence in 1962 leaving six municipalities in the county.

3. Vanderbilt University, George Peabody College, Tennessee State University, and Fisk University are the largest of the educational institu- tions in the county.

4. These problems are described in: A Future for Nashville (Nash- ville: Community Services Commission for Davidson County and The City of Nashville, 1952); Daniel R. Grant, "Metropolitics and Professional Political Leadership: The Case of Nashville," The Annals of the American Academy of Political and Social Science, 353:72-83, May, 1964; and Roscoe C. Martin, Metropolis in Transition, (Washington: Housing and Home Finance Agency, 1963), pp. 103-113.

5. A Future for Nashville, A Report of the Community Services Com- mission for Davidson County and the City of Nashville, 1952.

6. Article XI, Section 9, Tennessee Constitution.

7. The failure of the metro campaign has been analyzed by: David A. Booth, Metropolitics: The Nashville Consolidation (East Lansing: Institute for Community Development and Services, Michigan State University, 1963) and Daniel R. Grant, op. cit., p. 78.

8. Nashville City and Davidson County Planning Commissions, Organization of The Office of Metropolitan County Mayor, February, 1963, p. 2.

9. Nashville City and Davidson County Planning Commissions, Organization of The Office of Metropolitan County Mayor, February, 1963.

10. Ernst and Ernst, Management Services Division, Electronic Data Processing System Specifications for the Metropolitan Government of Nashville and Davidson County, Tennessee, 1963.

11. The functions of the County Judge and County Courts are described in: G. Hilton Butler, Your Tennessee Government (Nashville: Tennessee Department, The American Legion, 1963), pp. 156–158. The responsibilities of the County Judge before the passage of the Metropolitan Charter included: making a statement of the financial condition of the county, appointing a person to care for county property, and serving as the accounting and financial head of the county.

12. Metropolitan Government Charter Commission, The Metropolitan Government Charter for Nashville and Davidson County (Nashville: Metropolitan Government Charter Commission, April 1962), Section 16.04.

13. An excellent description of the history of planning in the Davidson County area may be found in A Future for Nashville (Nashville: Community Services Commission for Davidson County and The City of Nashville, 1952).

14. Chapter 330, Private Acts of 1959.

15. Daniel R. Grant, "Opinions Surveyed on Nashville Metro," National Civic Review, 54:375–377, July, 1965.

16. Ibid., p. 377.

Chapter 11

Milwaukee County

MILWAUKEE COUNTY, WISCONSIN is the center of a metropolitan area that extends beyond the county boundaries to the west
and included a population of nearly 1.2 million in 1960. Milwaukee
County itself had a 1960 population of 1,036,041 and is eighth in the
country in industrial production. It is the home of several of the
nation's leading breweries as well as electrical machinery, fabri-
cated metal products, farm machinery, and chemical plants. Milwaukee is an important grain and livestock center and has one of
the busiest ports on the Great Lakes.

The city of Milwaukee, with a 1960 population of 741,324, is
ringed by Lake Michigan on the east and by suburban cities and
villages on the north, west, and south. Thirty years ago, there
were large tracts of unincorporated land in Milwaukee County;
today, no part of the county is unincorporated. The eighteen cities
and villages that nearly surround Milwaukee range in population
from the city of West Allis (68,157) to the village of River Hills
(1,257). The suburban cities and the larger suburban villages have
extensive municipal services, and the county does not need to provide as many urban services as Montgomery and Davidson Counties.

The central business district of Milwaukee is larger than its
counterpart in Nashville. It is an area approximately 15 blocks
long and six blocks wide which straddles Wisconsin Avenue. At the
west end of this area is the civic center with its massive grey stone
county buildings, the newer Wisconsin state office building, the
Milwaukee library, and several small malls. Near the east end of
this district is the bridge which crosses the Milwaukee River, a
picturesque wooden promenade along the river bank, and the 22
floor modern Marine National Exchange Bank Building. East of the
central business district is Juneau Park and Milwaukee Harbor on
Lake Michigan. Directly south of the central business district is
the Menomonee River Valley containing the largest industrial area
in the county.

Milwaukee, like most urban areas, has densely populated poorer residential areas surrounding the central business district. Driving west from the central business district, one first sees apartment buildings and a belt of older three story homes subdivided into apartments. A mile or two west of the central business district, the homes begin to have modest lawns and by the time one reaches the border of the city of Wauwatosa, three miles from downtown, the homes are large and stately with trees and substantial lawns. The suburban area extends nearly to the county border on the south, several miles beyond the county border in places on the north, and ten miles into Waukesha County on the west. Waukesha County, with a 1960 population of 158,249, is considered part of the Milwaukee metropolitan area by the Bureau of the Census.

Milwaukee County was organized in 1835, and since 1842 has had a County Board of Supervisors.(1) It became apparent in the late 1950's that the County Board of Supervisors faced an increasingly difficult task in supervising the many county departments under its control. It became evident that there was a need for a county officer vested with the power to coordinate and direct county governmental functions under the general policy determination of the Board of Supervisors. To provide this executive leadership, the county adopted a County Executive form of government in 1958, and enabling State legislation was obtained in 1959. The first County Executive in Milwaukee County was elected in April, 1960.

Milwaukee County had 41 units of local government in 1962 — only one more than Latah County, Idaho with 2% of Milwaukee County's population. These included the county government, 19 municipal governments, 16 school districts, and five special districts.(2) The special districts were: three housing authorities (two of which are now operating as departments of city government rather than as special districts), a drainage district, and a sewerage district. The relatively small number of special districts in Milwaukee County is a tribute to the comprehensiveness of county and municipal services in the area.

FORM OF GOVERNMENT

Milwaukee County has a strong executive form of government similar in many respects to that of Nashville–Davidson County. The executive head of government, the County Executive, is elected for a term of four years at a salary of $25,000 per year. The county legislative body is a 24 member Board of Supervisors, each member elected for a four year term at a salary of $8,600 a year.(3) The County Executive prepares recommended legislation, submits an executive budget, and has overall responsibility for the conduct of the executive branch of county government. The Board of

Supervisors enacts county ordinances and resolutions, reviews the executive budget, and has general oversight of administration.

The Milwaukee County Executive has greater authority and responsibility than any executive official in Petroleum, Latah, or Montgomery Counties. The chief function of the County Executive is to "coordinate and direct the administrative and management affairs of the county government, and to prepare and present the annual program and budget to the county Board."(4) The coordination and direction of administration is facilitated by the comprehensive budget system of the county. Each August and September, the County Executive rolls up his sleeves and sits down with his budget examining staff and county agency officials to make a careful review of the budget of each spending agency. Making a systematic review of the programs, workload, and spending of each agency gives the County Executive a thorough knowledge of the functions of all county agencies and enables him to better direct coordination of county programs. This executive budget system, which will be described in greater detail later in the chapter, won national recognition when the county Budget Director received the 1960 award of the Municipal Finance Officers Association. The County Executive's role of administrative director is enhanced also by his wide appointment power shown by Table 1. He exercises leadership through his annual message in which he describes accomplishments of the previous year and recommends changes in county ordinances and changes in administration for the coming year. The County Executive has the power to issue executive orders and to give directives to officials, boards and commissions under his supervision.

The County Executive is not a member of the County Board of Supervisors, and, for a time, his authority to veto an ordinance or resolution passed by the County Board was questioned by the courts. A 1962 amendment to the Constitution of the State of Wisconsin made the County Executive a constitutional office and clearly gave him the right to veto any proposed county ordinance or resolution.

In addition to his budget, administrative, and veto powers, the County Executive serves as spokesman for the county on many ceremonial and intergovernmental public occasions. He is at the airport to welcome prominent visitors to Milwaukee County, flies to Washington to represent the interests of the Milwaukee area in a nation civil defense meeting, represents the interests of his area at state legislative committee hearings, and makes many speeches in the county to explain the functions and services performed by county government. The County Executive runs on a nonpartisan ballot. The present County Executive is the first to hold this office in the county, and he has become so well-known and popular in the area that he was re-elected for a four year term in 1964 without opposition.

Table 1
STRUCTURE OF MILWAUKEE COUNTY GOVERNMENT

1. Form of county government	Strong executive
2. Legislative body	Board of Supervisors of 24 members elected by the voters
3. Chief administrative officer	County Executive elected by the voters
4. Agencies headed by a director appointed by the County Executive from civil service eligibility lists	Air Pollution Control Airports Auditor Corporation Counsel House of Correction Law and Reference Library Management and Budget Analysis Medical Examiner Public Works Purchasing Veterans' Service Officer
5. Agencies headed by a board or commission whose members are appointed by the County Executive	Civil Service Election Commission Parks Public Welfare Safety
6. Agencies headed by appointees of the County Board	Historical Museum
7. Other county elected officials	Circuit Court Clerk of Courts Coroner County Clerk County Court District Attorney Register of Deeds Sheriff Superintendent of Schools Surveyor Treasurer

The 24 members of the Milwaukee County Board of Supervisors are elected from 24 separate election districts. The Board elects its own chairman who presides over meetings of the Board and appoints the members of the 15 standing committees. The Board also elects a first vice-chairman and second vice-chairman who serve in the absence of the chairman. Regular board meetings are held every few weeks. However, members of the Board meet much more frequently in committee or other special meetings. An ordinance is normally given its first reading by the Board and then assigned by the Chairman to one of the 15 standing committees. This committee reviews the proposed ordinance thoroughly, holds hearings, frequently revises it, and returns it to the Board. If it is passed, the ordinance is sent to the County Executive. The County Executive may veto an ordinance or resolution, but it may be re-passed over his veto by a 2/3 vote of the Board. The budget proposed by the County Executive is extensively reviewed by the Finance Committee which holds several weeks of hearings. The Board also exercises a continuing oversight of administration through the day to day hearings of its standing committees.

Independently elected officials play a less important role in Milwaukee County government than in many counties. Most of these officials are judges or perform duties closely related to the court system. The Sheriff has the largest staff of the noncourt elected officials. The Sheriff for many years provided police protection in the unincorporated areas of the county. Now that all of the county is incorporated, his staff mainly patrols the county expressways. The Sheriff's office also makes over 100,000 process services each year and operates a county jail with an average daily population of 350 prisoners. The Sheriff is elected for a two year term, and the employees of his office are under civil service. The county voters also elect a Treasurer, County Clerk, Register of Deeds, Coroner, and Surveyor for two year terms. The County Treasurer collects many county taxes, invests county funds, and accounts for county receipts and expenditures. The County Clerk issues thousands of wedding licenses, dog tags, and entertainment licenses each year, and the Register of Deeds records certificates of incorporation, deeds, mortgages, and other legal papers. The positions of Coroner and Surveyor are of nominal importance and these positions will be abolished on December 31, 1966.

COUNTY FINANCES

Milwaukee County depends heavily upon the property tax as do most other counties. In 1965, 37% of the total county-collected revenues came from the property tax. Other major sources of county income include: state and federal aid; the state shared income, public utility, and occupation taxes; departmental fees and service charges; and income from bond issues. About 17-1/2% of the revenue of Milwaukee County consists of money collected for other subdivisions of local government within the county, principally the Metropolitan Sewerage District.

Property taxes are assessed by municipalities in Milwaukee County, and the ratio of assessed to true valuation is not the same in all areas of the county. There has been dissatisfaction with municipal assessment and collection of property taxes, and the Mayor of Milwaukee in April, 1964 proposed that these functions be transferred to the county. He stated that, "A single uniform assessment system for the entire county would provide greater efficiency in assessment procedures and eliminate unnecessary costs resulting from duplication."(5) He felt also that county assessment would bring about more uniform assessment of property.

STAFF AND AUXILIARY SERVICES

Milwaukee County has well developed staff and auxiliary services. The county has a comprehensive civil service system which covers more than 95% of all county employees. The main exclusions from the civil service system are elected officials and their deputies, members of county commissions and boards, and some student trainee positions. The Milwaukee County Civil Service Commission is headed by five citizens appointed by the County Executive and confirmed by the County Board of Supervisors. The Commission appoints a chief examiner who is responsible for the operation of the personnel staff of more than twenty persons. The civil service staff holds an average of 20 examinations monthly, classifies positions, and has an extensive training program.

The Management and Budget Analysis Department is a key staff arm of the County Executive. The budget staff of six analysts reviews in detail the requests of each county agency in July and August of each year. In late August and in September, the County Executive chairs a series of budget conferences in which departmental officials present and defend their requests. In October, the County Executive submits to the Board of Supervisors a five volume county budget containing extensive information on the programs and workload of each county agency. During October, the Finance Committee of the County Board of Supervisors makes a thorough review of the budget, and in November the budget is considered by the entire County Board. During the fiscal year, the budget staff keeps a continuing check on the expenditure trends of county agencies through monthly expenditure statements. Recognizing the importance of keeping a close check on agency spending, the County Executive has monthly expenditure trend data on all county agencies recorded on a large board in back of his desk. An agency head, whose unit appears to be in danger of overspending its appropriation, can expect to be called in for questioning by the County Executive.

Management surveys are a second key function of the Management and Budget Analysis Department. Six management analysts are continually reviewing the organization and procedures of county agencies. One survey resulted in the establishment of a records management program to reduce the number of obsolete records taking valuable file and office space. A second survey resulted in the establishment of a forms control program and central duplicating service in the County Clerk's Office. All forms must be ordered through the County Clerk's Office, and the staff sometimes finds that an existing form can be used rather than a new form prepared. Moreover, similar forms are collected in a file and periodically a new form is prepared replacing as many as forty separate forms. The central duplicating service, established with the assistance of the management analysts, provides a quick, inexpensive photocopy service that makes it unnecessary for many county agencies to purchase this expensive equipment. One employee of the County Clerk's Office provides while-you-wait photocopy service to county agencies. Less than a minute is required to run off several copies of a letter, and less than ten minutes are needed to provide several hundred copies. The central duplicating service has many other office machines that are operated much more efficiently by a central unit than by separate county agencies. It has microfilm cameras, microfilm readers, a complete darkroom, and a huge machine that makes four foot long copies of highway and architectural drawings.

The management analysts have assisted the County Auditor in establishing a modern, centralized data processing center. This data processing center prepares the county payroll and performs many tax and accounting functions. Another management survey resulted in the development of standards to measure clerical workload and to improve paperwork operations. (6)

The Department of Purchasing has also produced savings for the county taxpayers. Six buyers of this unit are able to buy in large quantities at low prices. In 1963, the Department purchased more than ten thousand tons of salt to be used by the county and cooperating cities and villages within the county. Buying in boatload lots, it received a price of $2.41 per ton less than the price of carload lots. The savings, amounting to more than $25,000, were passed on to the county and to the participating cities and villages. Ingenuity by buyers has also resulted in other substantial savings to the county. Pencils on metal chains were formerly used in county election booths. A golfer on the purchasing staff thought of the idea of purchasing much less expensive stubs of pencils used by golfers and attaching them with string to the election booth. A savings of 89% of the anticipated cost of election booth pencils resulted. Purchasing in quantity has made it possible for the county to buy coffee and flour every several months when market prices are down. Officials of the Department of Purchasing make a careful inspection of products received.

In purchasing, as in many staff and auxiliary services, the county has a great advantage over other units of local government in the county. It is large enough to employ a specialized staff and to buy in large quantities. The other units of local government, with the exception of the City of Milwaukee, are not large enough to do this.

All of the major county staff and auxiliary services are under personnel appointed by the County Executive with the exception of the staff of the central duplicating service which is under the supervision of the County Clerk and the revenue collection staff under the County Treasurer. The Corporation Counsel, who provides legal services to the county, the County Auditor, the Management and Budget Director, the Director of Purchasing, and the members of the Civil Service Commission are all appointed by the County Executive. Thus, the County Executive is in a position to coordinate the work of county staff and auxiliary services.

COUNTY SERVICES

Milwaukee County provides its citizens with many more services than smaller, more rural counties such as Latah. As Appendix A shows, Milwaukee County provides 39 general types of services and has exclusive responsibility with respect to many of these functions.

General Government

Milwaukee County provides all the traditional, general governmental services except property tax assessment and collection. The cities and villages of the county assess and collect all property taxes, but there has been dissatisfaction with this arrangement. Although the county does not assess property, it does pay part of the costs of a state supervisor of assessments who assists local assessors in a five county area. The County also collects the property taxes which are in arrears. There is an extensive county program of selling the tax delinquent property.

Independently elected county officials play a less important role in providing general government services in Milwaukee County than in a more traditional county such as Latah. The constitutional office of Coroner, for example, has been stripped of all functions except that of acting as Sheriff in the absence of the Sheriff and serving process papers when the Sheriff is a party to the action. The traditional functions performed by the Coroner in many counties have been transferred in Milwaukee County to a professional Medical Examiner appointed by the County Executive. The office of Coroner will be abolished as of December 31, 1966.

The court system serving Milwaukee County was reorganized in 1962, and it provides the advantages of flexibility and a system of specialized courts. In the Wisconsin court system, the Supreme Court is the state's highest appellate court. Below the Supreme Court is a system of Circuit Courts having both original and appellate jurisdiction. The Criminal Division of the Circuit Court has original jurisdiction over felonies and other serious criminal cases with two judges assigned to criminal cases. The Civil Division of the Circuit Court has original jurisdiction over serious civil suits including those in which the damages claimed exceed $100,000. Two judges of the Civil Division handle divorce and other family court matters. These judges are assisted by the Family Conciliation Department. Through the efforts of its counselors and the Family Court Judges and Commissioners, 45% of all divorce cases filed in 1963 were dismissed before trial by agreement of the parties or for other reasons. This is far above the national average according to a Milwaukee County Family Court report.(7)

Below the Circuit Court system in Wisconsin is the system of County Courts. The Milwaukee County Court has five divisions. The Misdemeanor Division hears all charges of misdemeanors arising within the county which are punishable by less than a year in prison or a fine of less than $1,000. The Civil Division handles small claims and less serious civil suits. The Probate Division handles the probating of wills, the appointment of guardians, and the administration of the estates of county citizens who die intestate. The Children's Division has jurisdiction in proceedings involving delinquent, neglected or dependent children and the termination of parental rights. There is also a Traffic Division with exclusive jurisdiction over traffic cases.

Serving the court system are court reporters, the staff of the law library, clerks of court, and separate probation staffs for adults and children. The Children's Division of the County Court also has a modern detention center which provides temporary care of children whose conduct or home conditions require their removal from the home pending further investigation or court review. This center, with a capacity of 64 children, provides recreation, arts and crafts, group counseling, medical care, and schooling.

Both the circuit and county court systems have the advantages of specialized courts. Flexibility is also provided through action of the County Board of Judges. The Chairman of the County Board of Judges, a Circuit Court judge elected by the other judges, can transfer cases between the circuit and county courts to more evenly distribute workloads.

Agriculture

What does an agricultural extension service do in a county in which there is not one acre of unincorporated land? In Milwaukee

County, the agricultural extension service shifts its program to meet the needs of its more urban population. Its professional staff of seven includes: an Agri-Business Agent, a 4-H Club Agent, a 4-H Club Home Economist, and four other home economists. The Agri-Business Agent provides information to hot-house growers, truck gardeners, garden supply houses and home gardeners. He alerts growers, gardeners and garden supply houses to new insect pests through newspaper articles, radio, and television. The two 4-H club agents work with the more than 200 voluntary 4-H club leaders and more than one thousand 4-H club members in the county. Since 1961, the 4-H club agents have placed special emphasis on enrolling youth in low socio-economic levels and have worked closely with the Urban League in Negro areas. The objective of this work is to give boys and girls a greater appreciation of the appearance of their neighborhoods and respect for other people's property, as well as to provide an enriching experience in projects such as woodworking, home grounds improvement, gardening, conservation, foods and clothing.

Two of the four home economists provide home economics education similar to that provided in many other counties. One is responsible for newspaper articles and television and radio programs on home economics. The second works with the leaders of women's home demonstration clubs. The other two home economists provide specialized home management services for very low income families. These home economists established a pilot training program for fifty public assistance recipients to train them as home management aids. Upon completion of a two months' training program, the home management aides are assigned by the Department of Public Welfare to recipient homes where home management help is needed. Since the home management aides are welfare recipients, they are perhaps better able to understand the problems of a welfare family and to get their suggestions accepted. They receive no pay for this service but do receive a $12 a month increase in their allowances to pay for transportation and other costs. They also receive the satisfaction of helping other recipients. In 1963, 48 homemaker aides put in 5,465 hours in welfare homes helping recipients improve their meal planning, shopping, mending, child care, laundry, and nutrition.

Education and Libraries

There are 17 school districts in Milwaukee County including the city of Milwaukee. An elected County Superintendent of Schools and his staff provided teacher recruitment, supervision of instruction, counseling, and consultant services until this office was abolished on July 1, 1965. Many of these services are now provided by a State controlled Cooperative Educational Service Agency.

The cities and villages maintain their own library systems, and the city of Milwaukee has a large museum. The county government operates a law library but no general libraries. The county has a historical museum in a building donated by one of the Milwaukee banks.

Health and Welfare

Half the county budget is spent on health and welfare services. The county government provides general hospital care, tuberculosis hospital care, health clinics for indigents, air pollution control, mental hospitals, child guidance clinics, homes for the aged and public welfare. Municipal health departments are responsible for environmental sanitation, maternal and child health, and communicable disease control.

The county health and welfare program is under the supervision of a five member Board of Public Welfare appointed by the County Executive and confirmed by the County Board. One member is appointed from the County Board of Supervisors. The members serve for four year terms at a salary of $1,500 a year. The Board of Public Welfare appoints a Director of Institutions and Departments who employs other health and welfare officials according to civil service rules.

The hub of the county health and welfare services is a large tract of land located near the western border of the county in Wauwatosa. Located on this land across a beautifully landscaped pond and lagoon is the Milwaukee County General Hospital. Unit I of this hospital, a modern eight story building with a capacity of more than 600 patients, provides hospital care for indigent persons and emergency cases. Accident or other emergency cases who can afford to pay for their care are transferred to other hospitals after initial treatment. The hospital has very modern facilities and is accredited for intern training, postgraduate instruction in medicine and surgery, and the training of dentists and dietitians. Attached to the hospital is one of the largest nursing schools in the state. There are 28 outpatient clinics located in the hospital.

Unit II of the Milwaukee County General Hospital, located close to Unit I, is a chronic illness and convalescent hospital caring for patients who require continuing care of a less demanding and expensive type than that given in Unit I. Elderly patients having a slow convalescence are transferred from Unit I to Unit II as soon as practical after their operation or treatment. The county also operates a small emergency hospital in the city of Milwaukee which gives first aid treatment and emergency operations particularly in accident cases.

The county operates a large tuberculosis sanitarium, Muirdale, which has a capacity of more than 550 patients. Successful treatment of tuberculosis has resulted in a reduction in the number of tuberculosis patients treated and has left idle capacity at Muirdale. Two of the floors at Muirdale and a ward in Unit I of the General Hospital are used for tuberculosis patients. The other two floors of Muirdale are used for patients with chronic illnesses.

The Milwaukee County Mental Health Center consists of two groups of buildings on the Wauwatosa grounds. The North Division building group, providing for about 900 patients, has a diagnostic and treatment center, psychiatric clinic, child guidance clinic, mental hospital wards and rooms for serious mental cases. There are about 11,000 calls for treatment and diagnosis in the Psychiatry Clinic alone. The South Division building group furnishes care and treatment primarily for the mentally ill patient who must stay longer in the institution. It has an average daily population of almost 2,800 patients.

Milwaukee County operates an infirmary, with an average daily population of about 600, for aged and infirm residents who are unable to care for themselves. The county has a Children's Home for about 230 dependent and neglected children. On an average day, there will be more than 5,500 persons occupying beds in county institutions.

Public assistance is another important function of the Board of Public Welfare. County government provides grants to old age assistance, aid to the blind, disability assistance, aid to families with dependent children, and general assistance recipients. In addition, the county provides veterans' aid and foster home and institutional care for children. Hospitalization and drugs for indigent patients are provided through the county general hospital. Municipalities in the county are not responsible for public assistance.

Among the noteworthy features of county public welfare are the work relief program, the use of hired housekeepers, the home management training program, and the cooperative training program with the Milwaukee Vocational Service and the Wisconsin State Employment Service. Hired housekeepers are used when one or both parents are absent from the home. The housekeepers provide cooking, cleaning and housekeeping services until the woman in the family is again able to handle these duties.

Air pollution control and inspection, another important county function, is under a director appointed by the County Executive. This agency tests the air in some seventy locations around the county to determine the extent of pollution. Air and dust samples are brought into a modern laboratory and analyzed for pollutants and irritants. Inspectors check chimneys, smokestacks, fuel burning equipment and open fires to determine whether they are unduly

polluting the air. A mobile trailer laboratory is taken to the industrial site, and the company is required to comply with the
pollution control ordinance if too much smoke or dust is being
emitted from its chimneys. The active air pollution control program of the county, one of the best in the nation, is one reason that
the heavily industrial county of Milwaukee does not have a serious
smoke, dust, and soot problem.

Parks and Recreation

The comprehensive parks program of Milwaukee County is under
the direction of a seven member, unsalaried Park Commission appointed by the County Executive and confirmed by the County Board.
The Park Commission owns more than 13,000 acres of land in the
county of which about one-fourth is in the city of Milwaukee. There
are more than 80 separate parks. Some, like Back Bay Park, are
small parks offering picnicking, shuffleboard, and a tot lot playground; others, like 30 acre Baran Park, provide a number of
baseball, football, and soccer fields. Milwaukee County also has
several large regional parks, like Brown Deer Park, which provides a one-fourth mile hard surfaced bicycle track, boating, a
bridle path, a cross country running course, a duck sanctuary and
nature study area, model boating, horseshoe courts, and an 18 hole
golf course as well as a number of picnic tables, play areas, football and baseball fields. In the winter, the park is used for skiing,
skating, tobogganing and coasting. There are other county parks
which provide archery, badminton, overnight camping, square
dancing, curling, tennis, fishing, model plane flying, swimming,
and social center buildings. There are small fees for the use of
park facilities which partially defray the cost of the park program.
Admission to the county's ten pools, for example, is free until one
in the afternoon and there is a 10¢ charge for children under 16 and
a 25¢ charge for adults during the afternoon hours. The fees at the
county's six golf courses range from 25¢ for juniors at one 9 hole
golf course to $1.50 for adults at the 18 hole courses.

Besides a large number of park facilities, Milwaukee County
operates a zoo, a conservatory, a botanical gardens, a boat marina,
a musical amphitheater, and a huge stadium. The recently completed zoo covers 174 acres, and many of the animals are housed
in natural settings outdoors which are separated from spectators
by deep moats. The zoo grounds are beautifully landscaped, and a
zoo train ride around the grounds is popular. The conservatory
consists of three large domes 75 feet high which display plants
grown in tropical regions, desert plants and flower shows. The
musical amphitheater, the Emil Blatz Temple of Music, seats
15,000 people and is used for outdoor concerts and musicals in the
summer. The Milwaukee County stadium, where professional football and baseball is played, has a seating capacity of 47,000.

A few of the other municipalities have small parks, but the people in these communities depend mainly upon the county park system. The municipalities of the county, particularly Milwaukee, do provide comprehensive summer and year-round recreation programs using school playgrounds, their own parks and social centers, and the county's parks and social centers. Organized recreation programs are mainly a municipal rather than a county function. However, the County Park Commission does have Drop-In Centers with game rooms for senior citizens at some of its parks and sponsors a six week summer day camp program for retarded children in cooperation with the United Association of Mentally Retarded Children.

Physical Planning and Development

Comprehensive planning is not a function of Milwaukee County government, but the county is involved in planning for its expressways, parks, and other public facilities. Planning, zoning, subdivision regulations, urban renewal, and industrial development are functions of the city of Milwaukee and other municipalities. Some municipalities only provide part of these services. Furthermore, there is no regional planning for the entire Milwaukee metropolitan area other than the small, advisory Southeastern Wisconsin Regional Planning Commission.

Public Safety

Police and fire protection are both county and municipal functions in Milwaukee County. Milwaukee County has 46 firefighters and 15 guards at county institutions and 44 firefighters and 8 guards at the county airport. The County Executive plans to create a Department of Safety to administer these police and fire protection services. The county also has an elected Sheriff who provides police protection and ambulance services on county freeways, makes more than 100,000 legal process services each year, and maintains the county jail with an average prison population of about 350. The Sheriff is legally responsible for maintaining law and order within the county, but by custom he has limited his law enforcement activities to municipalities which do not have adequate police forces. With the expansion of municipal police protection to cover the entire county area, this function of the constitutionally elected Sheriff is diminishing in importance and will cease in the future.

Jail maintenance and civil defense are mainly county functions. Besides the County Jail, the county maintains a House of Correction on a 750 acre farm. The House of Correction is under the supervision of a Superintendent appointed by the County Executive and receives persons violating municipal ordinances, county ordinances, and state laws. The federal government contracts with the county to keep many of its prisoners in this institution. The House of Correction has a rehabilitative program for prisoners and also keeps the prisoners busy on the 750 acre farm. This farm produces nearly a million pounds of fruits and vegetables, more than a million pounds of dairy products, and a hundred thousand pounds of meat for county health, welfare, and correctional institutions. The House of Correction also has a special program for alcoholics.

The Civil Defense Department is responsible for training county employees and volunteers for civil defense work in case of an emergency. Personnel of municipal fire departments have been given training in radiological fallout, doctors and nurses have been given special training at the emergency hospital operated by the county, and many other types of personnel have been trained. In 1965, Wisconsin law was changed to make the County Executive head of civil defense in Milwaukee County.

Public Works and Transportation

The Department of Public Works is responsible for constructing a fifty mile expressway system in the county that will cost over $450 million. The Department is also responsible for maintaining about eight miles of county trunk roads and an additional 130 miles of state and federal highways including expressways. The county government was granted the responsibility for building an expressway system because no other unit of local government was large enough to plan and construct such a system for the entire area. The expressways are six-lane, limited access highways which provide quick access to the downtown areas of Milwaukee. Twenty-four miles of expressways are complete and sixteen additional miles will be completed by 1969.

Municipalities in Milwaukee County construct, maintain and provide traffic engineering on city streets. In addition, they are responsible for water, refuse collection, and refuse disposal. The city of Milwaukee operates extensive port facilities. Sewage disposal is provided by the city of Milwaukee for Milwaukee and South Milwaukee, and a Metropolitan Sewerage District is responsible for the remainder of the county. The county government maintains a land fill site but otherwise does not perform any of these municipal functions.

The Airport Department of Milwaukee County government operates two airports. General Mitchell Field is the modern commercial airline terminal serving the Milwaukee area. It is used by five airlines and is the home of units of the Wisconsin Air National Guard and U. S. Air Force Reserve. The county also operates the smaller Timmerman Airport used primarily by business and privately owned airplanes.

SUMMARY

Milwaukee County is the center of a metropolitan area of more than one million persons. Since the entire county is incorporated, the county government is not faced with the problem of large unincorporated areas which require municipal services. County government has undertaken many area-wide, urban functions which can be more economically and effectively administered at the county level than by 19 separate municipalities. These area-wide functions include: parks, expressways, welfare, air pollution control, and the maintenance of institutional care programs in the fields of mental health, tuberculosis, correction, and juvenile detention. The county has been given these responsibilities because it is the only unit of government in the area large enough to plan and construct a system for the entire area. It is more equitable, also, for residents of the entire county to pay for services such as parks, air pollution, and expressways that are used by nearly all county residents. Moreover, county government can effect economies in data processing, clerical, purchasing, and other operations that the smaller cities and villages cannot. Recognizing the greater economies of large scale county operation and the equity of a more uniform assessment policy, the Mayor of the city of Milwaukee proposed that the county, not the municipalities, be made responsible for property tax assessment and collection. The trend in Milwaukee County is for county government to be given responsibilities for the administration of more and more area-wide functions.

Effective county administration of area-wide functions depends upon strong executive leadership in county government. The county executive form of government has provided this leadership. The County Executive is elected by the voters of the county for a term of four years. He has strengthened the executive branch of government through his appointment powers and use of a professional budget and management staff. One indication of the popularity of the County Executive and the county executive form of government was the fact that the present County Executive was elected to a second four year term in 1964 without opposition.

REFERENCES

1. From 1838 to 1842 the County was governed by a Board of County Commissioners.

2. U. S. Bureau of the Census. Census of Governments: 1962, Vol. I, Governmental Organization (Washington: U. S. Government Printing Office, 1963), p. 242. Data on the nature of Milwaukee County's special districts was provided by letter from the Bureau of the Census.

3. In 1968, the number of members of the County Board of Supervisors will increase to 25 and the supervisors' salaries will rise to $10,000.

4. Milwaukee County. Government Report (Milwaukee County, Wisconsin, 1963), p. 29.

5. The Milwaukee Journal, April 21, 1964, p. 18.

6. The County Executive's annual message to the Milwaukee County Board of Supervisors in 1962 expressed the hope that the clerical work improvements program would save the county $200,000 to $300,000.

7. The Family Court of Milwaukee County, 1963 Annual Report.

4 / THE COUNTY OF THE FUTURE

"*Great variations will occur, of course, from state to state, and even within a state, but it seems likely that increasingly the center of responsibility for performing a great range of local government activities will gradually be shifted from cities to counties.... Two or three or four counties for a more manageable universe of general governing agencies than do twenty or thirty or fifty cities which ordinarily now exist within these sprawling urban giants.*"

York Willbern,

The Withering Away of the City

(Birmingham: University of Alabama Press, 1964), p. 120.

Chapter 12

The Future
Of American
County Government

COUNTY GOVERNMENT in 1966 stands at the crossroads. Before describing the alternative roads ahead, it is desirable to summarize the past history of county government and some of the problems that counties presently face. It is important also to study the county home rule movement. After reviewing past history and current trends, a look into the future will be attempted.

PAST TRENDS IN COUNTY GOVERNMENT

The county can trace its origins back one thousand years. During its entire history, its organization and functions have been evolving, sometimes very slowly, sometimes more rapidly, to meet the needs of changing generations. County government was brought to America by English colonists in the 1600's. By the time of the American Revolution, the main forms of local government had evolved. In New England, the county was not as prominent as the town. New York had both counties and towns with the county governing body being composed of elected town supervisors. In Pennsylvania, the county governing body consisted of a board of three county commissioners elected at large in the county. County government was strongest south of the Mason-Dixon line where there were no towns.

County government spread westward after the United States became a nation, and by the Civil War, counties had been established on the West Coast. During this period of rapid expansion, county government was greatly influenced by Jacksonian concepts of democracy. County governing bodies were weakened and many new elective offices created. In an era in which little specialized knowledge was essential to county office and county officials were known by most county citizens, this form of government was not out of place.

For half a century after the Civil War, there were extensive changes in American society and few changes in the structure and powers of county government. The tremendous growth of American cities brought increased demands for urban services. Political machines developed and used the traditional form of county government with its many elective officials as a means of diffusing responsibility and controlling counties. Counties, particularly metropolitan counties, did not adapt quickly enough to meet the needs of the time. By World War I, county government was being characterized as an archaic, inefficient "dark continent."(1)

Since World War I, counties have increasingly expanded their functions to meet the needs of their citizens. Parks, recreation, expressways, airports, water supply, sewage disposal, planning, zoning, and urban renewal are among the many county functions initiated, or greatly expanded, since 1918. With the decline in importance of townships, counties have assumed former township functions in Michigan, Indiana, and other states. As their functions have expanded, counties have hired more professional employees and have used centralized purchasing, automatic data processing, and modern management techniques more extensively. The structure of county government has changed more slowly. Only a few counties used the county manager, county executive, or county administrative officer form of government prior to World War II.

Since World War II, there has been increasing concern with the problems of metropolitan governments. The inability of many cities to expand through annexation to encompass the entire urbanized areas that surrounded them led to the creation of a jungle of overlapping special districts. The flight of higher income residents and newer factories to suburban areas has caused serious losses in tax base, and has made it financially difficult and increasingly inequitable for the central city to provide airport, park and other services to the entire metropolitan area. Many authorities on metropolitan government are taking an increased interest in the county as a key to resolving metropolitan problems.

In the last two decades, there has been an extensive change in the organization and functions of a number of metropolitan counties and less change in rural counties. Seven of the ten most populous counties have one of the executive or administrator forms of county government rather than the traditional plural executive form. A

number of metropolitan counties are providing urban services such
as water and sewage disposal to unincorporated areas, and parks,
expressways, airports and other facilities to the entire population
of the county. Some of the most serious problems that beset county
government are in metropolitan areas, and some of the greatest
opportunities for county government are in these areas.

METROPOLITAN PROBLEMS -- A CHALLENGE AND OPPORTUNITY FOR COUNTIES

Serious metropolitan problems include: (1) the lack of needed
services particularly in unincorporated areas, (2) the financial
squeeze of central cities which have lost tax base to the suburbs,
(3) the uneven distribution of tax resources between suburbs, (4)
the subsidization of suburban dwellers by the central city, (5) the
duplication of costly facilities such as sewage treatment plants, (6)
the inability of any one unit of government to provide solutions to
key transportation, air pollution, and other problems which require
area-wide solutions, (7) the cost and confusion of many layers of
local government and a multiplicity of special districts, (8) the
inability of citizens to place responsiblity for failures in finding
solutions to metropolitan problems. These problems, which are
described in detail by Victor Jones, Charles Adrian, and others, are
problems of all local governmental units within metropolitan areas,
including counties.(2)

Sixteen solutions to metropolitan problems have been suggested
by authorities in the field and listed by Roscoe Martin in Metropolis
in Transition.(3) Many of these solutions involve an important role
for counties, particularly where the entire metropolitan area is
encompassed within a single county as it is in half of all metropolitan
areas. In these counties, county government is usually the only unit
of local government having jurisdiction throughout the entire metropolitan area. A description of the sixteen solutions and comments
on them follows.(4)

1. Informal cooperation. Sharing of police teletype information
    and mutual aid in firefighting are examples of informal co-
    operation that takes place between cities, counties, and other
    units of local government. The effectiveness of this solution
    depends upon the willingness of all units of government to
    cooperate.

2. The service contract. Many cities and counties buy and sell
    water, library, and other services on contract. Los Angeles
    County has made very extensive use of service contracts to
    provide a full package of municipal services to a number of
    cities within the county.

3. Parallel action. Many counties and cities have joined to establish joint city-county agencies in fields where both formerly had similar or parallel agencies. Joint agencies are numerous particularly in the fields of health, mental health, and library service and provide an effective means of equitably distributing costs to incorporated and unincorporated areas within a county.

4. The conference approach. The voluntary regional conference is a device for bringing together the representatives of county and other local governments to exchange information and discuss common problems. Agreements reached are voluntary and not binding. The first of the major regional conferences, the Supervisors' Inter-County Committee of the Detroit area, was established by county officials. County officials are active in other regional conferences.

5. The compact. A compact has been described as a formal agreement under which two or more governments undertake certain mutual obligations. It may exist between local governments of the same or different states. Counties have been active in compacts such as the compact between Campbell and Kenton Counties in Kentucky to form the Northern Kentucky Area Planning Commission.

6. Transfer of functions. Extensive transfers of functions have occurred from cities, villages, and townships to counties. Roscoe Martin states that this "is one of the principal means by which a government limited in geographical scope, powers or resources seeks to deal with expanding needs, or with demands for more service."(5) Transfers of functions from cities to counties have sometimes been at the request of city officials to ease a city's financial burden or to produce more equity in administration or the distribution of costs.(6) In Milwaukee County, for example, the airport, expressway, and park systems have been transferred from the central city to county government.(7) Function by function, transfers to county government are one of the most promising solutions to metropolitan problems.

7. Extra-territorial jurisdiction. Extra-territorial powers are sometimes granted cities to control planning, pollution, and other functions beyond their borders. Residents in the areas controlled outside the city are deprived of the right to vote against city officials imposing the regulations. The use of extra-territorial powers by cities to establish airports, parks and other facilities outside city boundaries has been beneficial but often has resulted in suburban dwellers making extensive use of these facilities without paying for them.

8. Incorporation. Incorporation of new suburban cities makes possible added services but further increases the multiplicity of local governments within an area. Where a newly incorporated city contracts with the county to provide services, it may avoid duplicating facilities with other cities in the area. The existence of many small suburban satellite cities often creates rather than resolves metropolitan problems.

9. Annexation. Annexation provides a means for cities to expand their boundaries to include densely populated adjacent areas that require municipal services. However, many large cities are surrounded or nearly surrounded by incorporated suburban municipalities which they are not able to annex. Other cities, with extensive unincorporated areas on their borders, have failed to expand because suburbanites have voted against annexation. Forcing suburban dwellers into a city against their wishes can be criticized as undemocratic. Roscoe Martin concludes that "Annexation, therefore, whatever its virtues and its weaknesses, has lost much of its effectiveness as a means of areal adaptation to changing local needs."(8)

10. City-county separation. Baltimore, Denver, St. Louis and San Francisco were separated from their respective counties before 1902 and perform both city and county functions. Since that time the only city-county separations have been in Virginia. Although it may have been possible to separate urban and rural areas in past decades and establish an appropriate unit for each, this is no longer practical. The urban area soon expands beyond the borders of the city creating new metropolitan problems in the surrounding areas. Roscoe Martin states that "city-county separation was essentially a product of a bygone rural age."(9)

11. Geographic consolidation. Consolidating county government with one or more cities in the county is another way of eliminating one layer of local government and establishing a strong government with powers to resolve metropolitan problems within a county-wide area. This provides a particularly good solution in metropolitan areas encompassed within a single county. In multi-county metropolitan areas, it may be possible to use this method to consolidate two or more counties. City-county consolidation was used to create Boston, Philadelphia, New Orleans and New York during the 1800's and has been used since World War II to consolidate Baton Rouge with East Baton Rouge Parish and Nashville with Davidson County.(10)

12. Functional consolidation. Consolidation of functions of one or more counties and/or cities into a single agency is a means of achieving some of the benefits of geographic consolidation

for a single governmental function. The transfer of city functions to county departments, the creation of joint city-county agencies, and the establishment of multi-county agencies are among the means that have been used to achieve functional consolidation.

13. Special districts. Small, single purpose special districts have been used to provide services to unincorporated areas. These districts provide, for the most part, only one service of government and each requires its own government and overhead expense.(11) Special districts add to the number of layers of local government in an area and further splinter governmental authority.(12)

14. Authorities. Authorities, which have the power to borrow funds beyond the debt limits of cities and counties, have been used increasingly for construction of public facilities. Authorities have been extensively criticized by Robert Smith and others as government by bond resolution with little or no control by local voters.(13)

15. Metropolitan government. Metropolitan government in its broadest sense may result from geographic consolidation of city and county or extensive transfers of functions to county government which elevate the county to a position of dominance in the metropolitan area. The three examples of metropolitan government in the United States, cited by Roscoe Martin, are of these two types.(14) A third approach is the creation of a federated metropolitan government composed of local government officials. This plan has been used successfully in Toronto, Canada and other foreign cities but has never been fully utilized in the United States. The Municipality of Metropolitan Seattle has a federated metropolitan form of government involving representatives of King County and municipalities within the county, but it presently provides only sewage disposal functions. When it undertakes other functions, it will become more fully a metropolitan government.(15)

16. Regional agencies. Regional agencies, such as the Delaware River Basin Commission, are devices for intergovernmental cooperation where governmental problems span state lines and several metropolitan areas. They have been utilized to study water supply needs, control air and water pollution, and develop transportation plans, but they have not been widely used.

Although county government may actively participate in resolving metropolitan problems in many of these sixteen proposed solutions, the greatest challenge to county government is in geographic city-county consolidation and in the transfer of functions to counties.

Chapter 10 illustrates the apparent success of the Nashville-Davidson County city-county consolidation. Chapter 9 on Montgomery County and chapter 11 on Milwaukee County describe counties which are successfully providing urban services. To fully utilize its potential for leadership in metropolitan areas, county government is dependent upon enabling legislation and constitutional provisions.

NON-METROPOLITAN COUNTIES -- PROBLEMS OF AREA, ORGANIZATION AND POWERS

Metropolitan counties are not the only ones facing a challenge in the decades ahead. Counties without a city of 50,000 or more, classified as non-metropolitan, will be facing several serious problems. A number of the smaller counties in the nation are losing population and tax base. It is becoming increasingly difficult to provide normal county services in many of these counties without exceeding state imposed county tax limits. A few counties may face bankruptcy as Petroleum County, Montana did during World War II. Unable to finance a full slate of county elective officials in the face of declining property tax revenues, Petroleum County adopted the county manager plan and greatly reduced payrolls and costs.

Two other possible solutions to declining county revenues are geographic and functional county consolidation. There have been few cases of geographic consolidation of counties since World War I. Rural James County in Tennessee consolidated with urban Hamilton County in 1919, and two rural counties near Atlanta consolidated with Fulton County, Georgia in 1932.(16) Clyde Snider reports that there have been no other consolidations of organized county governments since World War I.(17) Geographic consolidation of counties has been deterred not only by restrictive requirements in state constitutions but also by political opposition to consolidation. County officials and many citizens in the county which will lose its identity usually oppose consolidation.(18) County officers fear loss of their jobs. Store owners in the municipality which will lose its status as county seat fear loss of business. Ordinary citizens often oppose county consolidation from a sense of county pride. Where a two-third vote is required in both counties considering consolidation, as in Idaho, it is politically almost impossible to secure geographic consolidation.

Functional consolidation is politically more practical and is more widespread. Counties may reduce costs by establishing joint health, welfare, library, highway and other agencies with other counties. Smaller counties might consider contracting with larger counties to provide a variety of county services.

Counties on the fringes of metropolitan areas and counties with expanding populations face differing types of problems. Land values, assessments, and revenues are rising in these counties but so are land-use, health, highway and other problems. Many of these counties are given inadequate planning and zoning powers by state constitutions and laws. The cost of building approaches to new interstate highways may take an important part of county road-building funds in some counties. The number of overlapping special districts is increasing on the fringe of metropolitan areas and expanding small cities. An arsenal of optional planning, zoning, and other powers is needed by these counties.

Non-metropolitan counties face problems common to almost all counties—the lack of adequate authority to frame their own powers, organization and internal policies. These problems will be discussed more fully in the next two sections of this chapter.

LEGAL AND FISCAL ROADBLOCKS

County government is not free to shape its organization and functions to meet the needs of county citizens. Legal and fiscal roadblocks include:

1. Constitutional provisions which make it extremely difficult for counties to consolidate or change their boundaries. The Idaho Constitution, for example, requires a two-thirds vote in each county consolidated.

2. Lack of statutory or constitutional authority for city-county consolidation. It is significant that an amendment to the Tennessee Constitution was necessary to enable Nashville and Davidson County to consolidate.

3. Constitutional provisions which limit counties to a single form of government.

4. Constitutional or statutory limits on property tax rates.

5. Limitations on county use of non-property taxes such as sales and selective sales taxes.

6. Unnecessarily low county debt limitations.

7. Constitutional and statutory limitations on the functions and powers of counties. To secure additional powers, counties normally must get a change in state law.

Two outmoded legal concepts underlie many of the roadblocks to county government. One is the concept that all counties should be uniform throughout the state. The Wisconsin Constitution states, for example, that: "The legislature shall establish but one system of town and county government, which shall be as nearly uniform as practicable."(19) The Idaho Constitution states: "The legislature shall establish, subject to the provisions of this article, a system of county government which shall be uniform throughout the state."(20) These and similar constitutional provisions imply that there is some advantage for all counties to have the same organization, functions, and fiscal structure. But why should all counties be required to conform to the same mold? A Wisconsin report states:

"The Constitution requires a uniform system of county government in Wisconsin. The idea of uniformity implies that the units in the uniform system be alike, or at least very largely alike, yet it is a familiar fact that the counties are not alike and have not been alike for a long time, whether they have ever been."(21)

The case studies in chapters six through ten provide insight into the absurdity of attempting to require uniform county government. Why should a county of less than a thousand people and a population density of less than one-half person per square mile be required to have the same form of government, tax structure and functions as a county of a million people such as Milwaukee County, Wisconsin? The ranchers on the rolling treeless prairies of Petroleum County, Montana have differing needs for county services than the corporation executives, brewers, and construction workers of Milwaukee County. Even among counties of relatively the same population such as Nashville-Davidson County, Tennessee and Montgomery County, Maryland there are significant differences in needs. Urban renewal is much more vital to the blighted areas near the center of Nashville than to the suburban subdivisions of Montgomery County. The five case study counties are located in different states, but if they were located in the same state and subject to strict uniformity requirements of the state constitution, Petroleum, Montgomery, Davidson, and Milwaukee Counties could not meet as adequately the varied needs of their citizens. All four of these counties received the benefit of constitutional amendments which gave them added flexibility in government.

A second outmoded legal viewpoint is the concept of the county as a quasi-municipal corporation which serves merely as an arm of state government. This concept was most strongly expressed by the Ohio Supreme Court in 1857 when it stated that: "counties are created by the sovereign power of the state, of its own sovereign will" and stated that: "with scarcely an exception, all the powers and functions of county organization have a direct and exclusive reference to the general policy of the state, and are, in fact, but a branch of the general administration of that policy."(22) The concept of the county as an arm of the state was more true in the mid-1800's than today, but the legal fiction lingers on. In 1938, an Alabama Court termed the county: "an arm of the state, through which the state operates for convenience in the performance of its governmental function."(23) This court also stated that: "while a county has corporate characteristics, it is not, strictly speaking, a municipal corporation as is a city or town."

Contrary to legal opinion, many counties were established at the instigation of local inhabitants.(24) Moreover, counties have been granted an increasing number of powers to undertake planning, zoning, subdivision regulations, parks, airports, water supply, sewage disposal and many other functions which were formerly considered municipal functions. As Clyde Snider has pointed out, counties and townships have increasingly been authorized to perform functions similar to cities and "their differentiation from genuine municipal corporations has become progressively less distinct."(25)

COUNTY HOME RULE

County home rule is a reform movement designed to free counties from legal restrictions imposed by state legislatures. From the War of 1812 to the Civil War, local government officials in many areas became involved in fraudulent speculative schemes and burdensome local improvements.(26) State governments were called upon to prevent abuses in local government and passed increasingly restrictive limitations on the powers of local officials. The Dillion Rule, a rule of municipal law written in 1872, made clear that plenary power resided with the state government and that local governments possessed only powers expressly granted them, necessarily implied, or essential to the local government.(27) By the 1870's, the reaction to the restrictive effects of state legislative action crystallized in the home rule movement.

The home rule movement had its greatest success in the municipal field. Missouri incorporated home rule provisions in its constitution in 1875, and by 1930 fifteen state constitutions had home rule provisions pertaining to municipalities.(28) The first constitutional home rule provisions for counties were adopted by California in 1911 and Maryland in 1915.(29)

The California home rule constitutional amendment permits any county to create a home rule charter commission after an election called by a 3/5 vote of the Board of Supervisors or a petition signed by voters equal to 15% or more of those who voted in the county for governor in the last election.(30) The charter commission is composed of fifteen members elected by the voters of the county. After the charter is drafted, it is submitted to the voters and must be approved by a majority vote. The charter must then be approved by the State Legislature, but the Legislature has always given its approval to county charters approved by the voters. By 1961, ten California counties had approved home rule charters including Los Angeles (1913), Alameda (1927), Sacramento (1933), San Diego (1933), and Santa Clara (1951).(31) The provisions of county charters in California must not conflict with general state law with respect to activities that counties perform as administrative subdivisions of the state.(32) Although the exact extent of county powers has not been determined by the courts, they are apparently not as inclusive as the powers granted charter cities in California.

The Maryland home rule constitutional provision permits counties to create a charter commission by a petition signed by 20% of the county's registered voters followed by an election. After the charter is prepared, it must be ratified by a majority vote in the county. Montgomery County, Maryland adopted a home rule charter in 1948; Baltimore County followed in 1956; Wicomico and Anne Arundel Counties adopted charters in 1964. In 1965, the Maryland State General Assembly initiated a constitutional amendment for an alternative form of home rule called "code home rule."(33) Under this proposed constitutional amendment, a county may become a code county by a favorable vote of at least two-thirds of the members of the county governing board and a majority vote within the county. Code counties would be grouped in four classes and be given broad powers to enact local laws.

Eleven other states have county home rule provisions in their constitutions.(34) Ohio and Texas adopted county home rule amendments in 1933, but as yet no county has been successful in adopting a home rule charter. In the case of Ohio, the requirement that the charter must obtain majorities both inside and outside the central city of the county blocked the adoption of a charter in Cuyahoga County (Cleveland). Missouri adopted a home rule amendment pertaining to counties of more than 85,000 people in 1945, and St. Louis County obtained a home rule charter in 1951. The Louisiana Constitution authorized home rule charters for East Baton Rouge Parish in 1946 and Jefferson Parish in 1956, and both counties now have home rule charters. States which have more recently adopted county home rule constitutional amendments are: Washington (1948), Florida (for Dade County only, 1956), Minnesota, New York and Oregon (1958), Alaska (for boroughs, 1959), and Hawaii (1959). At least eleven counties in these states have home rule charters. Dade County, Florida adopted a home rule charter in 1957, and there were eight New York counties with home rule charters by the end of 1965.(35) In Oregon, twelve counties appointed county charter committees; nine counties prepared home rule charters; and two counties (Hood River and Washington) had home rule charters in 1965.

The increasing number of counties which have adopted home rule charters since 1960 has been encouraging to advocates of county home rule. While only about 1% of the nation's counties have home rule charters, these counties include seven having a 1960 population of 800,000 or more.(36) The trend appears favorable to much greater extension of county home rule in the next decade.

County charters have allowed counties considerable flexibility in organization, and there are county managers, county executives, and county administrative officers in charter counties. Most of the county charters provide merit systems, many establish budget procedures, and some have reduced the number of independently elected officials. County charters have been credited by Clyde Snider with giving counties a greater range of discretion to shorten the ballot, institute merit systems, establish scientific budgeting systems, and effect substantial improvements in governmental machinery.(37)

Optional county charters provide some of the same benefits of a full home rule charter. These charters provide principally for discretion by counties in choosing their form of organization. A 1928 Virginia constitutional amendment permits the Virginia General Assembly to enact optional forms of county government, and it has authorized, by law, the appointed county manager and county executive forms.(38) A 1935 New York constitutional amendment gives counties discretion in framing optional charters. Counties may adopt a county president, county manager, county director or county administrator form of county government as well as the traditional form. Under these provisions, Monroe County (Rochester) has adopted a county manager form of government, and six New York counties have adopted an elected county executive (or president) form.(39) North Carolina, North Dakota, and Montana also have made use of state constitutional provisions for optional forms of county government.

Underlying the county home rule and optional charter movements is the philosophy of local self-determination. This philosophy is expressed as follows by the American County Platform adopted in 1965 by the National Association of Counties:

"We in county government believe that Home Rule, or the right of local self determination, is a cornerstone of our American Democracy. Our state legislatures have not always recognized this and have been notoriously slow to delegate adequate authority to local officials to solve purely local problems. Counties have been hamstrung by antiquated state statutes and constitutional provisions that make it extremely difficult for elected county officials to act effectively, with the result that counties have often been forced to abandon functions to state and national government that could be discharged more efficiently and economically at the county level. . ."(40)

The National Association of Counties went on to recommend the following principles as the basis for an effective home rule movement.(41)

1. State constitutions should grant by popular referendum action to selected units of local government all functional and financing powers not expressly reserved, pre-empted, or restricted by the legislature.

2. Statewide standards and state supervision are justified where counties act primarily as agents of the state and do so with substantial state financing. Counties should be free to devise their own operating policies in all governmental programs not financed wholly or substantially by federal or state funds subject to a requirement that such policies be definitely set forth in writing.

3. Counties should be free to determine the scope and extent of the governmental service each will render, subject to the recognized need for some uniformity in standards for national and statewide services.

4. The degree of uniformity required of counties should be reexamined so that uniformity will not be for uniformity's sake but in each case will serve a specific beneficial purpose.

5. Counties should be free to devise their own internal organization.

6. Counties should be more free to devise their own operating policies such as in purchasing, capital outlay, personnel and should be free to establish rates of compensation and procedures for employment for all employees who are not responsible for programs which the county is undertaking as an agent of the State.

7. General control of county government should be placed wholly in the county legislative body.

The arguments for local self determination of county organization and internal operating policies are particularly convincing. Why should a state constitution, adopted 50 to 100 years ago, dictate the form of government which counties in some states can have? Why should not the citizens of a county be free to determine their own form of county government through popular vote as long as it meets general standards for democratic government? Citizens in many counties may wish to retain the familiar traditional form of county government with many independently elected officials. Citizens of other counties may wish to adopt a county manager, county executive, or county administrative officer plan. Why should county citizens be barred from voting for any of these plans of county organization? Similarly, why not permit all counties to frame their own purchasing, accounting, and other internal procedures as long as they meet general state standards? The right of local self determination is one of the cornerstones of democracy, yet it is being denied by obsolete provisions of state constitutions and law.

FUTURE TRENDS

Future trends in the rapidly changing field of American local government cannot be predicted with certainty or even a high degree of confidence. New inventions, space exploration, and the future course of race relations will affect American life and local government in ways that are difficult to foresee. More easily predictable is the continuation of current population and governmental trends into the future.

Population Trends

Barring the cataclysmic effect of nuclear war, the continued population increase in the United States seems assured in the next few decades. If present trends continue, an increasing proportion of Americans will live in the urban and suburban areas of metropolitan counties rather than in rural counties. This will cause, not only a further shift of power from rural to metropolitan counties, but also further increases in county expenditures for urban services. There will undoubtedly be many more counties engaged in planning, zoning, subdivision regulation, urban renewal, and other urban functions. Moreover, as Americans gain increased leisure time, additional county expenditures for parks, recreation, and community colleges may be anticipated. Increasing concentrations of population in suburban areas and changes in transportation patterns can be expected to increase county expenditures for expressways, airports, helioports, and perhaps, rapid transit.

The effect on county government of increasing population and greater demand for urban services cannot be fully predicted. Counties will, of course, supply only part of America's increased needs for urban services but, if present trends continue, they will provide a slowly increasing proporation of the cost of these services. From 1957 to 1962, the last five year period covered by a detailed census of local governments, the number of county government employees increased 29% while the number of federal civilian, state, and municipal employees increased 4%, 24% and 10% respectively.(42) During this same five year period, county expenditures increased 51% while federal, state, and municipal expenditures increased 14%, 50% and 35% respectively.(43) In 1957, 15.7% of all local government employees were county employees and in 1962, 16.7% were county employees. County government expenditures were 18.9% of all local government expenditures in 1957 and in 1962, they were 19.6%. As the nation grows in population and becomes increasingly urban, county officials can expect larger payrolls and expenditures.

Reapportionment

There are three aspects of reapportionment that have affected county government in the past and appear likely to have an increasing effect in the future. Two of these aspects of reapportionment seem certain to strengthen county government and one will probably weaken the county as a political unit.

The reapportionment of county governing bodies is almost certain to strengthen county government.(44) As urban and suburban residents gain increased representation on county boards, they will be less likely to consider county government as rural government and more likely to favor expansion of county services, increased county taxes, and a greater measure of county home rule. Furthermore, county government is more likely to meet the needs of its citizens if all sections of the county are more equitably represented on the county board.

The reapportionment of state and federal legislatures will probably weaken the county as a political unit. In many cases, reapportionment has meant the redrawing of legislative district boundaries in ways that divide populous counties into legislative districts and combine many rural counties into single districts. As a result, there will undoubtedly be more political organization on a state legislative district and Congressional district basis. This does not mean the political demise of the county. In the State of Washington, for example, larger counties have been divided into legislative districts for years, and county political organizations are still strong. However, in many states reapportionment may decrease the power of county chairmen and county committees.

The reapportionment of state and federal legislatures is likely to strengthen the county as a unit of government. The greatest population growth in our nation in the past decade has been in suburban areas, and suburban counties are likely to gain most in representation from reapportionment.(45) The county is the principal unit of government in most large suburban areas, and state legislators and

Congressmen from suburban counties have been among the strongest supporters of county government.(46) Counties, having extensive suburban areas, have traditionally provided the most favorable enviroment for county home rule and the newer executive and administrative forms of county government. As suburban delegations to state legislatures increase, more of the legal and fiscal roadblocks to stronger county government are likely to be removed.

Furthermore, reapportionment may cause a reappraisal of county home rule by rural county voters and legislators.(47) Previously many rural counties had their own state representative and/or state senator who could help shape state laws to meet their county's specific needs. When counties are combined into larger legislative districts, rural county officials will lose some of their contacts with the state capital and may find necessary state laws which give county government greater flexibility. The combining of counties into state legislative districts may also strengthen rural county government by encouraging geographic consolidation of sparsely settled rural counties or the creation of multi-county administrative agencies.

The effect of reapportionment in city areas is more difficult to predict. The county seems likely to gain in strength as a unit of government and to lose power as a political unit. Throughout the nation, counties probably have more to gain from reapportionment than they have to lose.

Interdependent Federalism (48)

If past trends continue, the future will bring more extensive federal and state involvement in metropolitan and urban problems. Not only are the number, complexity, and amount of federal aid programs affecting counties likely to increase, but contacts between federal and county personnel will become more numerous. Similarly, as state governments establish offices for local affairs and expand both grant and technical assistance programs to local government, closer ties between state and county officials will develop. Counties will need to learn how to make the best use of federal and state advisers, recognizing that some advisers may view county problems from their own limited viewpoint as specialists rather than from the standpoint of the entire needs of the county. Counties will need to gain maximum financial benefit from federal and state aid programs without disrupting the proper balance between grant and non-grant county programs. The more populous county may find it advisable to establish the position of grant-in-aid coordinator or urban adviser to serve as county liaison officer with state and federal agencies and to help the county receive the most benefit from its federal and state relationships.(49) There may be many times when county decision-making will be influenced by federal and state grant programs and advisers, but counties, acting together through the National Association of Counties and state associations of county officials, may also be able to influence federal and state decision–making.

As ties between the county courthouse and national and state agencies become closer, a shift in emphasis may occur in the concept of county home rule. County officials will continue to struggle for freedom from obsolete constitutional and legal restrictions which prevent county government reorganization, impair the ordinance making powers of counties, and limit the services counties can provide. The objective of county home rule will not be county autonomy, but greater flexibility to serve as a more effective partner in a combined federal, state, and local effort to solve the serious urban and rural problems of our times. The shift in the emphasis of the county home rule movement has begun. The National Association of Counties has taken the lead in emphasizing to county officials that: "the concept of separate levels of government, operating with exclusive responsibilities and exclusive sources of revenue, is now obsolete."(50) In stressing the importance of federal–state–local partnership programs in solving basic problems, the National Association of Counties is recognizing the growing interdependence of our federal system, and the necessity for the county to prepare itself for its role as a local government leader in this partnership.

Local Intergovernmental Relations

The past two decades have seen expansion of local intergovernmental agreements, service contracts, joint purchasing, regional councils of local governments, and other forms of intergovernmental cooperation. This trend is likely to continue with added impetus being provided by federal and state aid programs which encourage intergovernmental cooperation. This cooperation has enhanced county government in many areas. In Los Angeles County, the Lakewood plan of service contracts has not only put county services at the disposal of many cities within the county, but has strengthened the ties between suburban dwellers and county government. The role of the county as a senior partner in local intergovernmental relations has also been enhanced by joint purchasing agreements in which county purchasing agencies buy in quantity for other units of local government.

Future trends in the field of local intergovernmental cooperation may be indicated by the most recent legislative program of the Advisory Commission on Intergovernmental Relations.(51) This program includes model acts to facilitate state assistance for intergovernmental cooperation, to provide greater statutory authority for interlocal agreements, and to encourage the establishment of regional councils of public officials. The Commission's legislative program also includes a bill to permit the establishment of a county commission with powers to review proposals for the establishment, merger, and dissolution of special districts.(52) Further legislation proposed by the Commission provides authority for county urban renewal, county-wide vocational schools, and county planning and zoning in smaller cities and unincorporated areas. The trend in local intergovernmental relations is towards greater intergovernmental cooperation and a more important role for counties particularly in relation to special districts.

The Urban County

The most promising trend for the future of county government is the trend towards the urban county. Henry Schmandt predicts incremental change in the existing local governmental system including the gradual assumption of more urban-type functions by the county.(53) As Victor Jones has pointed out, there are five reasons why attention should given to developing the county into the central agency of local government in some metropolitan areas:

"1. The urban and metropolitan county is already assuming functions that can be distinguished only by legal definition from municipal functions.

2. Other means of integrating local government in metropolitan areas have either been inadequate or have evoked intense opposition.

3. The county has shown a persistent vitality even in urban communities. . . .

4. The central county, short of an area-wide unit of government, is more likely than any other jurisdiction to include all, or at least the major portion, of the metropolitan area. . . .

5. A 'federal' form of metropolitan government can be built around the county and the municipalities" (within the county). (54)

In the most of the metropolitan areas that lie within a single county, it is possible for county government to become, if it is not already, the main unit of local government. As Norman Beckman, Assistant Director for Metropolitan Areas of the Advisory Commission on Intergovernmental Relations, points out:

"Excepting New England, county government is on the move in urban sections of the country; and it will ride the wave of the future with regard to metropolitan governmental organization and political power. The reason for this is that county government has a priceless asset which many municipalities do not have—what students of government would term 'adequate areal jurisdiction'—but what can better be described by the word 'space.'

. . . .In addition to 'space' the county has high political feasibility (it exists, therefore it is feasible). It is directly accountable to an electorate that, under recent court decisions, will be reasonably representative. Finanlly, it has a broad tax base and well established working relations with the state and federal governments on the one hand and the cities on the other."(55)

There are important challenges for counties in larger metropolitan areas. John Bebout writes: "Even in metropolitan areas embracing several counties there is reason to believe that strong county governments in which the people have substantial confidence may provide a more viable basis for some form of metropolitan federation or metropolitan-wide intergovernmental cooperation than the more numerous and more diverse municipal units."(56) W. Brooke, Graves and Mark H. Freeman point out that: "Even in those instances in which the metropolitan area spills over into two or more counties, the task of coordinating the efforts of a small number of counties is far simpler than that of coordinating the dozens or scores of small local units to be found within most metropolitan areas."(57)

The ability of metropolitan counties to undertake greater responsibility in metropolitan areas depends upon the freedom given counties to shape their organization and powers to meet the needs of their citizens. It depends also upon the adequacy of county revenue sources and the confidence of citizens in county government. Too frequently, county government is associated in the minds of citizens with the archaic government of the Gilbertson era. The image of county government is improving as the achievements of county government are reported by authorities on local government and by the press. Institutes and conferences called to acquaint college students with recent trends and career opportunities in county government are also improving the image of county government.(58)

CONCLUSION

American county government has made substantial strides in the past fifty years, but continued progress requires further change in the organization, services, finances, and intergovernmental relations of county government. The rapidity with which counties can adjust to the changing needs of their citizens will depend, in part, upon the flexibility and authority granted them by state constitutions and state laws. It will depend, in part, on the willingness of county officials to support necessary changes in the functions, organization, and intergovernmental relationships of their counties. It will depend also on a better public understanding of the achievements and potentialities of county government.

REFERENCES

1. Henry S. Gilbertson, The County, The 'Dark Continent' of American Politics (New York: The National Short Ballot Association, 1917).

2. See Victor Jones, Metropolitan Government (Chicago: University of Chicago Press, 1942), pp. 52–84; Charles Adrian, State and Local Governments (New York: McGraw Hill, Inc., 1960), pp. 237–247; Jewell Cass Phillips, Municipal Government and Administration in America (New York: The Macmillan Company, 1960), pp. 143–148; Victor Jones "Local Government Organization in Metropolitan Areas: Its Relation to Urban Development" in Coleman Woodbury, The Future of Cities and Urban Development (Chicago: University of Chicago Press, 1953), pp. 508–526; John C. Bollens and Henry J. Schmandt, The Metropolis (New York: Harper and Row, 1965), pp. 308–370; and Daniel Grant and H. C. Nixon, State and Local Government in America (Boston: Allyn and Bacon, Inc., 1963), pp. 338–341.

3. Roscoe C. Martin, Metropolis in Transition (Washington: Housing and Home Finance Agency, 1963), p. 3.

4. For a more extensive description of these approaches, see Roscoe Martin, op. cit., pp. 5–11. The comments on these approaches are the writer's and not, necessarily, Professor Martin's.

5. Ibid., p. 7.

6. The Mayor of Milwaukee favored transfer of assessment functions from city to county government in Milwaukee County because it would provide greater efficiency in assessment procedures and eliminate unnecessary costs from duplication. The Milwaukee Journal, April 21, 1964, p. 18.

7. See chapter 11 for a more extensive description of the transfers in Milwaukee County.

8. Roscoe C. Martin, op. cit., pp. 8, 9.

9. Ibid., p. 9.

10. The Nashville–Davidson County consolidation is described in chapter 10. An excellent description of the Baton Rouge–East Baton Rouge Parish consolidation in Louisiana may be found in: William C. Havard and Floyd L. Corty, Rural–Urban Consolidation (Baton Rouge: Louisiana State University Press, 1964).

11. One exception, is the Metropolitan Water District of Southern California which provides a metropolitan-wide approach to water supply problems.

12. Many authorities on local government have been critical of the proliferation of special districts. W. Brooke Graves and Mark H. Freeman write "A strong case can be made for using the counties rather than continuing to create more special districts to perform functions which can be performed satisfactorily by the counties." W. Brooke Graves and Mark H. Freeman, County Government: Origins, Development, Present Status, Future Prospects with Special Reference to West Virginia (Washington: The Library of Congress Legislative Reference Service, 1962), p. 51.

13. Robert G. Smith, Public Authorities, Special Districts and Local Government (Washington: National Association of Counties Research Foundation. 1964).

14. Roscoe C. Martin, op. cit., p. 11. The governments of Nashville-Davidson County and Baton Rouge–East Baton Rouge Parish are of the first type and the government of Dade County, Florida is of the second type.

15. Roscoe Martin terms the Municipality of Metropolitan Seattle a special district and describes it in detail in Metropolis in Transition, pp. 75–87.

16. Clyde F. Snider, Local Government in Rural America (New York: Appleton–Century–Crofts, Inc., 1957), p. 533.

17. Ibid. However, two of South Dakota's unorganized counties have been eliminated by annexation and consolidation.

18. This opposition has been described in detail by Clyde F. Snider, op. cit., p. 534.

19. Constitution of the State of Wisconsin, Article IV, Section 23. The Wisconsin Constitution had to be amended to permit the election of a chief executive officer in counties of 500,000 or more people.

20. Constitution of the State of Idaho. Article XVIII, Section 5.

21. Bureau of Government, University Extension Division, The University of Wisconsin, County Government and the Problems of Urban Expansion (Madison: University of Wisconsin, 1959), p. 14.

22. Commissioners of Hamilton County v. Mighels, 7 Ohio St. 109, 118–119 (1857).

23. Moore v. Walker County, 236 Ala. 688, 690 (1938).

24. Clyde F. Snider, op. cit., pp. 60, 61.

25. Ibid., p. 61.

26. Advisory Commission on Intergovernmental Relations, State Constitutional and Statutory Restrictions Upon the Structural, Functional, and Personnel Powers of Local Government (Washington: Advisory Commission on Intergovernmental Relations, 1962), p. 6.

27. Ibid., p. 23. The Dillon Rule states: "It is the general and undisputed proposition of law that a municipal corporation possess, and can

exercise the following powers, and no others: First, those granted in express words; second, those necessarily or fairly implied in, or incident to, the powers expressly granted; third, those essential to the declared objects and purposes of the corporation — not simply convenient, but indispensible."

28. Ibid., p. 8.

29. Clyde F. Snider, op. cit., p. 106.

30. Ibid., pp. 106, 107.

31. Arthur Bromage, Municipal and County Home Rule for Michigan (Detroit: Citizens Research Council of Michigan, 1961), pp. 17, 18.

32. Ibid., p. 18.

33. This proposed constitutional amendment will be placed on the ballot in Maryland in November, 1966.

34. For recent descriptions of the adoption of county home rule constitutional amendments and charters see: Arthur Bromage, "Local Government" in W. Brooke Graves, Major Problems in State Constitutional Revision (Chicago: Public Administration Service, 1960), pp. 244-246.

35. Erie, Monroe, Nassau, Oneida, Onondaga, Schenectady, Suffolk, and Westchester Counties have home rule charters. For a detailed description of all but the most recent of these charters, see: New York State, Office for Local Government, County Charters in New York State (Albany, N. Y.: Office for Local Government, 1963).

36. These are Los Angeles, San Diego and Alameda Counties in California, Dade County in Florida, and Erie, Nassau and Westchester Counties in New York.

37. Clyde F. Snider, op. cit., p. 111.

38. For a more extensive description of optional charters see: Arthur Bromage, Municipal and County Home Rule for Michigan, pp. 21, 22.

39. New York State, Office for Local Government, County Charters in New York State, p. iv.

40. A copy of the American County Platform may be found in American County Government, 31:27-46, January, 1966. This platform was adopted on July 14, 1965 at the annual meeting of the National Association of Counties.

41. Ibid., p. 30.

42. U. S. Bureau of the Census, Census of Governments: 1957. Summary of Public Employment (Washington: U. S. Government Printing Office, 1958), p. 13 and U. S. Bureau of the Census, Census of Governments: 1962, Compendium of Public Employment (Washington: U. S. Government Printing Office, 1963), p. 19.

43. U. S. Bureau of the Census, Census of Governments: 1957, Compendium of Government Finances (Washington: U. S. Government Printing Office, 1959), p. 19 and U. S. Bureau of the Census, Census of Governments: 1962, Compendium of Government Finances (Washington: U. S. Government Printing Office, 1964), p. 27. Statistics on revenues show similar trends.

44. See chapter 3 for a more detailed description of current trends in the apportionment of county governing bodies.

45. From 1950 to 1960, the population of the central cities of all metropolitan areas in the nation increased 10.8% or 5.6 million people. During the same period, the population of these metropolitan areas outside the central city (mainly suburban areas) increased 48.5% or 17.9 million people. Advisory Commission on Intergovernmental Relations, Metropolitan Social and Economic Disparities: Implications for Intergovernmental Relations in Central Cities and Suburbs (Washington: Advisory Commission on Intergovernmental Relations, 1965), p. 36.

46. Bernard Hillenbrand, "Is Reapportionment a Threat to Counties?" The County Officer, 29:471, November, 1964 describes the suburbanite's stake in county government.

47. This idea has been developed in greater detail by Bernard Hillenbrand, "Reapportionment and Home Rule," The County Officer, 29:335, August, 1964.

48. The writer is indebted to Alan K. Campbell, Director of the Metropolitan Studies Program of Syracuse University for the concept of "interdependent federalism".

49. For a further description of the role of the county urban adviser, see Bernard Hillenbrand, "A County Urban Adviser and Federal Aid," American County Government, 31:6, January, 1966.

50. This policy statement of the National Association of Counties, quoted more fully in chapter 6, may be found in American County Government, 30:15, May, 1965.

51. Advisory Commission on Intergovernmental Relations, The 1966 State Legislative Program (Washington: Advisory Commission on Intergovernmental Relations, 1965).

52. The commission would be composed of two members appointed by the county governing board, two appointed by city officials, and a fifth member appointed by the other four members. Ibid., p. 423. The legislation is similar to that used in California and described in chapter 6.

53. Henry J. Schmandt, "Changing Directions," National Civic Review, 54:534, November, 1965.

54. Victor Jones, "Local Government in Metropolitan Areas," in The Future of Cities and Urban Redevelopment, by Coleman Woodbury (Chicago: University of Chicago Press, 1953), pp. 592, 593.

55. Norman Beckman, "Taking Account of Urban Counties," American County Government 30:68, October, 1965.

56. John Bebout in Model County Charter (Washington: National Municipal League, 1956), p. xxxvii.

57. W. Brooke Graves and Mark H. Freeman, op. cit., p. 51.

58. The California County Supervisors Association invited senior and graduate students from 32 California colleges to several conferences on county government. The purpose of the meetings was to acquaint the college students with California county government and to show them that counties offer them exiciting, career employment. American County Government, 30:18, August, 1965.

5/APPENDICES AND BIBLIOGRAPHY

Appendix A

SERVICES PROVIDED BY FIVE COUNTY GOVERNMENTS

Services	Petro-leum	Latah	Mont-gomery	Nashville-Davidson	Mil-waukee
General Government					
Assessment of property taxes	x	x	x	x	
Collection of property taxes	x	x	x	x	x
Coroner or medical examiner	x	x	x	x	x
Courts		x	x	x	x
Election supervision	x	x	x*	x	x
Liquor sales			x		
Prosecuting attorney	x	x	x	x	x
Recording legal documents	x	x	x	x	x
Serving legal papers	x	x	x	x	x
Agriculture					
Extension		x	x	x	x
Fair		x		x	
Weed eradication		x		x	
Education and Library					
Citizenship Commission (special citizenship training program)					x
Community college			x		
Libraries			x	x	
Museum (adult or children's)				x*	x
Schools			x	x	
Health and Welfare					
Air pollution control			x	x	x
Alcoholics clinic			x		x
Child guidance center		x	x	x	x
Children's home				x	x
Emergency hospital care				x	x

259

SERVICES PROVIDED BY FIVE COUNTY GOVERNMENTS (Contd.)

Services	Petro-leum	Latah	Mont-gomery	Nashville-Davidson	Mil-waukee
Health and Welfare (contd.)					
General hospital care				x	x
Health	x	x	x	x	x
Home for the aged		x		x	x
Mental hospital or hospital wing				x	x
Public assistance		x	x	x	x
Tuberculosis hospital				x	x
Parks and Recreation					
Auditorium				x	
Botanical gardens					x
Children's Theater				x*	
Concert stage				x	x
Parks		x	x	x	x
Recreation			x	x	x
Social centers			x	x	x
Stadium					x
Symphony Orchestra				x*	
Zoo					x
Physical Development					
Code Enforcement			x	x	x
Industrial development			x	x	
Planning		x		x	x
Subdivision regulations			x	x	
Urban Renewal			x	x	
Zoning			x	x	
Public Safety					
Civil Defense		x	x	x	x
Fire protection			x	x	x**
Jail		x	x	x	x
Police	x	x	x	x	x
Public works					
Airports			x	x	x
County roads	x		x	x	x
Expressways					x
Ports					
Refuse collection				x	
Refuse disposal			x	x	x
River terminal				x	
Sewage				x	
Streets			x	x	
Traffic engineering			x	x	x
Water				x	
Total number of functions	10	20	35	50	40

*The county contributes partial financial support with respect to these services but does not directly administer the service.
**Milwaukee County provides fire protection only at the county airport and county institutions.

Appendix B

State Associations of Counties

State	State Association and Address	Name and Title of Executive Director
Alabama	Association of County Commissioners of Alabama, 660 Adams Ave., Montgomery, Alabama	Winston Stewart Executive Director
Arizona	Arizona Supervisors & Clerks Association, Graham Co. Courthouse, Safford, Arizona	H. C. Gietz Secretary-Treasurer
Arkansas	Arkansas Association of County Judges, Russelville, Arkansas	R. D. Howell Secretary-Treasurer
California	County Supervisors Association of California, 1100 Elks Building, Sacramento, California	Wm. R. MacDougall General Counsel & Manager
Colorado	Colorado State Association of County Commissioners, 904 Majestic Bldg., Denver, Colorado	J. Fred Schneider General Counsel & Secretary-Treasurer
Florida	Florida State Association of County Commissioners, P. O. Box 549, Tallahassee, Florida	E. R. Hafner Executive Secretary
Georgia	Association County Commissioners of Georgia, 205 Forsyth Building, Atlanta, Georgia	Hill R. Healan Executive Director
Hawaii	Hawaii Association of Counties, County Building, Lihue, Hawaii	George R. Pascua President

State	State Association and Address	Name and Title of Executive Director
Idaho	Idaho Association of Commis- sioners & Clerks, Preston, Idaho	C. L. Swenson Executive Secretary
Illinois	Illinois Association of County Su- pervisors & Commissioners, 415 Ridgely Bldg., Springfield, Illinois	James M. Walsh Executive Secretary
Indiana	Association of Indiana Counties, 521 Board of Trade Building Indianapolis, Indiana	Claude Hodson Executive Director
Iowa	Iowa State Association of County Officers, County Courthouse, Independence, Iowa	Leslie Fry President
Kansas	Kansas County Commissioners Association, 112 West Seventh Street, Topeka, Kansas	E. A. Mosher Executive Director
Louisiana	Police Jury Association of Louisiana, P. O. Box 755, Natchitoches, La.	W. A. Breedlove Executive Secretary
Maine	Maine Counties Association, Kennebec County Courthouse, Vassalboro, Maine	Forrest Brown Secretary-Treasurer
Maryland	Maryland County Commissioners Association, P. O. Box 362, College Park, Maryland	William S. Ratchford Executive Secretary
Massachusetts	Massachusetts Association of County Officials, Hampden County Courthouse, Springfield, Massachusetts	Daniel Walsh Secretary-Treasurer
Michigan	Michigan State Association of Supervisors, 319 West Lenawee Street, Lansing, Michigan	W. E. Dennison Executive Director
Minnesota	Association of Minnesota Counties, 375 Griggs-Midway Building, St. Paul, Minnesota	Ralph T. Keyes Executive Secretary
Mississippi	Mississippi Association of Super- visors, Moss Point, Mississippi	Eddie A. Khayat Secretary-Treasurer
Missouri	Association of County Judges of Missouri, Benton County Court- house, Warsaw, Missouri	R. J. Behrens Secretary-Treasurer

State	State Association and Address	Name and Title of Executive Director
Montana	Montana Association of County Commissioners, County Court-house, Bozeman, Montana	Ralph Aaker Secretary-Treasurer
Nebraska	Nebraska Association of County Officials, Ravenna, Nebraska	Carl A. Stark Secretary-Treasurer
Nevada	Nevada Association of County Commissioners, P. O. Box 507, Winnemucca, Nevada	Frank Bengochea Executive Secretary
New Hampshire	State Association of County Commissioners of New Hampshire, Carroll County Courthouse, Sandwich, New Hampshire	Arthur B. Brown President
New Jersey	New Jersey Association of Chosen Freeholders, Mercer County Courthouse, Trenton, New Jersey	Jack Lamping Executive Director
New Mexico	New Mexico Association of County Officials, 1855 La Jolla, Las Cruces, New Mexico	Mike Frietze, Jr. President
New York	County Officers Association of the State of New York, 248 State Street, Albany, New York	C. L. Chamberlain Executive Director
North Carolina	North Carolina Association of County Commissioners, 205 Lennox Bldg., Chapel Hill, N. C.	John Morrisey General Counsel
North Dakota	North Dakota Auditors Association, Hettinger, North Dakota	Thomas B. Stevens President
Ohio	County Commissioners Association of Ohio, 41 S. High Street, Columbus, Ohio	Adolph Maslar Secretary
Oregon	Association of Oregon Counties, P. O. Box 2051, Salem, Oregon	Ward Armstrong Executive Secretary
Pennsylvania	Pennsylvania State Association of County Commissioners, County Courthouse, Butler, Pennsylvania	James Green Secretary-Treasurer
South Carolina	South Carolina Association of County Road Officials, County Highway Bldg., Aiken, South Carolina	Fred W. Scott Secretary-Treasurer
South Dakota	South Dakota Association of County Commissioners, Pierpoint, South Dakota	Edwin C. Lee Executive Director

State	State Association and Address	Name and Title of Executive Director
Tennessee	Tennessee County Services Assn. YMCA Building, Nashville, Tennessee	James Tipton Executive Secretary
Texas	County Judges and Commissioners Association of Texas, County Courthouse, San Angelo, Texas	Harold Green Secretary-Treasurer
Utah	Utah Assn. of Counties, Newhouse Hotel, Salt Lake City, Utah	C. A. Grant Executive Director
Virginia	Virginia Assn. of Counties, 402 County Office Building, Charlottesville, Virginia	George R. Long Executive Director
Washington	Washington State Association of County Commissioners, 106 Maple Park, Olympia, Washington	John L. Chamber Executive Secretary
Washington	Washington State Association of Elected County Officials, 1063 Capitol Way, Olympia, Washington	Lyle T. Watson Executive Secretary
West Virginia	West Virginia Assn. of County Officials, 207-1/2 Duffy Street, Charleston, W. Virginia	Richard Shelton Executive Director
Wisconsin	Wisconsin Co. Boards Assn., 1 West Main St., Madison, Wisconsin	A. J. Thelan Executive Secretary
Wyoming	Wyoming Assn. of County Officials, Fremont County Courthouse, Lander, Wyoming	James A. Farthing Secretary-Treasurer

For Supplementary Reading

The following list of references provides further information on county government. Included as general references are books on county government, books on local or metropolitan government which have sections on county government, and other publications which provide insight into some facet of county government or its problems. A few exceptional articles, government reports or other sources are also included as general references.

Studies of county government in selected states have also been included as references since they provide an invaluable source of detailed information on county government. Sources are also provided for further study of county government in eight selected counties described in chapters six through eleven.

General References

Adrian, Charles R. State and Local Governments, A Study in the Political Process. New York: McGraw-Hill, Inc., 1960.

Advisory Commission on Intergovernmental Relations. Alternative Approaches to Governmental Reorganization in Metropolitan Areas. Washington: Advisory Commission on Intergovernmental Relations, 1962.

_____. Governmental Structure, Organization and Planning in Metropolitan Areas. Washington: Advisory Commission on Intergovernmental Relations, 1961.

_____. Performance of Urban Functions: Local and Areawide. Washington: Advisory Commission on Intergovernmental Relations, 1963.

_____. State Constitutional and Statutory Restrictions on Local Government Debt. Washington: Advisory Commission on Intergovernmental Relations, 1961.

_____. State Constitutional and Statutory Restrictions on Local Taxing Powers. Washington: Advisory Commission on Intergovernmental Relations, 1962.

_____. State Constitutional and Statutory Restrictions Upon the Structural, Functional, and Personnel Powers of Local Government. Washington: Advisory Commission on Intergovernmental Relations, 1962.

_____. Tax Overlapping in the United States. Washington: Advisory Commission on Intergovernmental Relations, 1964.

_____. The Role of the States in Strengthening the Property Tax. Washington: Advisory Commission on Intergovernmental Relations, 1963.

Alderfer, Harold F. American Local Government and Administration. New York: The Macmillan Company, 1956.

American Municipal Association and National Association of Counties. Voluntary City-County Regional Cooperation. Washington: American Municipal Association and National Associaton of Counties, 1963.

Bebout, John E. Model County Charter. New York: National Municipal League, 1956.

Blair, George S. American Local Government. New York: Harper and Row, 1964.

Bollens, John C. Special District Governments in the United States. Berkeley: University of California Press, 1957.

_____, and Henry J. Schmandt. The Metropolis. New York: Harper and Row, 1965.

Bromage, Arthur W. Municipal and County Home Rule for Michigan. Detroit: Citizens Research Council of Michigan, 1961.

_____. American County Government. New York: Sears Publishing Company, 1933.

Casella, William N. "County Government in Transition." Public Administration Review, 16:223-231, Summer, 1956.

Fairlie, John A. Local Government in Counties, Towns and Villages. New York: The Century Company, 1914.

_____, and Charles M. Kneier. County Government and Administration. New York: The Century Company, 1930.

Gilbertson, H. S. The County, the 'Dark Continent' of American Politics. New York: The National Short Ballot Organization, 1917.

Grant, Daniel R. and H. C. Nixon. State and Local Government in America. Boston: Allyn and Bacon, Inc., 1963.

Graves, W. Brooke. American Intergovernmental Relations: Their Origins, Historical Development and Current Status. New York: Scribner's Sons, 1964.

_____. Intergovernmental Relations in the United States: A Selected Bibliography on Interlevel and Interjurisdictional Relations. Washington: Commission on Intergovernmental Relations, 1955.

_____. (ed.). Major Problems in State Constitutional Revision. Chicago: Public Administration Service, 1960.

Hillenbrand, Bernard F. "County Government is Reborn," Readings in State and Local Government, Joseph F. Zimmerman, (ed.). New York: Holt, Rinehart and Winston, Inc., 1964.

_____. "Urban Counties in 1964," The Municipal Yearbook, 1965. Chicago: International City Managers' Association, 1965. Similar articles have been written by Mr. Hillenbrand for prior issues of The Municipal Yearbook.

Hodgson, James G. The Official Publications of American Counties. Fort Collins: Colorado State College, 1937.

James, Herman G. Local Government in the United States. New York: D. Appleton and Company, 1921.

Jones, Victor. Metropolitan Government. Chicago: University of Chicago Press, 1942.

_____. "Local Government Organization in Metropolitan Areas: Its Relation to Urban Redevelopment," The Future of Cities and Urban Redevelopment, Coleman Woodbury, (ed.). Chicago: University of Chicago Press, 1953.

Kammerer, Gladys M. County Home Rule. Gainesville: Public Administration Clearing Service, University of Florida, 1959.

_____. The Changing Urban County. Gainesville: Public Administration Clearing Service, University of Florida, 1963.

Kane, Joseph N. The American Counties; A Record of the Origin of the Names of the 3,072 Counties, Dates of Creation and Organization. Revised Edition. New York: Scarecrow Press, 1962.

Kneier, Charles M. "Development of Newer County Functions," American Political Science Review, 24:134–140, February, 1930.

_____. "The Legal Nature and Status of the American County," Minnesota Law Review, 14:141–156, 1930.

Lancaster, Lane W. Government in Rural America. New York: D. Van Nostrand Company, Inc., 1952.

Martin, Roscoe, C. Metropolis in Transition. Washington: U. S. Housing and Home Finance Agency, 1963.

Maddox, Russell W. and Robert F. Fuquay. State and Local Government. Princeton, N. J.: D. Van Nostrand Company, Inc., 1962.

McArthur, Alastair. "State Associations of County Officials in 1964," The Municipal Yearbook, 1965. Chicago: International City Managers' Association, 1965. Similar articles have been written by Mr. McArthur for the prior issues of The Municipal Yearbook.

Morlan, Robert. Capital, Courthouse and City Hall. Cambridge: Riverside Press Co., 1960.

National Association of Counties. American County Government. Published monthly. Washington: National Association of Counties.

_____. The County Officer. Published monthly until it was renamed American County Government in April, 1965. Washington: National Association of Counties.

_____. Information and Education Service Reports. A series of reports published on the functions of county government. Washington: National Association of Counties.

_____. The American County Action Program for Home Rule. Washington: National Association of Counties, 1962.

_____. The County Finance Congress. Washington: National Association of Counties, 1960.

_____. The County Letter. A newsletter on county activities circulated to County Information Service subscribers. Washington: National Association of Counties.

_____. The County Planning Congress. Washington: National Association of Counties, 1963.

_____. The Urban County Congress. Washington: National Association of Counties, 1961.

Pate, James E. Local Government and Administration. New York: American Book Company, 1954.

Porter, Kirk H. County and Township Government in the United States. New York: The Macmillan Company, 1922.

Smith, Robert G. Public Authorities, Special Districts and Local Government. Washington: National Association of Counties, Research Foundation, 1964.

Snider, Clyde F. "American County Government: A Mid-Century Review," American Political Science Review, 46:66-80, March, 1952.

_____. American State and Local Government. New York: Appleton-Century-Crofts, Inc., 1950.

_____. Local Government in Rural America. New York: Appleton-Century-Crofts, Inc., 1957.

United States Bureau of the Census. Census of Governments, 1962. Vol. 1, Governmental Organization. Washington: U. S. Government Printing Office, 1963.

_____. Census of Governments, 1962. Vol. IV, No. 2, Finances of County Governments. Washington: U. S. Government Printing Office, 1964.

_____. Governing Boards of County Governments: 1965. Washington: U. S. Government Printing Office, 1965.

Wager, Paul. County Government Across the Nation. Chapel Hill: The University of North Carolina Press, 1950.

Webster, Donald. Urban Planning and Municipal Public Policy. New York: Harper and Brothers, 1958.

Weidner, Edward W. American County Government — Patchwork of Boards. New York: National Municipal League, 1946.

Studies of County Government in Selected States and Counties

Alabama

Thomas, James D. A Manual for Alabama County Commissioners. University, Alabama: University of Alabama, 1963.

Arkansas

Alexander, Henry M. Organization and Function of State and Local Government in Arkansas. Fayetteville: Bureau of Research, University of Arkansas, 1947.

Reed, Edward W. and Henry M. Alexander. The Government and Finance of Counties in Arkansas. Fayetteville: Bureau of Business and Economic Research, University of Arkansas, 1953.

California

Bigger, Richard and others. County Government in California. Third Edition. Sacramento: County Supervisors Association of California, 1958.

Bollens, John C. and others. County Government Organization in California. Berkeley: Bureau of Public Administration, University of California, 1947.

Crouch, Winston W. and others. California Government and Politics. Third Edition. Englewood Cliffs, N. J.: Prentice-Hall, Inc., 1964.

Hall, Stuart C. County Supervisorial Districting in California. Berkeley: Bureau of Public Administration, University of California, 1961.

Los Angeles County

Crouch, Winston W. and Beatrice Dinerman. Southern California Metropolis. Los Angeles: University of California Press, 1963.

Ford, John A. Thirty Explosive Years in Los Angeles County. San Marino: Huntington Library, 1961.

Gove, Samuel K. The Lakewood Plan. Urbana: Institute of Government and Public Affairs, University of Illinois, 1960.

Martin, Roscoe C. "The Service Contract: Practice in Los Angeles County," in Metropolis in Transition. Washington: Housing and Home Finance Agency, 1963, pp. 13–25.

Colorado

Allen, Harry S. Duties and Functions of Colorado County Officials; A Manual for County Officials. Denver: Colorado Information, 1963.

McBride, Conrad I. County Road Administration in Colorado. Boulder: Bureau of State and Community Service, University of Colorado, 1958.

Connecticut

Faeth, Henry J. The Connecticut County; A Description of Its Organization, Function and Relationship with Other Governmental Units. Storrs: Institute of Public Service, University of Connecticut, 1949.

Delaware

Dolan, Paul. The Government and Administration of Delaware, Chapter 24. New York: Crowell, 1956, American Commonwealths Series, Vol. 7.

Florida

Dovell, Junius E. Florida's County Government. Gainesville: Public Administration Clearing Service, University of Florida, 1952.

University of Miami Bureau of Business and Economic Research. Handbook of Florida Counties. Miami: University of Miami, 1959.

Willis, Bryan and John L. Berry. Manual for County Commissioners of Florida; A Comprehensive Guide for the Operation of the Office. Tallahassee: State Auditor, 1958.

Dade County

Campbell, O. W. "The Dade County Approach — Administrative Aspects." The Urban County Congress. Washington: National Association of Counties, 1961.

Serino, Gustave. Miami's Metropolitan Experiment. Gainesville: Public Administration Clearing Service, University of Florida, 1958.

Sofen, Edward. The Miami Metropolitan Experiment. Bloomington: Indiana University Press, 1963.

———. "The Politics of Metropolitan Leadership: The Miami Experience," Midwest Journal of Political Science, 5:18-38, February, 1961.

Wolff, Reinhold P. Miami Metro: The Road to Urban Unity. Coral Gables: University of Miami Bureau of Business and Economic Research, 1960.

Georgia

Hughes, M. Clyde. County Government in Georgia. Athens: University of Georgia Press, 1944.

Styles, Robert L., Jr. Handbook for County Commissioners. Athens: Institute of Law and Government, University of Georgia, 1962.

Hawaii

Hoppes, Muriel. Guide to Government in Hawaii. Honolulu: Legislative Reference Bureau, University of Hawaii, 1963.

Idaho

Duncombe, Herbert Sydney and Katherine D. Pell. Handbook for County Officials in Idaho. Moscow: Bureau of Public Affairs Research, University of Idaho, 1966.

Latah County

League of Women Voters. This is Latah County, Idaho. Moscow: League of Women of Voters, 1957.

Illinois

Howards, Irving. "County and Township Functions in Illinois," Illinois Local Government, Lois M. Lelekoudas, (ed.). Urbana: University of Illinois, 1961.

Snider, Clyde F. and Irving Howards. County Government in Illinois. Carbondale: Southern Illinois University Press, 1960.

Indiana

Erb, Emerson C. Administrative Practices in Indiana County Highway Departments. Bloomington: Bureau of Government Research, Indiana University, 1959.

Iowa

Smith, Harry R. A Handbook for County Supervisors. Iowa City: Institute of Public Affairs, State University of Iowa, 1962.

Wessel, Robert I. Iowa Rural Government Since 1900. Ames: Agricultural Experiment Station, State University of Science and Technology, 1963. (Special Report No. 32.)

Kansas

Cape, William H. County Government in Kansas. Lawrence: Governmental Research Center, University of Kansas, 1958.

Drury, James W. Government of Kansas, Chapter 24. Lawrence: University of Kansas Press, 1961. (Originally planned for American Commonwealths Series, Vol. 14.)

Kentucky

Biggs, William E., and Nathan S. Lord. Compensation of Kentucky County Officials. Frankfort: Legislative Research Commission, 1964. (Research Report No. 22).

Manning, John W. Government in Kentucky Counties. Lexington: Bureau of Governmental Research, University of Kentucky, 1937.

Louisiana

Chandler, L. E. A Study of Parish Government in Louisiana. Hammond: Southeastern Louisiana College, 1960.

Baton-Rouge — East Baton Rouge Parish

Havard, William C. and Floyd L. Corty. Rural-Urban Consolidation. Baton Rouge: Louisiana State University Press, 1964.

Kean, Gordon. "The Plan of Government for the Parish of East Baton Rouge and the City of Baton Rouge, Louisiana," The Urban County Congress. Washington: National Association of Counties, 1961.

Maryland

Bowen, Don L. and Robert S. Friedman. Local Government in Maryland. College Park: Bureau of Governmental Research, University of Maryland, 1955.

Spencer, Jean E. Contemporary Local Government in Maryland. College Park: Bureau of Governmental Research, University of Maryland, 1965.

Montgomery County

Charter of Montgomery County, Maryland. Rockville: Montgomery County, n.d.

League of Women Voters of Montgomery County, Maryland. The Government of Montgomery County, Maryland. Silver Spring: League of Women Voters, 1963.

Maryland Department of Economic Development in cooperation with the Montgomery County Department of Information and Economic Development. Community Economic Inventory, Montgomery County, Maryland. Rockville: Montgomery County Department of Information and Economic Development, 1964.

Public Administration Service. The Government of Montgomery County, Maryland. Chicago: Public Administration Service, 1962.

Massachusetts

Conley, Arthur C. A Study of County Government. Boston: Massachusetts Federation of Taxpayers Associations, 1941.

General Court. Legislative Research Bureau. Report Relative to County Government in Massachusetts. House Document No. 3131. Boston: Legislative Research Bureau, 1962.

Michigan

Brake, D. Hale. The Michigan County; An Outline of the Structure and Functions of County Government. East Lansing: Institute for Community Development, Michigan State University, 1962.

Bureau of Social and Political Research, College of Business and Public Service, Michigan State University. The County Board of Supervisors, Its Powers and Duties. East Lansing: Michigan State University, 1959.

Minnesota

Legislature. Commission to Study the Organization, Function and Structure of County and Township Governments. Report to the Legislature. St. Paul: Minnesota Legislature, 1961.

Mississippi

Brammer, Dana B. <u>A Manual for Mississippi County Supervisors</u>. University: Bureau of Governmental Research, University of Mississippi, 1966.

Missouri

Missouri Public Expenditure Council. <u>Toward Better County Government</u>. Jefferson City: Missouri Public Expenditure Council, 1947.

Montana

Renne, Roland R. <u>The Government and Administration of Montana</u>, Chapter 24. New York: Crowell, 1958. American Commonwealths Series, Vol. 24.

<u>Petroleum County</u>

Halcrow, Harold G. <u>County Manager Government in Montana: Presenting a Case Study of Petroleum County</u>. Bozeman: Agricultural Experiment Station, Montana State College, 1949.

Renne, Roland R. "Rural County Can be Efficient," <u>National Municipal Review</u>, 33:448–451, October, 1944.

_____. "Too Small to be Efficient," <u>National Municipal Review</u>, 36:78–82, February, 1947.

Nebraska

Shumate, Roger V. <u>Reorganization of County Government</u>. Lincoln: Nebraska Legislative Council, 1950.

Nevada

Legislative Counsel Bureau. <u>County Consolidation and Reorganization in Nevada</u>. Carson City: Legislative Counsel Bureau, 1948.

New Jersey

Collier, James M. <u>County Government in New Jersey</u>. New Brunswick: Rutgers University Press, 1952.

Rich, Bennett M. The Government and Administration of New Jersey, Chapter 25. New York: Crowell, 1957. American Commonwealths Series, Vol. 28.

New Mexico

Goldberg, Edward M. The County Commission in New Mexico. Albuquerque: Division of Government Research, University of New Mexico, 1962.

New York

Caldwell, Lynton K. The Government and Administration of New York, Chapter 7. New York: Crowell, 1954. American Commonwealths Series, Vol. 30.

Office for Local Government, State of New York. County Charters in New York State. Albany: Office for Local Government, State of New York, 1963.

North Carolina

Coltrane, George A. (ed.). County Government in North Carolina. Chapel Hill: Institute of Government, University of North Carolina, 1965.

McMahon, John A. (ed.). County Yearbook. Chapel Hill: Association of County Commissioners, published annually.

Rankin, Robert S. The Government and Administration of North Carolina, Chapter 25. New York: Crowell, 1955. American Commonwealths Series, Vol. 31.

North Dakota

Legislative Assembly. Legislative Research Commission. County Government Reorganization Study. Bismarck: Legislative Research Commission, 1965. (In Report, pp. 95-113).

Ohio

Aumann, Francis R. and Harvey Walker. The Government and Administration of Ohio, Chapter 24. New York: Crowell, 1956. American Commonwealths Series, Vol. 33.

Holden, Matthew, County Government in Ohio. Cleveland: Cleveland Metropolitan Services Commission, 1958.

Oklahoma

Bureau of Government Research. Duties and Powers of County Officers in Oklahoma. Norman: Bureau of Government Research, University of Oklahoma, 1952.

Oregon

Lamb, Bromleigh S. The Units of Local Government in Oregon, 1961. Eugene: Bureau of Municipal Research and Service, University of Oregon, 1962.

Willamette University, Institute of State Affairs. A Report on County Government in Oregon. Salem: Institute of State Affairs, Willamette University, 1956.

Pennsylvania

Department of Commerce. Comparative County Data for Pennsylvania. Harrisburg: Bureau of Community Development, Department of Commerce, 1955.

South Dakota

Cape, William H. Handbook for South Dakota County Officials. Vermillion: Extension Division, State University of South Dakota, 1961.

Tennessee

Greene, Lee S. and Robert S. Avery. Government in Tennessee, Chapter 22. Knoxville: University of Tennessee Press, 1962. (Originally undertaken for the American Commonwealths Series).

Nashville-Davidson County

Booth, David A. Metropolitics: The Nashville Consolidation. East Lansing: Institute for Community Development and Services, Michigan State University, 1963.

Grant, Daniel R. "Metropolitics and Professional Political Leadership: The Case of Nashville," The Annals of the American Academy of Political and Social Science, 353:72-83, May, 1964.

_____, and Lee S. Greene. "Surveys, Dust, Action," National Civic Review, 50:466–471, October, 1961.

Martin, Roscoe C. "Metropolitan Government: The Case of Nashville and Davidson County," in Metropolis in Transition. Washington: Housing and Home Finance Agency, 1963, pp. 103–113.

The Community Services Commission for Davidson County and the City of Nashville, Tennessee. A Future for Nashville. Nashville: The Community Services Commission, 1952.

The Metropolitan Government Charter Commission. The Charter of the Metropolitan Government of Nashville and Davidson County, Tennessee. Nashville: The Metropolitan Government Charter Commission, 1962.

Texas

Benton, Wilbourne E. Texas: Its Government and Politics. Englewood Cliffs, N. J.: Prentice-Hall Inc., 1963.

Keith, John P. City and County Home Rule in Texas. Austin: Institute of Public Affairs, University of Texas, 1951.

Virginia

Gibson, Frank K. and Edward S. Overman. County Government in Virginia. Charlottesville: Bureau of Public Administration, University of Virginia, 1961.

Spicer, George W. Fifteen Years of County Manager Government in Virginia. Charlottesville: Division of Extension, University of Virginia, 1952.

Washington

Byers, Barbara. County Government in Washington State. Olympia: Washington State Association of County Commissioners, 1957.

Campbell, Ernest H. and Herbert H. Legg, Jr. County Government in the State of Washington. Seattle: Bureau of Governmental Research, University of Washington, 1948.

West Virginia

Graves, W. Brooke and Mark H. Freeman. County Government: Origins, Development, Present Status, Future Prospects With Special Reference to West Virginia. Washington: Legislative Reference Service, Library of Congress, 1962.

Shamberger, Harold J. County Government and Administration in West Virginia. Morgantown: Bureau of Government Research, West Virginia University, 1952.

Wisconsin

Bureau of Government, University Extension Division, University of Wisconsin. County Government Activities in Wisconsin. Madison: University of Wisconsin, 1961.

_____. The County in Wisconsin. Madison: University of Wisconsin, 1962.

Milwaukee County

County of Milwaukee. Milwaukee County. Second Edition. Milwaukee: County of Milwaukee, 1963.

Public Administration Service. The Government of Milwaukee County: A Concluding Report. Chicago: Public Administration Service, 1956. (Prepared for the County Board of Supervisors).

Wyoming

Trachsel, Herman H. and Ralph M. Wade. The Government and Administration of Wyoming, Chapter 2. New York: Crowell, 1953. American Commonwealths Series, Vol. 48.

Index